# JOHN ANTROBUS

# THREE PLAYS FOR THE STAGE

## OF GOOD REPORT

## LACK OF MORAL FIBRE

## THE LOONEYS

Also by John Antrobus for BearManor Media

**GOON BUT NOT FORGOTTEN**
Mad recollections and television sketches that worry Sherlock Holmes

**THE MILLIGAN PAPERS**
Six BBC Radio comedy scripts
(The last series Spike Milligan did for the BBC)

**INVITATION TO A PLAGUE**
A murder has occurred in an incurables ward. All the patients will die within a few weeks so it makes an investigation pretty meaningless, as Inspector Hedge points out to his Superintendent. However, he might discover a germ warfare experiment has leaked into the community...

**THE HORSE MUTINY**
The stories of three horses in World War One

This volume: © 2022 John Antrobus. All Rights Reserved.

No portion of this publication may be reproduced, stored and/or copied electronically (except for academic use as a source), nor transmitted in any form or by any means without the prior written permission of the publisher and/or author.

Published in the USA by
BearManor Media
1317 Edgewater Dr. #110
Orlando, FL 32804
www.BearManorMedia.com

Paperback edition: ISBN: 978-1-62933-875-0
Hardcover edition: ISBN: 978-1-62933-876-7

# ACKNOWLEDGEMENTS

A big thanks to Peter Embling who proof read and laid out the pages and with whom I could always converse over any matters relating to content of the book.

More big thanks to my publisher Ben Ohmart without whom... Ben is a constant source of wonder over his enthusiasm for my writing.

All in all these acknowledgements are once again thanks for the encouragement that sees us all to the Promised Land!

**PERFORMING RIGHTS**

For all permissions relating to performance and production please refer to:
Jean Diamond, Diamond Management: jd@diman.co.uk

# INTRODUCTION

These three plays travel back through time from 2004 to 1971. They have been chosen not quite at random as signposts of part of my journey as a writer. I could easily have chosen other plays and I may get the opportunity to do so in another volume or several volumes.

What do these three plays have in common? If anything, that is, apart from the fact that I wrote them.

Well to start with OF GOOD REPORT, 2004, is an impression of how I began my employment becoming a quickly rising star as a writer. It all came so easily, was so much fun and so much laughter in the company particularly of Johnny Speight but also of other celebrity writers in Associated London Scripts. We were on top of the world though true Spike Milligan would have his bouts of depression and hospitalisation. I thought for me it would never end just get better and better, more and more...

THE LOONEYS, 1971, which I constantly rewrote into different versions over the years was my play that would rescue the falling star of my fortunes. I wrote and rewrote THE LOONEYS, seeing it as a West End comedy hit. I am still waiting. The play does echo the pain I felt, particularly in the ever-hopeful Arnold Gosport, fallen from the Heavens of film stardom, alcoholic father of the family and instrument of his own demise.

LACK OF MORAL FIBRE, was again often rewritten as it developed over the years, the two main characters of Skipper, Wing Commander Teddy Wilmot and his barman, Dennis, remaining in my heart and in my mind. The play reflects my love/hatred of my experience of military affairs and is one of several World War Two plays I have written and that I may yet have the privilege of publishing.

So here I am again, always at a new beginning in the ever-renewing Cosmic Day. I have always loved to go out to play! That is why I am blessed to be known as a playwright...

# OF GOOD REPORT

## by

# JOHN ANTROBUS

The play opened 5th December, 2004, at White Bear Theatre, London.
Director: John Antrobus.

In the mid fifties JOHN (Antrobus), fresh out of RMA, Sandhurst, after abandoning an army career, joins the agency, Associated London Scripts and is teamed up with JOHNNY (Speight).

They join up with Terry Nation and Dick Barry to write the *Frankie Howerd Radio Show*.

Though it is a comedy show, JOHN is drawn into the darker corridors of the BBC who are determined to root out left wing elements. Their bomb-happy producer, ex-army officer, BEVERLEY, is determined that JOHN shall get his hair cut. The producer likes to think of himself as very modern as he entertains a ménage à trois with his wife at home into which complications that JOHN, rather unworldly, and the more experienced and cynical (not to say Stalinist) JOHNNY are drawn one weekend.

# OF GOOD REPORT

TIME: mid-fifties, height of the Cold War

CAST:

    JOHN ANTROBUS: a comedy writer

    BERYL VERTUE: an agent

    JOHNNY SPEIGHT: a comedy writer

    BEVERLEY: BBC radio producer

    TESSA

    GILBERT HARDING

    FRANKIE HOWERD

    SHANI

    FX MAN

    JUDY: wife of Beverley

    TEA LADY

    GEORGE: George Beckett, BBC Controller – man in the corridor

    TERRY: Terry Nation, comedy writer

    DICK: Dick Barry, comedy writer

    THREE TRAMPS

# ACT I

## SCENE 1

*Enter JOHN, conversing with a skull.*

**JOHN**
Oh come, clouds of monstrous words and form not character mincing so that some actor chappie may say, "I don't think my character would say this". What character? There are no characters. I am set free in this blizzard of words, snatched phrases on the wind, howling indignation. Who from? No character, I assure you. No characters in this piece. So just say simply what is writ. But surely, subject? Topic? Focus? Drama? Structure? Have you all there? No, I have words, that's all. For actors. So let them speak and be glad of the employment or be gone. As to directors, kindly stop people thinking, that will be enough. But, this play, surely – is it topical? I know not? Historical? Possibly. Factual? Hardly. Light entertainment? Oh definitely. Hell's a popping. Zany is the word you're looking for, isn't it? A zany piece. Now we have our butterfly pinned down and in the cabinet. Happy, are you?

*Enter BERYL.*

**BERYL**
What have we here? A man with an umbrella. It hasn't rained for weeks. A herring-boned suit... Hello?

**JOHN**
Hello. Where do I start? Where do I sit?

**BERYL**
Pardon?

**JOHN**
I've come here to write. I'd rather like to get on with it. Plunge in.

BERYL
You're?

JOHN
Yes.

BERYL
John Antrobus.

JOHN
You were expecting me.

BERYL
Not quite like this.

JOHN
I'm longing to write. Have you a desk free? Available. I've so many ideas.

BERYL
Would you like a cup of tea?

JOHN
Is that how one starts? A career? Do the others? Did they? Start that way? Is that the secret?

BERYL
Our other writers are out to lunch, *to audience*: I've got a weird one here. I feel safe with him but good heavens! If he'd submitted himself instead of the scripts he would never have got inside the door.

JOHN
Where is the tea?

BERYL
Imagine it.

JOHN
Right. *MIMES DRINKING CUP OF TEA*.

BERYL
Where are you from?

JOHN
I don't know. That is I don't know where it all started. Or whether there was a beginning – for any of us – I don't know these things. I came from an egg. I'm new laid, that's it. Scratching around in the farmyard. It's my first day out of the egg. I stand. I move around. Peck. There's a lot of light. Bustle. I'll soon be at home. Actually I'm from Sandhurst. The Royal Military Academy. I asked to leave because I didn't want to kill people.

BERYL
The pen is mightier than the sword.

JOHN
We hope so. Where are the others? Where is Spike Milligan?

BERYL
Behind that door.

JOHN
*Reads the sign.* "Do not disturb. I am disturbed enough already." I like that. God, it's lonely without… a parade or something. I'm used to more people…

BERYL
Beryl.

JOHN
Beryl. And a military band. But I'll settle down. Where's Eric Sykes?

BERYL
He's having egg and chips. He always has three eggs. At the local cafe.

JOHN
That's wonderful. So close. Eric Sykes is a brilliant writer, yes. He wrote all those monologues for Frankie Howerd I used to listen to when I was, well – was I anything ?

BERYL
Younger ? When you were younger ?

JOHN
I was never younger. I was – listening.

BERYL
You were a listener ?

JOHN
Yes…

BERYL
We're going to team you up with another new writer called Johnny Speight.

JOHN
How tall is he?

BERYL
Well, I don't know. He should be tall enough.

JOHN
Only the best writing partnerships are tall, aren't they. Galton and Simpson.

BERYL
They're very tall, yes.

JOHN
They had the kindness to read my scripts. Muir and Norden, they're tall as well.

BERYL
We don't represent them.

JOHN
Pity. You represent…

BERYL
All sorts. All shapes and sizes.

JOHN
And this Johnny Speight?

BERYL
He's quite short.

JOHN
I – really – I really don't know. Have you got anybody taller. How tall is Spike Milligan?

BERYL
He's not as tall as Galton and Simpson. But they're exceptional.

JOHN
They are exceptional, yes. Very exceptional. *Looking at framed cheque.* 'In case of bankruptcy break glass and cash million pound cheque immediately'. I hope this is going to work. What year is it?

BERYL
1954.

JOHN
It's getting late.

## SCENE 2

JOHN
That same afternoon I found myself working with Johnny Speight.

*JOHNNY SPEIGHT and JOHN.*
*JOHNNY is tapping painfully – two fingers – on an imaginary typewriter.*

JOHN
What are you writing?

JOHNNY
What?

JOHN
I don't know what you're putting down.

JOHNNY
So?

JOHN
Well is this a collaboration. An act of co-authorship – shouldn't I know what's going on?

JOHNNY
You can read it later.

JOHN
Is that how it works?

JOHNNY
I don't know. *He stops typing.* Where were you during the General Election? At Tory party headquarters?

JOHN
I was in Trafalgar Square. Cheering on the Tory victory, yes. Not at their headquarters. I'm not that well known.

JOHNNY
Churchill's a fucking bastard who ordered the troops to fire at the workers.

JOHN
Did he?

JOHNNY
Fucking right he did.

JOHN
I didn't fucking well know that. Well I'm against killing.

JOHNNY
What?

JOHN
That's why I left Sandhurst. I asked the general if I could leave. I said I don't want to kill people because somebody else tells me to. It's going to be too late when we're under orders so I'd rather say no now.

JOHNNY
Are you a fucking pacifist?

JOHN
Pardon?

JOHNNY
Against killing on principle, are you?

JOHN
Well I haven't gone into it a lot.

JOHNNY
People have to be killed if they get in the way of human progress.

JOHN
Do they?

JOHNNY
Or we'll stay fucking ignorant, won't we? The slums, matey, are in the minds of people.

JOHN
I dare say they are – Johnny.

JOHNNY
Stalin's right.

JOHN
Good.

JOHNNY
And fuck Churchill.

JOHN
If you insist.

JOHNNY
Haven't you read The Siege Of Sidney Street?

JOHN
No. At Sandhurst we did a lot of military history. I know quite a lot about Stonewall Jackson.

JOHNNY
Fuck Stonewall Jackson.

JOHN
He was a Southern general.

JOHNNY
So fucking what? Who's going to make the tea?

JOHN
I am. But you'll have to mime it. THEY MIME DRINKING TEA.

JOHN
How many sugars did you put in your tea?

JOHNNY
Five.

JOHN
You'll ruin your teeth.

JOHNNY
These aren't my teeth. *He takes teeth out. Shows them to John.* These fucking teeth are fucking National Health teeth. Fucking National Ill-health they should call it, cos that's what we got. You know how we won the war?

JOHN
No. Well Monty had a lot to do with it.

JOHNNY
Monty's a cunt.

JOHN
Right. I didn't know that.

JOHNNY
We won the war because we were stupid. We didn't know we was beaten in 1940 that's how stupid we were. Hitler let our troops get off the beaches at Dunkirk – a demoralised rabble – so that they could go home and tell the others to pack it in. To fucking pack it in cos we were up against the well-oiled machinery of the Wehrmacht and we didn't have a chance. But they get back to Dover and some berk gives 'em a wet woodbine – and some fucking idiot starts cheering like they've won the fucking war when all they've done is escape by their arse – and some other fucking idiot starts singing *There'll Always Be An England* – and suddenly fucking Dunkirk, the beaches littered with equipment, weapons, tanks, Bren gun carriers, letters home, a scene of desolation – becomes a major victory.

JOHN
Yes, well I wasn't in Dunkirk company at Sandhurst but that was one of the names. I was in Somme company.

JOHNNY
Somme? You were in Somme company? Was that another fucking victory, was it? Lions led by donkeys, they were. Do me a favour. Do you want to type?

JOHN
I don't know how to.

JOHNNY
Nor do I. The only fucking war we've got to win, mate, is the class war.

## SCENE 3

BERYL
How are you getting on with Johnny?

JOHN
Oh very fucking well, thank you.

BERYL
How's the script coming along?

JOHN
It's long enough but it lacks width. As to height… we're not really matched. How tall is Spike? Did you get a chance …?

BERYL
To measure him? No. One doesn't think of him as tall. Or short. He's just – Spike!
*She laughs.*

JOHN
I suppose one could think of him any way one liked. Where are Ray and Alan today?

BERYL
They're recording.

JOHN
I like them. They're brilliant writers. I think they noticed me. They said hello anyway. But the next time Alan didn't seem to know who I was. He asked me again. So I told him again… I offered to take over writing Hancock's Half Hour so that they could go on holiday. Have a break, you know. They thought I was joking. They told Eric Sykes and everyone laughed a lot.

BERYL
I'm sure you were joking.

JOHN
Are you?

BERYL
Nobody's serious here.

JOHN
I must remember that.

BERYL
We were described in a daily paper recently as a Fun Factory.

JOHN
How terrible. Do they think we manufacture jokes all day long? Johnny Speight and I, we talk about George Bernard Shaw – who I've started reading, he's very good – and Henri Bergson's Fucking Theory Of Creative Fucking Evolution. I've bought that. I'll get round to that.

BERYL
Not much time for jokes then, in that?

JOHN
No. It's character we write. And absurdity. Don't you find life to be absurd, Beryl?

BERYL
Oh, pretty much all the time. One's bound to working here…

# SCENE 4

*JOHNNY mimes tearing page from typewriter.*

JOHN
It's blank.

JOHNNY
That's why I threw the f-fucking page away. I wouldn't throw it away if there was any f-fucking words on it, would I?

JOHN
No. Never. It's a terrible waste of paper. We always used to save all our paper bags. Of course there was a war on.

JOHNNY
You know the funny thing is…

JOHN
What's that, Johnny?

JOHNNY
Galton and Simpson. Ray and Alan, when I met them. When I first met them, I had them down as a couple of fucking pooftahs. I mean you know how Ray dresses.

JOHN
Well Edwardian modern. Teddy boy. Drainpipe. Razor. Razor.

JOHNNY
What are you talking about? Off your fucking head, are you?

JOHN
Ray's always well dressed. He's always dressed. You mean you thought you were coming into a den of iniquity.

JOHNNY
I'm saying fucking shirt-lifters. They're in show business, right? They're everywhere. They're attracted to the glamour. It's a freer world, isn't it? You got to look after yourself. After three days at sea everything's fucking legal.

JOHN
But surely not Ray and Alan?

JOHNNY
No, course not! I'm telling you what I thought.

JOHN
I think they have a platonic liking for each other. Like you and me, I suppose.

JOHNNY
Oh, fuck off! I'm just telling you an impression I had.

JOHN
Well I never had that impression.

JOHNNY
Because you never have any impressions. You don't notice anything, do you?

JOHN
What are you trying to tell me?

JOHNNY
I'm saying Ray and Alan are pudding merchants! Right?

JOHN
You mean they like girls?

JOHNNY
Course they fucking do.

JOHN
Well Ray's married to one.

JOHNNY
That doesn't mean anything. That could be fucking cover, couldn't it?

JOHN
But not in Ray's case...

JOHNNY
Of course not in Ray's case. I'm just telling you of a fucking impression I had when I first met him.

JOHN
What about Alan?

JOHNNY
What?

JOHN
What was your first impression of Alan?

JOHNNY
I didn't fucking know, did I? I thought if I'm going in that fucking agency I better watch my arse. That's all.

JOHN
But you don't need to watch your arse.

JOHNNY
I know I don't need to watch my fucking arse.

JOHN
Do you regard yourself as attractive then?

JOHNNY
What's that supposed to fucking well mean? Attractive? Course I'm fucking attractive. I'm not a fucking corpse, am I? What more do they need ?

JOHN
Who?

JOHNNY
Wake up, John. That's all. Watch your arse when we go up the BBC. That's all.

JOHN
Well I'm going to ask Beryl.

JOHNNY
What are you going to ask her?

JOHN
I don't know.

JOHNNY
It's no good asking her if she's running a male brothel, is it? It's a fucking script agency.

JOHN
Well that's what I thought.

JOHNNY
So don't complicate things.

JOHN
Alright.

JOHNNY
Don't go asking Beryl if she's introducing young boys to her clients.

JOHN
I've come here on the understanding that my scripts are acceptable – the samples I wrote – and that I'm a funny writer.

JOHNNY
You are, John, you are.

JOHN
So…

JOHNNY
So don't get paranoid. Fucking nut case. Think everyone's after your arse.

JOHN
I don't.

JOHNNY
Then don't keep talking about it. Okay? We've got a fucking script to write

here. We've got a script to deliver to those fucking idiots at the Beeb. That twerp, Captain Beverley Houghton-Twist, who's one ambition is to take the salute at the Remembrance Day parade in his village.

JOHN
Yes. When he reads his name on the war memorial he'll realise he's dead.

JOHNNY
He can't fucking read, don't worry. All I'm saying is when we go up there – to Aeolian Hall – to the Beeb – watch your fucking arse, right. Cos it's full of brown hatters up there.

# SCENE 5

*BEVERLEY, ex-army officer type. Regimental blazer, toothbrush moustache. In front of his desk, JOHN and JOHNNY are seated – while he thumbs through their script.*

BEVERLEY
I've got one thing to say to you lads. One thing. And one thing only. I want to go on record *Off to his secretary:* you hear that, Tessa?

*TESSA enters.*

TESSA
What ?

BEVERLEY
On record with this simple comment about Johnny Speight's and John Thingermebob's pilot script for a series based on a private eye. A Dick! Tessa, take note. Here it comes. This script is absolutely… wait for it. Don't jump the gun… This script commissioned by my office to encourage the work of new writers! My God, the country needs them. The life blood of the BBC is the talent of new writers. We risk thirty guineas in the hope of getting that blood transfusion. Right, thanks for coming in.

JOHNNY
You haven't told us what you think of the script, Beverley.

BEVERLEY
I haven't? Tessa? What have you written down?

TESSA
Nothing much, so far.

BEVERLEY
Are you sure?

TESSA
Perfectly sure, Beverley.

BEVERLEY
Show me.

TESSA
No.

BEVERLEY
Oh. Well this 'ere script is either complete and utter drivel...

JOHNNY
Fuck off!

BEVERLEY
Or... it's brilliant. It is obviously the result of two fevered minds thinking alike. I would have to say this script is before it's time.

JOHNNY
We haven't got any other fucking time, Beverley.

BEVERLEY
By some weeks. At least. This 'ere missive could be utterly incomprehensible to my Aunt Enid listening in Bexhill-On-Sea. And that's who we must be aiming our scripts at. All the Aunt Enids!

JOHN
Sitting in Bexhill. In droves. Crouched round their radio sets in covens. Aunt Enids screeching, "I don't like that!"

BEVERLEY
That's right, Antrobus. To put this script on – Nick The Dick – in the current climate which is very clammy – we would risk being laughed at.

JOHNNY
It is a fucking comedy.

BEVERLEY
True. I'll bear that in mind. Leave it with me, boys. At the moment it's too hot to handle. I'm going to put it between asbestos covers and file under D for Dangerous. *Gives script to Tessa.*

TESSA
Wilco Sunray.

BEVERLEY
Over and out.

*TESSA exits.*

BEVERLEY
Unexploded New Work by promising authors. *He stands up. Holds out his hand.* Goodbye.

JOHNNY
Well are we going to make a fucking pilot or not?

BEVERLEY
Good question, Johnny. You're asking all the right questions. Keep asking those sort of questions. You know where the lift is. Kindly leave the premises in good order. Do not write on the walls. I should warn you that any abusive behaviour will be noted in your files.

JOHN
What files?

BEVERLEY
What files? Good question. *Calls off.* Do you know of any files, Tessa?

TESSA
*Pokes her head in for a moment.* No!

BEVERLEY
There you are. You've nothing to worry about. *Seeing them out.* And Antrobus, a word in your ear. A haircut would be advisable before your next visit to Aeolian Hall.

JOHN
Is that an order?

JOHNNY
You can't give him fucking orders, Beverley. You're not at fucking Alamein

now. A bomb happy Captain with shit-stained shorts.

BEVERLEY
True, Johnny, very true. Stand down. Steady the Buffs. Good bye, chaps. You have my absolute trust. You are front line material, both of you.

*JOHN salutes, exits. JOHNNY gives Hitler's salute and exits, goose-stepping.*

BEVERLEY
Sar'n Major! Give those men a 48 hour pass…

*He marches across stage, exits.*

## SCENE 6

JOHN
We eventually got work on a Frankie Howerd radio series. That is Johnny Speight and I, along with Terry Nation and Dick Barry. Full credit there but my memory favours Johnny and myself. I do not even care about memory except as this or that fragment surfaces, insists it has a place in a story. Each week we interviewed a guest for the radio show, then wrote a sketch for them to play with Frankie Howerd. So far, so good… It was thus that we arrived at the town seat of Gilbert Harding, a noted celebrity of that era.

*Gilbert Harding enters holding glass. To portrait of mother…*

GILBERT
Bung-ho mother.

JOHN
Ding.

JOHNNY
Dong.

*GILBERT crosses to imaginary front door.*

GILBERT
The war's been over ten years and we're still making our own sound effects.

*He mimes opening one door – lots of bolts and locks. Then he looks through spy hole at John and Johnny and mimes opening second door.*

GILBERT
Welcome to my humble abode. Come in, come in! No, don't close the doors – we'll be here all bloody night! *He crosses to drinks cabinet and pours drinks.* A Scottish malt whisky is ready to leap into the glass, like a spawning salmon, spawning conversation we hope. But don't let my mind run away with the evening. Chuck your coats anywhere. Now which one is Speight?

JOHNNY
Me. Hello Gilbert.

GILBERT
*As they shake hands.* Ah, this is the brilliant Mr Speight... *He holds up his hand.* I won't wash that for a fortnight. I might have guessed it was you. A savage intelligence rests upon his brow. A veritable Jonathan Swift working on the Frankie Howerd radio show. Never mind. How are the mighty fallen. I too have signed to perform on this show. A buffoon must make his living. It's either that or the hell of Christmas pantomime in Cheltenham playing Widow Twankey. Tormenting genius. As ever... and you would be ?

JOHN
John Antrobus.
*They shake hands. GILBERT keeps hold of JOHN's hand.*

GILBERT
Let me look at you. Come into the light. Yes, I want to remember this first meeting. Of such scraps is a life put together. Forgive me, Johnny.

JOHNNY
No, I'm Johnny. He's John.

GILBERT
Of course. Well it's done. The hand is shook. *He brusquely throws aside the handshake.* Lead on Macduff. The scotch in crystal tumblers. No ice, for God's sake.

JOHNNY
OK.

JOHN
OK.

GILBERT
A little bracken water myself gathered from the moors. Now let's see. Here's a glass and cheers. To new life. To comedy. To that humiliation to which we are called – the guest spot on the Frankie Howerd Show – the poking of the bear. Cheers.

JOHN and JOHNNY
Cheers.

*They clink glasses and drink.*

GILBERT
Sit down. Let's get down to business. Enough of the pleasantries. Now which one of you is the genius (*camp*) and which one's the typist?

JOHN
We're co-authors.

GILBERT
Oh, pull the other one. Beauty hath not brains. You're telling me with your looks you can write as well. Is that possible? Dumbfound me.

JOHN
Well…

GILBERT
I can see him as a star, a film star, can't you, Johnny? You're the Johnny one.

JOHNNY
Yeah, he's got a good profile. But he wasn't chosen for his looks. He can write.

GILBERT
Amazing. I am prostrate, John Antrobus, before such genius imbuing – imbued of beauty – a marvel. So what crap have you brought me to perform? I'll do anything. I'm shameless. For seventy guineas I'm all yours.

JOHNNY
First of all Gilbert, I want you to fucking know that we don't write fucking crap.

GILBERT
I'm greatly relieved to hear it. So why do you want me? I am the original crap artist. I've told you I'm the performing bear. It's my living.

JOHNNY
In this fucking philistine society, what else can you be?

GILBERT
Precisely. A kindred spirit. A fellow traveller.

JOHNNY
I was brought up in the slums. In the East End, right.

GILBERT
I think none the worse of you.

JOHNNY
But the worst slums I come across was the slums in their fucking minds.

GILBERT
A conversation when I least expected it. More whisky, gentlemen. John! You pour. And liberally, please.

JOHN
Right-ho, Gilbert.

GILBERT
So by what subterfuge do you intend to wreak havoc with the thinking of our nation, Johnny, in this little sketch you have in mind? Fuck 'em, is that what I'm hearing?

JOHNNY
Fuck the lot of them. I tell you, John, he can fucking think. Don't underestimate him. Just cos he's fucking beautiful.

GILBERT
I don't. I was carried away for the moment.

JOHNNY
He's out of fucking Sandhurst, he is. The fucking Royal Military Academy.

GILBERT
Good heavens. Are you well connected?

JOHNNY
He's fucking disconnected.

JOHN
I didn't want to kill people so I asked to leave.

GILBERT
Are you vegetarian?

JOHN
No. I didn't want to eat people.

GILBERT
Good. Then my hors d'oeuvres will not offend. Little sausages on sticks. Like shriven penii. I prefer that as a plural to penis, don't you? What use words without wordplay? So what's the idea behind this sketch that I'm to perform with Frankie? That I'm so looking forward to, now I've met you both. My word I am. Though slightly disappointed it's to be an intellectual piece.

JOHN
We haven't written it yet.

GILBERT
Oh, haven't you?

JOHN
We meet you first. We get an idea of who you are.

GILBERT
Well if you find that out, let me know. What are you, a couple of psychiatrists? Couple of shrinks? Where's your white coats? I thought you were going to write a sketch full of crass jokes and sexual innuendo. Why do you need to know who I am? You think you can find that out in five minutes? Do you? When the best trained minds in Vienna have failed. Nobody understands me! Now get out. No, stay, please, stay... The moment has passed, my darlings. My doves.

JOHN
It's to get an impression, Gilbert, that's all.

GILBERT
Well I'm not an impressionist, am I, Johnny? You tell him.

JOHNNY
No, and you don't play the musical saw, Gilbert.

GILBERT
Precisely. Why is he taunting me? Get to know me? Not bloody likely. Want me to strip naked in front of you, do you? Bare my wounds. Are they self-inflicted? What word springs to mind when you say Mother? Is that it? I've done all that. What shapes do you see when we show you this pattern?

JOHNNY
Gilbert, listen, mate, we're all wounded. We're all crippled. But some of us can see it, that's the difference. And the rest are fucking ignorant.

GILBERT
Well tell your pal that. And get him off my back. John, what's your name?

JOHN
Antrobus.

GILBERT
Why are you persecuting me? Beauty and the beast, is that it? Don't answer. Pour more drinks, there's a love… They know not what they do. The innocence of youth. It's sheer cruelty. You know John, you have the indifference of cold marble. Pour the drinks, there's a love. Go on. No-one's to blame. We're all trapped, selling our arse for a penny. Now about this sketch? Will it be funny? Johnny?

JOHNNY
Yes, Gilbert.

GILBERT
That's a relief. Because I think it should be, Johnny. We're not going to solve the world's problems in a five minute piece in a Frankie Howerd show. My advise is don't mention Weitgenstein.

JOHNNY
Eight minutes.

GILBERT
I should have asked for more money.

*JOHN has poured more drinks.*

GILBERT
Prost!

JOHN and JOHNNY
Cheers!

*They drink.*

JOHNNY
Stalin's got the right idea.

GILBERT
Indeed, he has!

JOHNNY
You've got to purge the Establishment.

GILBERT
Even if it means shooting the wrong people.

JOHNNY
There are no wrong people. There are no wrong fucking people, Gilbert.

## SCENE 7

JOHN
Terry Nation with a bottle of milk...

*Enter TERRY with a bottle of milk*

JOHN
Dick Barry with a bag of apples...

*The actor turns and mimes to eat an apple, as DICK... He wears half a costume as TERRY and half as DICK.*

JOHN
Johnny scratching his leg. His neurotic safety valve...

*JOHNNY at the typewriter, scratching his leg.*

JOHN
Me taking up space. The next Frankie Howerd radio show script to be delivered Friday morning to Captain Beverley Houghton-Twist in his producer dugout at Aeolian Hall. After poncing around all week we eventually got down to writing late Thursday evening and worked all night. As per usual...

*TERRY AND DICK (one actor) slumps on the floor and falls asleep.*

*JOHNNY, at desk, silent.*

*JOHN at window.*
*Turns back to room.*

JOHN
It's raining outside.

JOHNNY
Better than inside. What's the time?

JOHN
It's three o'clock in the morning, Johnny. Shall I wake the others up?

JOHNNY
No, it's better the two of us.

JOHN
But we are a team.

JOHNNY
I know we're a fucking team. What do you want, jerseys?
*He stands up and stretches.*
Just the Gilbert Harding sketch to do. The guest spot. Bleedin' pooftah.

JOHN
You think everyone's a pooftah, Johnny.

JOHNNY
Until proved otherwise, yes. So what? It's only sex. They'll make breathing illegal next. Fucking Oscar Wilde was worth more than a thousand Queensburys. What did he invent? Rules of fucking boxing. Cunt. Now we've got a police state in the lavatories of England.

JOHN
Yes, Clapham Junction's pretty bad. Gilbert shared your Stalinist views, didn't he?

JOHNNY
Your Gilbert he's a fucking Trotskyist not a fucking Stalinist. Can't you tell the difference?

JOHN
No.

JOHNNY
Gilbert's an idealist, like Trotsky. Which was why your Trotsky merited an ice pick in his nut. Trotsky could see the good in human nature. Stalin knew there isn't any.

JOHN
So what's the point?

JOHNNY
What do you mean, what's the point?

JOHN
Well what's the point of having a fucking revolution if we're all rubbish anyway?

JOHNNY
We're making way for the superman.

JOHN
It's going to take a superman to work out a sketch for Gilbert Harding and Frankie Howerd tonight…

*They both fall silent, until JOHN gets an idea.*

JOHN
So!… I went to the doctor…

*JOHN AND JOHNNY improvise as FRANKIE HOWERD upon the following monologue.*

JOHN AND JOHNNY
… He said what do you want mush? Eh? Mush? They have no respect do they? These days. And I mean he had three cigarettes on the go. The surgery was full of smoke. And he smelt of brandy. I said shall I open the window? He said if you can find it yes… Oh, I thought, I've got a right one here. He said how many people are out in the waiting room? I said it's packed. He said I'll turn the heating off, that'll get rid of 'em. Then he looked at me, he said I suppose you want a sick note don't you, like all the others, bringing the country to rack and ruin. I said hang on doctor, please, I require a consultation. He said do you want it privately or on the National Health? I said yes privately on the National Health please. Ha! Cos I can be cheeky too… You have to be don't you, sometimes, or they'll walk all over you. So I said to him shall I remove my overcoat? He said which one? Well I was wearing my wardrobe at the time because I was in between lodgings. It can happen to all of us. You can imagine my chagrin. My in had never been so shagged. Ha! Oh, that's better… I said doctor if you can stand up would you please examine me. He said right ! He looked down my throat

he said your shoe laces are undone. That was it. I took my germs elsewhere. What?

## SCENE 8

*SPOTLIGHT*
*SHANI WALLIS enters – sings few bars of a fifties number, ending on long note.*
*FRANKIE HOWERD (Johnny). Looks at his watch, as she holds note. At last she finishes with a flourish.*
*Lights up.*

FRANKIE
Have you finished ?

SHANI
Yes, Mr Howerd.

FRANKIE
I don't know where she gets the breath. Thank you Shani Wallis. The face that launched a thousand canoes. What a lovely singer. A lovely girl. She gets it from her mother. I don't know where her mother gets it from.

*SHANI exits.*

FRANKIE
Now, hang on, just get meself comfy. Oh this elastic is tight. They don't care, do they? They don't think of us when they make them, that's for sure. You've got the same problem, have you madam ? Wriggle. Go on… *improv*. Now my next guest. Straight from *What's My Line*. The one who isn't Isabel Barnett. The renowned, the illustrious, the one and only – I know that cos I counted him – ladies and gentlemen, Gilbert Harding!

*Enter GILBERT HARDING.*

GILBERT
Thank you, Frankie. I will just make myself comfortable. Oh, that didn't get much of a laugh.

FRANKIE
No, it's the way you say it, Gilbert. And the wriggle.

GILBERT
Oh, I'm not very good at wriggling. Or any other outdoor sport. Mind you I was an Oxford blue. Oars was my speciality.

FRANKIE
Was they? No comment.

GILBERT
What sketch are we going to do this week, Frankie?

FRANKIE
The one we rehearsed this afternoon, mate. While you were still sober.

GILBERT
I did have one quickie in the Green Room.

FRANKIE
Did you? Well I've heard it's not green any more, so I don't know what you've been doing in there.

*Enter SHANI and FX MAN.*

SHANI
In the heart of darkest Africa...

*FX MAN: Tom Tom noises.*

SHANI
Through dense jungle, plagued by mosquitoes...

*FX MAN: Mosquitos*

SHANI
Frightened by tigers...

*FX MAN: Tiger.*

SHANI
Trampled upon by elephants...

*FX MAN: Elephant.*

SHANI
Hissed at by snakes…

*FX MAN: Snake.*

SHANI
Bitten by alligators…

*FX MAN: puzzled. Tries to impersonate alligator.*

FRANKIE
Oh, get on with it! We haven't got all day! We know the jungle's full of animals.

SHANI
Sorry. Cutting his way through the undergrowth with only a machete in his hand…

*FX MAN: cutting undergrowth with machete.*

FRANKIE
Well that's a relief.

SHANI
Looking for the fabled lost city of Southampton.

GILBERT
Southampton must be lost if it's in darkest Africa.

FRANKIE
We gave him that line. Poor old devil. To encourage him.

SHANI
Worn to a frazzle by his endeavours was the intrepid explorer, renowned for his previous trip…

FRANKIE
Up the Thames. Go on!

SHANI
We find our intrepid explorer, sweat stained, his clothes torn to ribbons by brambles...

FX MAN: clothes tearing.

SHANI
His hair falling out.

FX MAN
My hair's falling out.

FRANKIE
Yes. For only five pounds a bottle you too can restore your bald bounce. Order today, the Frankie Howerd way to re-thatch your roof.

SHANI
May I complete my announcement, Mr Howerd? I'm nearly finished.

FRANKIE
Your career is.

SHANI
I'm only reading what's written in the script.

FRANKIE
Well don't tell everyone. They think we're ad-libbing.

SHANI
Staggering into a clearing, and falling onto his knees – wanting only to die –

FX MAN
I want to die.

SHANI
Was...

OMNES
The intrepid explorer!

SHANI
Francis C Howerd.

FRANKIE
What's the C for?

SHANI
For all the little boats to sail on!

FRANKIE
Oh, the satire's biting tonight.

GILBERT
Why don't we try my sketch, Frankie? It's about discovering the North Pole. I'll distribute copies. Here you are everyone. *Distributing copies acting...*

FRANKIE
What a liberty! He comes in here as if he owns the place. He even gave me a rent book. I said 'book'. Hang on, Gilbert! Show a modicum of restraint, if you please. Oh do what you like! He knows we're desperate. Continue...

*FX MAN: Whistling gale.*

SHANI
Having eaten the last of their huskies...

*FX MAN: Burps.*

SHANI
The two intrepid...

OMNES
Intrepid, intrepid, intrepid.

FRANKIE
Oh Gawd. Anyone not intrepid tonight?

SHANI
Through the eyes, nose, ears and teeth of a snow blizzard...

*FX MAN: Snow blizzard noise.*

**SHANI**
Blinding them to the perilous ice crevices...

**FX MAN**
I can't see.

**SHANI**
They stumbled exhausted tripping over their two months growth of beard...

**FX MAN**
I must shave when I get home.

**FRANKIE**
I'll have a two months growth of beard if I wait for him to finish. Move on a couple of pages! We've all got buses to catch. Homes to go to. In Gilbert's case an Old People's Home.

**GILBERT**
Right. My turn. Stand back. Oh, look there's the North Pole over there. Hello! Hello! Anyone at home. Is this the North Pole?

**FRANKIE**
No, it's the South Pole. I told you to turn right at Clapham Junction. Where did you get this rubbish? This mere scribble on the back of an envelope?

**GILBERT**
I bought it from Morecambe and Wise. It was a bargain lot with two pairs of socks.

**FRANKIE**
I've only one thing to say to you, Gilbert.

**GILBERT**
What's that?

**FRANKIE**
Good night. Oh, I wonder if we can get Dame Edith Evans next week? If she's not still on the game.

## SCENE 9

*CHORUS enters.*

CHORUS
Well! Well! Well! Well!
That will be the day…..

*JOHN enters. He is wearing jeans and leather jacket, like James Dean.*

*JUDY enters. She sits, makes up her face.*

*JOHN confronts JUDY – as singing suddenly stops.*

JOHN
Oh. Wrong office. Sorry.

*CHORUS exits.*

JUDY
Who do you want?

JOHN
Beverley Houghton Twist.

JUDY
Come in and join the queue, darling. I'm Mrs Houghton-Bloomin' Twist, in case you were wondering. I met my husband during the war – in a blackout – it was frightfully romantic. Then someone turned the lights on and it's never been the same since.

JOHN
That's funny.

JUDY
Are you an expert on humour?

JOHN
I hardly ever trade in jokes. Situation is more my cup of tea. Character. What makes someone tick.

JUDY
You're an actor?

JOHN
A writer.

JUDY
On that's much better. Congratulations. You're so young as well. One doesn't expect young people to be funny. Witty, yes, but it's not the same, is it?

JOHN
I don't know. I don't know what I am.

JUDY
One takes you as one finds you then?

JOHN
I spend my life imitating people. It's difficult not to have a class image. That's where Hollywood comes to the rescue. James Dean for instance.

JUDY
You look like James Dean.

JOHN
Thank you.

JUDY
Don't you find London frightfully boring? I can't wait to get home. It's a mistake to get dressed in the morning, darling. It means you're going out and something disastrous is bound to happen. It's safer to stay in bed and take another pill.

JOHN
There are the London shops.

JUDY
While the money lasts.

JOHN
There's theatre in the West End.

JUDY
Never go.

JOHN
Are you against it?

JUDY
It's like knitting, darling, I never do it. I'm not against it.

JOHN
There are lots of restaurants in London.

JUDY
I don't eat. Any other suggestions?
*Obviously upset, she mimes taking a pill from her real handbag.*

JOHN
Would you like a glass of water ?

JUDY
Yes please.

JOHN
You'll have to mime it.

JUDY
Of course, darling, BBC cuts. *She mimes taking pill drinking water .*

JOHN
You've got a place in the country, haven't you? Do you find that more interesting?

JUDY
Hardly. But I breed.

JOHN
Oh.

JUDY
Dogs. Alsatians, darling.

JOHN
Of course. Do you have a radio? You must do. Do you listen to the Frankie Howerd radio show?

JUDY
My husband's show. Yes.

JOHN
Because that's what I write on.

JUDY
Oh, it's the only thing I listen to. Apart from the Brain's Trust. You are clever.

JOHN
It's a gift.

JUDY
There's no point in being modest. I do have a secret life. I read books. That way I can stay in bed all day.

JOHN
I love reading. Who are your favourite authors?

JUDY
PG Wodehouse. Evelyn Waugh. George Simenon. Dorothy L Sayers. Anybody who can give me a giggle or a thrill.

JOHN
I'm reading Jean-Paul Sartre, Albert Camus and Henri Bergson's Theory Of Fucking Evolution, recommended by Johnny Speight.

JUDY
Yes, well I'm sure fucking is essential to evolution.

JOHN
What were you doing in the war? I mean how did you meet Beverley? I mean, I expect…

JUDY
Yes, I was old enough, darling. I was an ambulance driver. Killed more people in the blackout than I ever rescued. We used to knock them over and chuck them in the back with the others.

JOHN
Did you knock Beverley over in the blackout?

JUDY
No, he knocked me over. Emotionally. He'd just been to the Palace for his medal. He'd been so brave. Or drunk. I thought I should marry him immediately because I was sure he was going to get killed on his next mission. I hate long relationships. But he survived, poor lamb, and I mustn't hold it against him. So…

JOHN
What?

JUDY
Hello? Have I lost you?

JOHN
No. I didn't sleep last night. We were working. It's all a bit disjointed.

JUDY
What is?

JOHN
This conversation. It doesn't nourish me, I just get more and more nervous.

JUDY
You get nervous ?

JOHN
The more you say the less is said. I mean it's all very smart, isn't it? You've got it off pat. It's all pseudo Noel Coward. You're good at it. I'm not. I can't cope with it. What do you want? Why are you talking to me?

JUDY
I'm passing the time, darling.

JOHN
Well don't pass the time with me. I'm not a time passer. I'm not a time server. It's getting late. If you've got something to say, Mrs Houghton Twist, then bloody well say it.

JUDY
I'm sorry. I didn't realise.

JOHN
I haven't slept…

JUDY
I know. I know. Don't worry, that's all.

JOHN
I can't play a role if I don't have a character. What am I? A feed? To all the comedians?

JUDY
I'll make it alright. Don't worry.

*Enter BEVERLEY.*

BEVERLEY
Oh hello, darling.

JUDY
*She allows BEVERLEY a peck on the check…* Mind my bloody make up, Beverley.

BEVERLEY
Sorry. You've met young erm Antrobus, have you?

JUDY
You don't need to be so condescending. He has got a christian name.

BEVERLEY
Yes, well he's errm – not the Johnny one…

JOHN
John Antrobus.

BEVERLEY
That's it. This is my wife, Judy.

JUDY
His Old Woman. Comfortable as a pair of slippers. Beverley. Beverley. BEVERLEY!
*She gets his attention.*
Invite John down for the weekend. He reads books.

BEVERLEY
Does he, bai jove? Right-ho. Antrobus, Company Orders. You are to proceed to the cottage on the earliest possible weekend. With Johnny and Terry and Dick. Any Sunday you like, except Sunday's not a good idea because I'm umpiring cricket on Sundays. So it will have to be a Saturday. Any Saturday you like except it will have to be in two weeks time because there's a reason which I can't remember at the moment. Like we're recording the Frankie Howerd show. Tessa will provide you with a map. Expected time of arrival, ETA, let's say noon. Start lines to the river will be marked out by guides. Silence is essential…

JUDY
For God's sake.

BEVERLEY
No, it's not. Have you had a nice morning in town, Judy?

JUDY
I saved myself from suicide by shopping heavily, darling. And I've spent all our money.

BEVERLEY
So I see. Well done, darling. We can only hope that mummy croaks it and we get the inheritance before Harrods send the next bill. Antrobus, give the script to Tessa. She'll be here in a minute.

JOHN
Don't you want to go through it?

BEVERLEY
No. Any rude words I'll take out at rehearsal. Like bum. And 'brown stain'. Brown's alright and stain's alright, but don't put them together. Apart from that you have my total trust. The audience ratings are on the up. Tell the others. Very satisfactory. And put on a suit for the recording, Antrobus. Or I won't introduce you to the audience, as one of the writers, at the beginning of the show. It's more important to be smart than to be funny.

JUDY
Why?

BEVERLEY
Good question. Morale, that's why. If I hadn't shaved before Alamein…

JUDY
You were in Cairo that morning, darling.

BEVERLEY
Rommel wasn't.

## SCENE 10

JOHN
It was a day of odd encounters. Having started with Judy – Mrs Houghton-Bloomin' Twist, about whom I felt vaguely excited… but so what? She must have been at least ten years older than me, and married. One did not readily admit to feelings in those days. Feely, touchy had not arrived. There were outbursts of emotions, as there had to be, usually after boozing… But all our critical faculties looked outwards. Then again I was also broody, a loner, self-obsessed in an Albert Camus, The Outsider, sort of way. I might even have been an Existentialist but I wasn't sure what it was. At the Beeb that day, in the corridor…

*TEA LADY with trolley enters. Bumps her way past JOHN.*

TEA LADY
Tea up!

*Ensemble mime opening their office doors – with a burst of noise – as they queue up like penguins at the tea trolley.*
*They congregate for a moment or two, incomprehensibly babbling, with lots of 'darlings' – then suddenly return to their offices closing the doors. This cuts off the sound. One man steps out of his office again.*

MAN
Sorry! Wrong office!

*MAN changes offices with the woman next to him.*
*All in ensemble mime. They exit like clockwork penguins, saying « BBC BBC BBC BBC BBC … »*

JOHN
In the corridor I bumped into a programme controller. Or was he? Nobody quite knew what he was, a man named George Beckett…

*JOHN and GEORGE brush past each other in the corridor.*

BECKETT
*Vaguely Irish.* Hello John Antrobus. A rising star in the firmament. Dare I say it, a brilliant future beckons, and always with it the risk of self-

destruction. Stay simple and humble is my advice, John.

JOHN
Thank you George.

GEORGE
Look, let's go and have a weewee together and a quiet chat. If you've got a moment...

JOHN
Gripping my arm, George led me to the Gents. I was worried, but he made no move to molest me...

*They have moved into toilet. Go to urinals.*

GEORGE
How are you getting on with the rest of the team?

JOHN
Great.

GEORGE
We're grooming them all for success. Writers are the life-blood of Auntie. We watch them all closely. We know more than you would perhaps imagine.

JOHN
I don't know. I didn't know we were being watched.

GEORGE
Don't worry, John. Look at it this way. The BBC is the great bastion of free speech that must not be abused.

JOHN
Who's to judge, George? When it's being abused. If it's not being abused, it's not being used.

GEORGE
Good point. Well there's some as has to judge! Or the wreckers and reds would bring the lot down round our ears. And don't think they're not plotting

to do so, 'ere we speak. John. John Antrobus, because it is so. And need not concern you as much as some of us – who is paid to keep on eye on trouble-makers. So that you, Johnny boy, can practise your art. You have a vital organ to play with – the BBC. So if I ask you to lend a hand, don't be shy...

JOHN
George, I don't really know what you're going on about.

GEORGE
We've had you in our sights, Johnno, since you had your nervous breakdown when you left Sandhurst. The Royal Military Academy. You were doing so well there. Sword of Honour material. Top honours beckoning...

JOHN
George, I did not have a nervous breakdown.

GEORGE
Grammar school boy determined to make good. You were working too hard. You blew a fuse.

JOHN
I simply decided I didn't want to kill people. That's why I left Sandhurst.

GEORGE
You don't think that's strange?

JOHN
No.

GEORGE
Not wanting to kill people? Don't you think that's weird?

JOHN
Not really. Strikes me as quite normal.

GEORGE
But you're from a military family.

JOHN
I know. How do you know?

GEORGE
You're asking the question before you killed anyone that I asked after I killed my first Boche. A flaxen haired youth. Beautiful young man that I could have gone cycling with under different circumstances, across Europe.

JOHN
Exactly. I don't understand how you come to have all this information about me.

GEORGE
It's on a need to know basis.

JOHN
You need to know nothing about me, George.

GEORGE
I need to know everything about everybody.

JOHN
I don't see why…

GEORGE
Don't you, John? Don't you see that those who built this country have blood on their hands ? Those who defend it also. I've strangled and knifed men, John, so that we can have this bloody conversation. And are you telling me you won't help to keep the peace? Now we've got it. If we ask you to lend a hand?

*Cue : Fade up Russian Army choir.*
*Fade in red light FX…*

GEORGE
There's the bloody Red Army stacked up in Europe ready to roll. Ten thousand bloody tanks in East Germany. And van loads of KGB wallahs ready to follow them westward ho! Do you think they give a fuck about the BBC? They're waiting for us to fall apart and they'll just move in. They'll go through France like butter. And there'll be a fucking great Cossack with

snow on his boots standing next to you waving his joint, and by God or Lenin you won't be able to write a damn word for Frankie Howerd without it going before some commissar committee.

JOHN
It can't be worse than Captain Beverley-Houghton-Twist, retired, vetting our work.

*Cut music and light FX.*

GEORGE
Don't worry about Beverley. He got a bowler hat and a posting to the Beeb to make up the numbers. He's bomb happy, just right for Light Entertainment.

*They exit toilet.*

GEORGE
John, listen, you might have dropped out of Sandhurst but you're still on the firm. Got it?

JOHN
Queen and Country Limited? You must be joking, George.

GEORGE
What you have trained for is still your Primary Objective – The Defence Of The Realm. And as it happens, young Johnno, you're ideally placed to help us. Look where you've finished up?

JOHN
Aeolian Hall?

GEORGE
If we'd put you to sleep and sent you here it could not have worked out better. You've even got pacifist credentials.

JOHN
For what? A Warsaw peace conference? Me and Picasso? I'm not going, George.

GEORGE
Keep your ears to the ground. Listen. Report back. Give me a name when you have one.

JOHN
A name?

GEORGE
Keep up the good work, John. Onwards and upwards. Regards to Johnny Speight, Terry Nation and Dick Barry. Associated London Scripts! What a hot-bed of talent. All under one roof. Ideal. Easier to keep an eye on them. Anything you want, any time, let me know… won't you? Don't go short.

*GEORGE exits.*

END OF ACT I

## ACT II

## SCENE 11

JOHN
We were issued maps and gas masks and instructed to turn up at 13.00 hours at the Houghton-Twist love nest in the heart of the countryside. Johnny Speight was nervous to see so much grass and trees.

*Summer bird song. Cast make this and other sound FX.*
*Enter JOHN, JOHNNY, TERRY/ DICK.*

JOHNNY
It's like fucking Hyde Park has escaped. They should concrete over the lot and make some decent car parks.

*JOHNNY mimes pressing front door bell. It doesn't work.*
*TERRY/DICK mends it with a pocket screwdriver (mime of course) – presses bell.*

JOHN
Ding.

JOHNNY
Dong.

*Enter BEVERLEY, dressed in tropical army gear (Bridge Over The River Kwai). Incongruously he wears his usual shoes, socks and suspenders. He carries an officer's cane. He consults his watch and counts down.*

BEVERLEY
Four, three, two, one, zero…

*He opens front door.*

BEVERLEY
In you come lads ! Chop-chop !

*The visitors enter.*

BEVERLEY
Did you have a nice trip? Come through the village, did you?

JOHNNY
No, we dropped out of the fucking sky.

BEVERLEY
Like the Japs did in Kuala Lumpur. And they came up in submarines and from the left and the right in a pincer movement... It's a lovely spot, isn't it? Yes. without fear of contradiction let it be said... to Johnny foreigner or anyone else who may come selling pegs on our door step – or cleaning products, yes... oh, yes... this little village is a microcosm of England.

JOHNNY
So where's the little slums and the little factories belching smoke?

BEVERLEY
Ah, there Johnny you have me. Let me put it this way... We are the best that England has to offer...

JOHNNY
Based on the worst that England is trying to hide.

BEVERLEY
Good point, Johnny. We need a social conscience, and you are it. I see glimmerings too in John. But not in Terry, or in Dick. Terry is the silent type. You don't know what he's thinking. You don't know what he's dreaming up.

TERRY
Daleks.

BEVERLEY
There you are, Daleks. Nobody knows what that means. Well done, Terry. I am a good judge of character. You have to be when the lives of your men depend upon it. And were I giving a stripe to anyone – don't hold your breath – it would be to Dick Barry here. Trusty Dick.

DICK
Have you heard the one about...?

BEVERLEY
No, Dick. Not today, please. My corporal. Beware the barrack room lawyers.

JOHN
So what's so special about this village, Beverley? It's the sort of place you could expire in without anyone noticing.

BEVERLEY
Good point, John. This is the ideal place to fade away, like an old soldier. Yes, one day I shall start curling up at the edges like an old photograph…

JOHNNY
Or an old cheese sandwich.

BEVERLEY
Johnny, you are paid to lampoon the likes of me, and therefore I bear you no ill will. Sharpen your talents upon the image I present. By all means. It's not all of my self that you see. Yes… no… and yet again I say unto you… whatever is lovely and of good report; if there be any virtue, if there be any praise, think on these things. Fall out, Sergeant Major. Well done. Well done, chaps. We saw them off. The blighters. And when they come back – we'll see them off again.

JOHNNY
Fucking hell. It's like being buried inside a coffin without a bell.

BEVERLEY
Yes, indeed. Everything changes and nothing changes. We have had a death in the village recently. Nature taking it's course. Leaves shed. The Major – our local Major – has gone to meet his Maker.

JOHNNY
Who makes fucking Majors? Same fucking Maker who made fucking dinosaurs.

BEVERLEY
The upshot is that since the Major died last month, I am next in line in this 'ere village to take the salute at the war memorial. That's good news.

JOHN
How did he die? The Major?

BEVERLEY
It was a killing. A slaying on the doorstep.

JOHN
Did anyone see it?

BEVERLEY
I said the fly. With my little eye. I saw him die.

JOHNNY
You had everything to gain, Beverley, by his demise. Your heart's desire to take the fucking salute next Remembrance Sunday.

BEVERLEY
I know how this looks, Johnny, but you won't be able to pin it on me. Like the King did with my MC, God bless him.

JOHNNY
I hate all these medals and memorials. It's fucking glorifying war. They should give a medal for cowardice. I'd fucking take one.

BEVERLEY
I respect that point of view, Johnny. I know you did your bit.

JOHNNY
In the fucking cookhouse.

JOHN
You should have been cooking for the SS. We'd have won the war much quicker.

TERRY
You say we're having lunch at the pub?

BEVERLEY
Yes, Terry. Judy is indisposed, therefor the catering has been moved to the Blue Boar. See company orders.

JOHN
Will she be putting in an appearance?

BEVERLEY
It's doubtful, John. She has a migraine. Poor sweet ravished bird of youth. She cannot grow old nor shall the years decay. All the vanishing creams in the Kingdom must be summoned to her bedside. May I fill your glasses? Or in your case Terry, your bottle of milk?

TERRY
No thanks, Bev.

BEVERLEY
Are you sure you wouldn't prefer a glass?

TERRY
What's the point? Unless it makes you feel more comfortable.

BEVERLEY
No, no, Terry. I admire bohemians. And you, Dick, are you happy with your apple?

DICK
Yes, I'm content.

BEVERLEY
You can always put it aside and start a fresh one.

DICK
No, I like to finish what I've started.

BEVERLEY
That's a good trait. Believe me, Dick. I could be listening to General Montgomery. He always finished the job.

JOHNNY
He finished the fucking Airborne at Arnhem.

BEVERLEY
That's a bit below the belt, Johnny. *He moves to cocktail cabinet.*

Same again then.

JOHNNY
We haven't had the first fucking drink yet.

BEVERLEY
Haven't we? Difficult to tell when you're miming.
*He serves mime drinks.*
After which we might go and have a look at the Alsatians in the kennels.

JOHNNY
We saw the fucking Alsatians on the way in, Beverley.

BEVERLEY
Actually they're German Shepherds.

JOHNNY
Yeah, like our fucking Royal Family, they've changed their names too.

JOHNNY
I see you've got a flagpole in the garden.

BEVERLEY
For St George's Day. Yes. And occasionally it is flown at half mast. When a member of the Royal Family dies. Which they often do. Unfortunately.

JOHNNY
It's fucking incredible. It's like the Eagle's Nest in reverse. Alsatians. Fucking flag poles…

BEVERLEY
I hope you draw no comparison between Eva Braun and Judy. Though she does like making home movies… which could interest young John there.

JOHNNY
Nationalism is how wars start, Beverley.

BEVERLEY
I don't know how wars start, Johnny, but I jolly well know how to finish them.

## SCENE 12

JOHN
After a decent lunch at the Blue Boar, Terry and Dick motored back to London. Johnny and I decided to book at the Inn for the night, then walked back to the cottage with Beverley. Still no sign of Judy. We went to visit the kennels…

*Ensemble act as dogs in a line of kennels, barking.*
*Enter BEVERLEY, JOHNNY and JOHN.*

BEVERLEY
Betty looks after the kennels. She's a wholesome woman from the village whose husband fell into a threshing machine, unfortunately, widowing her.

*BEVERLEY mimes opening enclosure gate.*

BEVERLEY
In you come, then. Chop chop !

*They enter kennel enclosure. The dogs are not running free.*

BEVERLEY
Judy's lost interest in dogs, like she loses interest in everything I'm afraid. Me included. Never mind. Such is life…

*The dog barking is subdued under BEVERLEY's speech.*
*Now as JOHN and JOHNNY tickle the dogs they become noisy.*
*One dog takes interest in BEVERLEY's cane and takes it in his mouth.*
*Business.*

BEVERLEY
Johnny likes that puppy, don't you, old boy? Actually it's a golden Labrador. We had a small litter, that's the last one. Give it to Connie as a wedding present, if you like it. From me and Judy…

*BEVERLEY mimes giving the dog to JOHNNY. They exit the enclosure.*

BEVERLEY
It's had all the inoculations. So did I before I went to Burma and chased the

Japs back where they came from.

*JOHN and JOHNNY exit to house.*
*BEVERLEY stays behind a moment to address the dogs.*
*The dogs listen and bark attentively.*

BEVERLEY
They were fanatical, the Japanese, but we broke them. Me and Bill Slim. Like we'll break the spoilers at the BBC. My God, whoever thought of putting an Irishman in charge of Internal Security? George Beckett! He had an uncle died in the post office in O'Connell Street, 1916. That's the last man you want keeping your files.

*BEVERLEY exits to barking dogs.*
*Ensemble exit.*

## SCENE 13

**JOHN**
Johnny took the puppy and decided to go back to London after all. The fresh air had sobered him up. So I was left to catch the train in the morning. Because I didn't have anything to go back to… I was really making it all up as I went along. I decided to get pissed on my own. But you can't sometimes. It just won't come. In the Blue Boar that evening, quite late, I was sitting on my own…

*JUDY enters.*

**JUDY**
Hello. Mind if I join you?

**JOHN**
Mrs Houghton-Twist. I thought you were indisposed.

**JUDY**
I was. Now I'm disposed. And it's Judy. Beverley said you were down here on your own and might need cheering up. So here I am. Do you want me or not?

**JOHN**
Yes, alright, Judy, I'm just surprised. Is Beverley coming? Is he on the way?

**JUDY**
No, why should he be? Haven't you had enough of him? For one day? Why are you drinking on your own? Are you an alcoholic, darling?

**JOHN**
I don't know. I've never thought about it. You mean like Scott Fitzgerald? Or Brendan Behan? Or Hemingway?

**JUDY**
You don't have to copy people, do you?

**JOHN**
Yes. I do. It's quite important. I mean, I don't know any other way.

JUDY
You look utterly lost. Are you waiting for the right person to come along?

JOHN
I think I am.

JUDY
You think too much. You're far too serious for somebody who's writing comedy. Look, I don't want to interrupt anything. If you are about to make an important discovery. If something mind-shattering is coming to the surface ?

JOHN
No. I was wondering – can you have a nervous breakdown and not realise you've had one?

JUDY
They're the best sort, darling. Happens all the time. I've ordered tea for two, to get you on the wagon. Do you mind me looking after you for a few minutes? I don't want to smother you. To mother you.

JOHN
You're not old enough to be my mother.

JUDY
Thanks for mentioning it. So what has Beverley been telling you today? Has he been entertaining you with tales of village life?

JOHN
Yes, definitely. He was very chuffed about taking the salute at the next Remembrance Sunday parade because someone's shot the local major.

JUDY
Shot?

JOHN
Killed. As in murdered.

JUDY
Beverley told you that? He is lying again. No-one's shot the Major since the battle of The Somme.

JOHN
That's a coincidence. I was in Somme Company.

JUDY
Some company ?

JOHN
No, Somme Company. It was some company.

JUDY
The Major has been put into a twilight home by long-suffering relatives. Of course that's too dull a story for Beverley to tell.

JOHN
Why would he lie?

JUDY
He's a compulsive liar, darling.

JOHN
But what's his motive?

JUDY
To make everything madly entertaining. So that nobody will ever leave him. Beverley's worst fear is of boring people. The village becomes an Agatha Christie film set and… *She imitates Beverley smoking his pipe.* 'The BBC is a nest of spies and agitators, Judy'. He's even got poor old George Beckett down as a Commie mole. All George does is to shuffle paper all day long for Personnel.

JOHN
I don't know about that. Beverley says George Beckett had an uncle in the Easter Uprising.

JUDY
They're all plotting against each other at the BBC. It's a continuation of the

war by other means. They're children. They've never grown up. They all had a good war and they don't want it to end. They don't know how to live a normal life.

JOHN
Nor do I.

JUDY
Beverley longs to take the salute. It's his grand passion and it's utterly pathetic. It's pointless because there's another retired army wallah moving into the village of higher rank.

JOHN
Order of seniority.

JUDY
You know who's moving here? Don't you?

JOHN
Do I?

JUDY
George Beckett.

JOHN
Was he a major in the war?

JUDY
In the commandos, darling. He plays the piano divinely. And paints.

JOHN
But it's a deliberate provocation if George Beckett knows Beverley's feelings. Why this village? There are plenty of other villages with war memorials to move to. France is full of them. Is that what they fought for? The right to be so trivial?

JUDY
The trouble is darling, the army has trained them to be killers for years and now set them loose in the Home Counties. They're still quite dangerous. I

woke up the other night and Beverley was attempting to strangle me. He thought I was a Jap who'd got behind the lines.

JOHN
Not a Jap who'd got into bed with him?

JUDY
That would have been more interesting. Let's talk about you. What are you going to do with your life? Write jokes for ever?

JOHN
I don't write jokes.

JUDY
Sorry.

JOHN
I want to be a playwright. For the Royal Court. I'd like to be an Angry Young Man.

JUDY
You're far too good natured.

JOHN
There's a lot to be angry about.

JUDY
Can't you just keep writing for Light Entertainment? You'll make yourself ill writing plays, darling.

JOHN
It's about caring, Judy.

JUDY
It's about not fucking caring, darling.

JOHN
You don't have to be ill to write plays, do you?

JUDY
You probably do. Your role models are all alcoholics.

JOHN
Anyway what is ill? Was I ill to leave the army? I was not invalided out. Because I did not want to kill people? Does that mean I had a nervous breakdown? I made a rational decision.

JUDY
We rationalise after the fact, darling. We don't know what moves us. We don't know when we're heading for the rocks.

JOHN
Fuck me, Judy. What with Johnny Speight and his Ibsen. Read Ibsen, he says, read fucking Ibsen. Read The Fucking Dolls House. So I do. Then I come here and find it isn't an Agatha Christie thriller after all but Ghosts, Mrs Alving. Are you planning to throw yourself in the mill race?

JUDY
No, darling. We don't have one. I could jump off a footbridge onto the A1, but it's not the same thing, is it?

JOHN
No.

JUDY
Stick to overdose.

*BLACKOUT. LIGHTNING and THUNDER FX, (loud, real).*
*In lightning we see BEVERLEY in the storm wearing a poncho over his tropical gear.*
*Cut FX.*
*BEVERLEY is standing before JUDY and JOHN*

BEVERLEY
Greetings one and all. I was out for an evening stroll and I thought I'd just pop in and say 'Greetings one and all. Is everybody happy?'

JUDY
Yes we jolly well are. Now bugger off, Beverley.

BEVERLEY
Meaning what?

JUDY
You've come to spoil things, haven't you?

BEVERLEY
No, I haven't.

JUDY
Yes, you have.

BEVERLEY
What gave you that idea?

JUDY
Let me breath. Leave me alone. Can't I have a life of my own in this God forsaken village ?

BEVERLEY
Of course you can, my precious. You can have anything your heart desires. For I am the good wizard who with his wand casts magic spells to make your dreams come true.

JUDY
My dream is to have a night off from you, Beverley.

BEVERLEY
Granted. Overnight leave from barracks. Issue a pass, sergeant major.

JOHN
Look, excuse me, I'm in the way here.

BEVERLEY
Sit down, Antrobus. Fear not. All is well and all manner of things shall be well. I am merely doing the rounds. Orderly Officer. Checking the lines. Making sure the sentries are awake. That the post is secure.

JUDY
I'm going to the loo, Beverley. When I come back I expect to see a Big Hole

where you are standing, OK?

BEVERLEY
Wilco, Judy. Roger and out.

*JUDY exits.*

JOHN
I'm sorry. I mean, I'm not sorry. I'm never sorry. That's beside the point. But I cannot catch the last train because it's gone.

BEVERLEY
What's that?

JOHN
I'll be saying goodnight. I'm off to my room to read. Could you say goodnight to Judy?

BEVERLEY
Please, sit down. You don't understand, do you? No you don't. This is not a sleepy little hamlet where nothing happens. A sterile backwater for tadpoles. People here are alive, vibrant, modern. Controversial. As I am prone to say in my warm up before every show… Anything can happen and probably will. So sit back, relax, and enjoy the proceedings. And do be generous in putting your hands together to show your appreciation. Thank you. Good night, John.

*BEVERLEY exits, as JUDY enters.*

# SCENE 14

JOHN
I bought a motor. My first. It was a lot of fun in those days. Freedom of the road as Mr Toad says.

*JOHN and JOHNNY mime being on car journey – JOHN driving. Both singing. Zambesi…*

JOHNNY
Another fucking guest to visit in the heart of the fucking countryside. AE Matthews. He's dead, isn't he ?

JOHN
Yes.

JOHNNY
Then how's he going to learn his fucking lines ?

JOHN
He'll be better than Anthony Steele was last week.

JOHNNY
*Looking at passing scene.* What's that ?

JOHN
A cow.

JOHNNY
I can't believe you had it away. You had your leg over? You had your fucking oats? It's Beverley's wife, you twot.

JOHN
He doesn't have to know what actually happened.

JOHNNY
He set the whole fucking thing up, didn't he? Beverley. He sent her to see you, you Charlie. You know Beverley Twist's favourite film, don't you? Jules and fucking Jim ! He'd have you riding a bike round the village with her on the fucking handlebars. He's ruthless. Don't underestimate him.

JOHN
What do I do?

JOHNNY
Pretend it never happened. Deny everything, I can't believe you're such an idiot. You're naive, you are. You're fucking wet behind the ears.

JOHN
We're turning left. Stick your hand out.

*JOHNNY mimes knocking his hand against the window.*

JOHN
Wind the window down !

*JOHNNY winds window down and stick his arm out.*

JOHN
I think she's fond of me.

JOHNNY
Yeah, I'm fond of you, John. I don't invite you to fucking Eastcote for a ménage à trois. It never happened. And watch that fucking Gilbert Harding.

JOHN
Why?

JOHNNY
He wants you to go to supper with him and Nancy Spain.

JOHN
Yes, so? He's interested in my career. Left!

*JOHNNY stick his arm out.*

JOHN
Right...

*JOHNNY misunderstands JOHN and puts his right arm across.*

JOHN
It doesn't matter where I go you always think someone's after me.

JOHNNY
Well I'm not fucking jealous, if that's what you think. It's your arse, mate. I don't care what you do. I don't care what any twot does. I've got my own plans.

JOHN
What are they?

JOHNNY
Like Stalin mate, I work on a 'five year plan'.

JOHN
What, are you building a hydro-electric dam in Northolt and moving the population to the Isle of Wight?

JOHNNY
Something like that, yeah. This country's fucking finished, mate. It's getting worse.

JOHN
I thought you believed in progress, Johnny.

JOHNNY
Yes, I do. But... but sometimes things have to get worse before they get better. Which is why all those cunts giving money to charity are getting up my nose. They are merely covering up the blemishes of capitalism.

JOHN
Yes, well I don't give money to charity.

JOHNNY
I do. When it's clear it advances my fucking career. That is the only exception. Not to do good. That is an unfortunate by-product.

JOHN
'It is only by the outrageous excesses of capitalism that the workers will be brought to revolution'. Left!

*JOHNNY sticks his arm out.*

JOHNNY
And we have a part to play.

JOHN
What, in the revolution?

JOHNNY
Not at this stage. In being excessive capitalists, right? Not fucking do-gooders.

JOHN
But you bought a poppy last November.

JOHNNY
You don't have to stand out like a prat.

JOHN
So your five year plan is to become a successful capitalist?

JOHNNY
That is the first stage, yes. Johnny – Twenty Thousand Pound A Year – Speight.

JOHN
That's more than twice what the directors are earning today. Ray and Alan. Spike. Eric.

JOHNNY
You got to think big or you go backwards.

JOHN
Rolls Royce and a big cigar.

JOHNNY
Nothing wrong with that.

JOHN
It doesn't appeal to me. I do believe in sexual freedom.

JOHNNY
Sex is a joke. A cosmic fucking joke. We shouldn't have to procreate. There should be some other fucking way.

JOHN
Don't you mean some other fucking way? We're stuck with it. So we might as well enjoy it.

JOHNNY
*Looks at passing scene.* There's that cow again ?

JOHN
That's a different cow, Johnny.

JOHNNY
You'd be better off paying for it, mate, than what you're doing. Cos there'll be a price to pay, you can be fucking sure of that.

JOHN
Left !

JOHNNY
We're going round in fucking circles, you twot !

JOHN
Well who wants to see AE Matthews?

## SCENE 15

JOHN
Despite Speight's advice I continued to see Judy. It seemed simple enough. She would come to London on a shopping expedition and we would meet and go to the cinema and then back to my place. Judy said Beverley knew she was seeing me and approved – because she needed a pal for – sex, I suppose – but I don't know if she told him we went to the cinema. How do I know what went on between them? There was certainly no three in a bed nonsense – Johnny's fevered imagination, that was – always having to watch your arse. She didn't mind if I went out with other women, she said, so I felt quite liberated. She never stayed the night. I felt we were in a French movie actually, but then French movies – in those days – came to a climax. Like when I was invited to Judy's birthday party in the country…

*BEVERLEY enters wearing regimental blazer. He carries his cane between his teeth because both hands are occupied to put up a sign 'Happy Birthday'. JOHN helps him.*

BEVERLEY
*With stick in mouth:* I've booked you in at the Blue Boar.

JOHN
Thank you.

BEVERLEY
I've got you a special rate.

JOHN
I don't mind paying that.

BEVERLEY
On thirteen guineas a week plus overseas repeats I should jolly well think not.

*They sit down.*

BEVERLEY
It means a lot to me that you've come down to the country for Judy's birthday… *Realising that he still has the stick in his mouth, he takes it out.* It

means a lot to me that you've come down to the country for Judy's birthday It's the BIG FOUR O. At least we got that far.

JOHN
I've never been able to understand age. It's not something that really happens to me. The watcher. The observer.

BEVERLEY
Every year you have a birthday, Antrobus.

JOHN
I was never born. Look, let's not get into this, Beverley. You can choose. Life's a trap, none of us get out alive. I mean OK, if you want to buy it. It's tempting. I mean it's fucking pessimistic, what more do you want?

BEVERLEY
I fear The Frankie Howerd radio show has made inroads on your morale. Would you like another bottle of milk?

JOHN
No, I haven't touched this one. It's Terry Nation drinks milk. Not me.

BEVERLEY
Oh, right. I've got six pints in of dairy cream, so we won't go short. Are you sure you won't have an apple?

JOHN
That's Dick Barry. He eats apples all the time.

BEVERLEY
Well if you change your mind and decide you're either Dick Barry or Terry Nation, you are well catered for.

JOHN
Thank you. For the moment I'm content to be John Antrobus. But the moment is passing.

BEVERLEY
It's good to be able to live in your own skin.

*JUDY enters – dancing – singing « happy birthday to me ! »*
*The others join in.*
*She gives John a big lipstick kiss.*

JUDY
Hello, John.

JOHN
Hi Judy.

JUDY
What have you given him milk for? In a bottle? *To John.* Did you ask for that?

JOHN
Yes.

BEVERLEY
He's covering up for me. I thought he was Terry Nation. Or Dick Barry. All writers look alike to me.

JUDY
Of course he's not Terry Nation. You don't imagine I'd be snogging Terry Nation behind your back, do you? Once a week in town, darling. To the Odeon then back to his place.

BEVERLEY
I think Terry's the pick of the bunch. 'We will destroy you' I don't know why he keeps saying that.

*BEVERLEY takes the bottle of milk.*

JUDY
If you like him so much you snog him…

BEVERLEY
Perhaps I will. *He gives John a drink.*

JUDY
Don't give John that. He doesn't drink these days, do you?

*JUDY takes the drink from JOHN – gives it to BEVERLEY – who decides to drink it.*

JOHN
Only when I'm with Johnny Speight. Which is quite a lot. Or sometimes on my own. I go to Yates Wine Lodge in Portobello Road and drink a bottle of wine. They've got lots of mirrors. You see yourself at different angles. One receding to infinity.

JUDY
I'm keeping him on the wagon, Beverley.

BEVERLEY
Well done, Judy. Give him a lemonade. He wasn't born, he told me earlier. I don't know where that came from?

JOHN
It's mathematics. If you weren't born you can't die. You can't be eternal and mortal. You can't start off mortal then suddenly become eternal. Either you can measure something. It's got a beginning and an end. Or... you're looking at it. You are the measurer.

BEVERLEY
Well you're better to talk to the chaplain about that.

JOHN
I saw him at Sandhurst. I said I can't be confirmed because I'm not sure I believe in God and I don't want to kill people. He said the Bishop won't mind. Faith will come. I said, well I mind. It will be my finger on the trigger. Never mind the bishop! Or did I say that? Probably not. Anyway it's an anecdote. All characters have anecdotes to support them.

*He spins round and collapses onto the floor, from which position he enjoys the scene.*

BEVERLEY
I believe you left Sandhurst under a cloud, Antrobus. The Royal Military Academy. Now if you were buggering somebody, all well and good, but this pacifist talk...

JUDY
Oh leave him alone, Beverley. He's not a bugger.

BEVERLEY
I'll take your word for it, Judy.

JUDY
It's quite obvious being sober is not going to work tonight. So let's all get sloshed.

*JUDY pours big drinks for everyone. She downs her own drink in one go.*

BEVERLEY
Steady, Judy.

JUDY
And stop calling him Antrobus. His name is John.

*JUDY snatches the cane from under Beverley's arm, and points it at him.*

JUDY
You're not in the officers' mess.

*A chase ensues as BEVERLEY tries to retrieve his cane.*

JUDY
It was bloody nice of him to come all this way to see us.

JOHN
Bloody nice !

JUDY
On my bloody birthday !

JOHN
On her bloody birthday !

BEVERLEY
Another year younger! Forty? It's like having two twenty year old's skipping around the place!

*As JUDY skips over JOHN. JOHN makes a bigger obstacle for BEVERLEY to jump over.*

JUDY
Stop it. I don't need that sort of encouragement, Beverley! I know it's all falling to pieces. Everything is disintegrating.

BEVERLEY
With age comes the gaining of wisdom.

JUDY
And the sagging of breasts, darling.

BEVERLEY
Nonsense, darling. We made our dream come true. We built our little nest. *Sings.* We'll build a sweet little nest, somewhere in the West, and let the rest of the world go by!

JUDY
Shut up! You're boring us all again! John Antrobus could stay in London where there are still some exciting people.

BEVERLEY
The ones you didn't run over in the blackout.

JUDY
He doesn't have to spend his time with old farts like us! *She still has the stick.* You love this thing more than anything else in the world.

*JUDY throws the stick down and turns to exit.*

BEVERLEY
Play the game, old girl.

JUDY
The game is over, old boy.

*She exits.*

BEVERLEY
Emotional creatures, what? Cheers.

JOHN
Cheers.

BEVERLEY
Never could understand women. Big failing on my part. I look for an explanation in nature, Nation...

JOHN
Antrobus.

BEVERLEY
Yes. What I see is stags. They get on fine except when it comes to the rutting season. Then there's a clash of antlers. The young stag, he tries his luck, but the Old Un sees him off in a cloud of dust. Cos the Old Un, he has all the does to himself – at least for another year. And that's good enough for me. A year at a time. So you've come rutting, have you?

JOHN
I haven't had a chance to give Judy her present.

BEVERLEY
Oh, she'll be back. I shouldn't worry about her. You think a lot about her, don't you? Where she is? What she's doing? What she's up to now?

JOHN
I've bought her a negligee. Couldn't think what else to get.

BEVERLEY
Ideal. A negligee, yes. What a good idea.

JOHN
I wasn't quite sure of her size.

BEVERLEY
Oh. Weren't you?

JOHN
You can go back to Harrods and change it. I've got the receipt here.

BEVERLEY
All the bumph. All the paper work. Good show. Splendid. Miles and miles of red tape, eh? Stretching back to Whitehall. Well me and Bill Slim, in the jungle, we didn't have any time for that. We concentrated on the job in hand. Killing Japs. Not indenting for toilet rolls. Or paper clips. Like I have to do at the Beeb. You know, Antrobus, in some ways it was a damn sight easier to be a killing machine.

*Enter GEORGE BECKETT, miming carrying a gift.*

GEORGE
Am I late?

BEVERLEY
Not at all. Come in George. You came through the garden, did you? Know your way round the neighbourhood. George is a local now. He's bought the Grand Manor. I tug my forelock.

GEORGE
Hello there, Johnno. Nice to see you off parade. No names, no pack-drill, eh? Is that it? But I'm still waiting for you know what...
*Taps his nose. Takes a glass from Beverley.* Cheers. I've already had a few. Socialising does not come easy to one such as me. Unless I'm oiled like a sardine. Mind you, Beverley, there are some occasions which are extremely social and which need extreme oiling. I've brought your Missus a present. I hope you don't mind. It's a negligee.

BEVERLEY
Another negligee. Thank you. George. I'll put it on the pile of negligees. I'm glad I bought her a set of potting tools. To ring the changes.

JOHN
You're looking well, George.

GEORGE
It's all the bloody country air, Johnny boy. And the damn gossip. This is like

a dormitory village for the Beeb. Bloody Toytown it is, and I'm Larry The Lamb – Baaa!

BEVERLEY
It's good to have you aboard, George.

GEORGE
Oh we're changing metaphors, are we? Right me hearty! Break open a crate of fish fingers! So, Johnno, how goes the writing game?

JOHN
Thanks for asking, George. OK. George and Alfred Black have commissioned me to write some sketches for Arthur Haynes on ITV.

BEVERLEY
ITV.

GEORGE
Commercial television.

BEVERLEY
It will never work. It won't last. One television channel is enough for this country. Everyone will be going around with square eyes soon.

GEORGE
They have a chance, Bev. ITV. If they can poach enough talent from Auntie. We're overstaffed.

BEVERLEY
It's scandalous. I'd never go.

GEORGE
Well who'd ask you? You're radio.

BEVERLEY
It's true. I produce pictures of entertainment on a mattress of sound. But I could adapt. I choose not to.

JOHN
They pay well. £50 for a five minute sketch.

BEVERLEY
Who gave you your first break, you whipper snapper? Is that loyalty? To the Charter?

GEORGE
Hang on, Bev. He's not on a house contract.

BEVERLEY
Radio is story telling round the camp fire. It's an ancient art.

GEORGE
For ancient producers. We must move with the times, Beverley. Lord Reith is long gone. Of course I'm very grateful and very humble to remain in my corridor. I shall continue to serve my masters.

BEVERLEY
Where are they?

GEORGE
What?

BEVERLEY
What's one more act of treachery for you, George Beckett?

GEORGE
What do you mean by that, Beverley?

BEVERLEY
I mean this – I'll say it and I'll say no more – there are masters, old boy, and there are other masters. A dog has no calling but to serve he who fills his bowl.

GEORGE
My bowl is filled by the same hand as yours, Beverley. I bark to the same tune. I run to the same whistle.

BEVERLEY
And you've bought an exceedingly expensive kennel. Round these parts in which to rest your haunches.

GEORGE
The Manor House.

BEVERLEY
*Mock duffing his cap.* Which makes you rightfully the squire hereabouts.

GEORGE
Are you implying, by any chance, that my personal finances are dodgy?

BEVERLEY
You obviously have further funding. Perhaps from leaving messages under stones in Regent's Park. Or behind lavatory cisterns in Leicester Square.

GEORGE
I shall communicate with the BBC board of governors in any way I see fit. *Helps himself to another drink.* You've blown my cover, Beverley. It's the same damn conversation every time I come here. This time the performance is for the boy's benefit. However, we are here to celebrate the birthday of a wonderful woman…

*GEORGE fills the other glasses.*

GEORGE
I charge your glasses, gentlemen. I give you a toast. To Judy…

JOHN and BEVERLEY
To Judy.

*They drink.*

BEVERLEY
She'll be down in a minute.

GEORGE
She'll not be down again, Beverley. She's gone to the Manor House. She can take no more of you and the blooming Alsatians. She's bored out of her skull, Beverley. She can't take any more of you inventing yourself the way that you do.

BEVERLEY
She has fled the night? Through the wild lament?

GEORGE
Aye, and she's not coming back, Bev.

BEVERLEY
What are you attempting to transmit, George?

GEORGE
She's left you. For good.

BEVERLEY
On her birthday?

GEORGE
She's running out of time. Judy needs a new lease of life.

BEVERLEY
For you? She's gone?

GEORGE
I'm sorry, Bev. I could have wished for a kinder way to tell this.

BEVERLEY
No, no, I'd rather be pole-axed, thank you.

GEORGE
I wanted to make it more dramatic, Bev. I – I have a gun.

*GEORGE produces a revolver. It is real. He points it at BEVERLEY.*

BEVERLEY
I say, that is a really gun? Not mime? *He takes the gun.*

GEORGE
It is, Bev. It is.

BEVERLEY
Wonders will never cease. It has materialised, no doubt, to add dramatic effect to our scene. *He gives the gun back to George and resumes a threatened posture.*

GEORGE
I wanted to threaten you and say you must let her go or I'll kill you. I'd rehearsed it.

BEVERLEY
But my dear chap, I'm an expert at unarmed combat. I'd chop you down in a moment. I knew she'd go. I knew I couldn't hold her. I knew I'd ceased to interest her – no matter what I said. Or did. No repartee, at which art I pride myself and with which silvered tongue I won her, could now suffice. I was flogging a dead horse. How long has this been going on, George? Under my very nose.

GEORGE
Don't ask.

BEVERLEY
I would have spared young Terry's…

JOHN
John.

BEVERLEY
Yes. His tender ears. If she's gone, she's gone. I don't expect her to return. I hope that I can nurse this heart of stone back to some semblance of one that's beats… where was I? Yes, George, I would have enjoyed for you to come at me. With a knife preferably. Once a Jap dropped out of a tree right in front of Bill Slim.

*JOHN imitates Jap dropping from tree, making deathly shriek.*

BEVERLEY
Good show, John… In ten seconds he was dead. Strangled with his helmet strap. *He gives George the presents.* Take these presents to her. And tell her to stay north side of the village. The south is mine. And the green, where I umpire.

**GEORGE**
OK, Bev. I hope you won't cold shoulder me in the BBC club as a consequence of this night's shenanigans.

**BEVERLEY**
We don't mix work and pleasure, George.

**GEORGE**
There's no point hanging around. The dirty deed is done. If there's anything – anything at all I can do for you, Beverley…

**BEVERLEY**
There is one thing.

**GEORGE**
Name it.

**BEVERLEY**
You can resign from the British Legion so that I can take the march past the salute at the war memorial next Remembrance Day.

**GEORGE**
Done. I'm more concerned about preparing for the next war than mourning the previous ones. I don't want to remember the faces of fallen comrades, thanks. They haunt me enough as it is. Night after night marching past my bed. But behind that spirited platoon comes all sadness, Bev. The Jerry contingent. Those I have killed. And stared at staring back at me. In ditches. Yet sightless… Excuse me, I must go and play the piano, Bev.

*GEORGE exits.*

**BEVERLEY**
He's cracking, George. Did you notice? Playing Schubert's Nocturne in E minor by candlelight won't solve anything. He does not realise what he's taken on.

**JOHN**
It's shocking news.

BEVERLEY
What? What is?

JOHN
Judy. Walking out on you like that.

BEVERLEY
Oh, that, yes. Saw it coming, old boy. Defensive positions well established. Fall back. Give ground. Strategic withdrawal. Unbalance the enemy. Get him out in the open. Then counter attack. Classic manoeuvre.

JOHN
Do you think she'll come back?

BEVERLEY
Do you think I'll have her back? It's a storm in a teacup, old boy. Forget about it. The night is young. Full moon. Whatever happens one of us must stay awake. You never know when they're going to come. Tiptoeing across no mans land. Snipping the barbed wire. Don't shoot off at any shape in the dark. It might be a letter box.

JOHN
What? In no-man's land?

BEVERLEY
Oh yes. It's important that the chaps feel they can write home, wherever they are.

JOHN
I wouldn't want to crawl out into no man's land to post a letter.

BEVERLEY
That's hard on your mother. She'd want news.

## SCENE 16

JOHN
During that first summer at Associated London Scripts, Johnny and I would sometimes sit out on Shepherd's Bush Green across the road from our salubrious premises over a greengrocer's shop. Apart from two writers seeking inspiration, the Green offered sanctuary to office workers, alkies and pigeons...

*JOHNNY and JOHN sitting on a bench – JOHN feeding the pigeons.*

*Sound off : distant trumpet.*

JOHN
Spike's got his window open again. Playing the trumpet. He's good.

JOHNNY
He's no Dizzy fucking Gillespie. You know what he's doing? Spike. He's rewriting *Strinberg's The Father*. He plans to play The Father p-persecuted by women – and f-fucking finishing up in a straitjacket, helped into it by his old nurse. He's made for the part. He could start in a straitjacket, no one would notice.

JOHN
He's always rewriting.

JOHNNY
What ?

JOHN
Spike. Not like us.

JOHNNY
Eh ?

JOHN
Our wastepaper basket is always empty, Johnny.

JOHNNY
Meaning what?

JOHN
Meaning we never revise.

JOHNNY
So?

JOHN
Thus it can be deduced we are never wrong. The point I'm making, Johnny, is that we never alter a word, do we? It's like God has spoken. The tablets have been writ in stone.

JOHNNY
Moses couldn't fucking revise, could he? How much fucking revising are you going to do with a hammer and chisel? It was one fucking draft mate and get on with it you bastards. Ten fucking commandments. In your face. That'll bollocks your brains for a couple of thousand years. Cos you can't argue, can you? It's from God. Almighty. <u>He</u> said so. <u>Him</u>self.

JOHN
Yeah, but our Frankie Howerd script is not the word of God, is it?

JOHNNY
Yes it is.

JOHN
But God is dead.

JOHNNY
I don't need God to tell me what's… f… fucking funny. If we didn't think it was funny we wouldn't write it in the first place.

JOHN
All I said is, it's interesting that we can never be wrong.

JOHNNY
Look, John, I do not get up in the morning to be wrong. I did not look at myself in the fucking mirror this morning and say today Johnny Speight you are going to be wrong.

JOHN
So you're always right?

JOHNNY
I am beyond fucking right and fucking wrong. Right?

JOHN
Like Nietzsche?

JOHNNY
Yes. The judge and jury are inside your head, mate. Ask yourself. Who wrote the fucking rule book?

JOHN
They did. I've only recently realised that my parents are class enemies. I haven't told them yet.

JOHNNY
Oh leave off. Just get on with your own life, John. They've had theirs. Give them a fucking break.

JOHN
It's the truth, Johnny.

JOHNNY
You don't go round telling everyone the truth. It's too destructive. Read your Ibsen. Your Wild Duck. Fuck me, what's the matter with you?

JOHN
Well, there's some people think I had a nervous breakdown.

JOHNNY
You're fucking giving me one.

JOHN
I can give you an example where you have been fucking wrong.

JOHNNY
What?

JOHN
That newspaper interview you gave last week.

JOHNNY
What about it?

JOHN
You said you created the Arthur Haynes tramp character – in that article.

JOHNNY
So?

JOHN
Well I wrote the first Arthur Haynes tramp.

*Enter tramp N°1.*

JOHNNY
You didn't create his character though.

JOHN
Well he had a character.

JOHNNY
No he didn't.

JOHN
Yes he did.

1st TRAMP
Voices.

JOHNNY
He had the character you created for him. He didn't have the character I created for him.

JOHN
He had the character of a fucking tramp, Johnny.

1st TRAMP
I did, I did. I do.

JOHNNY
Well my character had the character of another fucking tramp.

*Enter 2nd TRAMP.*

JOHN
How many tramps are there? Arthur Haynes only played one tramp.

JOHNNY
No he didn't.

JOHN
Yes he did. They both dressed the same.

JOHNNY
Well tramps do. How the fuck do you think tramps dress? Do you think they have a tramps fucking fashion show? London tramp fashion week.

JOHN
I'm just saying you could have acknowledged that I wrote the first Arthur Haynes tramp sketch.

2nd TRAMP
You're laughable

1st TRAMP
I hope so. I've been writ by John Antrobus.

2nd TRAMP
Have you now?

1st TRAMP
Yes I have. With twitch !

2nd TRAMP
Well I been writ by Johnny Speight. Without twitch. But scratching. He has created my character and I am exceeding glad.

1st TRAMP
You don't have a character. Just a raving polemic are you. I know you. An endless tirade against the toffs.

2nd TRAMP
That suit's me fine. It's better than miming meths drinkers. You call that twitch a character?

1st TRAMP
It's a good twitch. It's a lovely twitch. It's the best twitch this side of Ipswich.

2nd TRAMP
No dialogue to speak of. Childish prattle.

1st TRAMP
I sleep in a doorway in Mayfair.

2nd TRAMP
Oh, I can't match that address. I have a skip in Islington. Do visit. My card. *Gives him card.*

1st TRAMP
It's blank.

2nd TRAMP
Yes, I have a bad memory.

*Enter 3rd TRAMP.*

1st TRAMP
Who are you, sir?

3rd TRAMP
Estragon.

2nd TRAMP
Who writ you?

3rd TRAMP
Samuel Beckett.

**1st and 2nd TRAMP**
Ooooh! Posh! Beckett!

**2nd TRAMP**
How literate!

**1st TRAMP**
How well writ he is. Indeed.

**2nd TRAMP**
With all mannerisms.

**1st TRAMP**
And such timing. Note the stillness from which proceeds action.

**3rd TRAMP**
What play, pray, am I in ?

**1st TRAMP**
Of Good Report.

**3rd TRAMP**
This is not Waiting For Godot?

**2nd TRAMP**
I fear not, sir.

**3rd TRAMP**
Then all is lost. I have strayed into amateur territory. What place be this ?

**1st TRAMP**
The White Bear, sir.

**3rd TRAMP**
The dreaded Fringe. And who writ you ?

**1st TRAMP**
John Antrobus

2nd TRAMP
Johnny Speight.

3rd TRAMP
Nothing but bad news. I must leave quickly.

*3rd TRAMP goes to door. Tries to leave. Knocks.*

VOICE OFF
Unless you are an undertaker, go away.

1st TRAMP
Perhaps we can come with you and be rewrit by Samuel Beckett.

2nd TRAMP
Rewrit, rewrit.

3rd TRAMP
Mr Beckett does not do rewrites. I'm sorry.

1st and 2nd TRAMP
Pity.

*1st and 2nd TRAMP embrace*

1st TRAMP
For money ?

3rd TRAMP
He fears success more than failure.

1st TRAMP
He could succeed to fail with us. I guarantee it.

3rd TRAMP
I'll speak to my author but I do not hold out much… hope.

1st TRAMP
With Beckett that's to be expected.

JOHNNY
Fuck Samuel Beckett! I'll fill the world with tramps!

*The TRAMPS scatter and exit.*

JOHNNY
Waiting For Godot – how many poncing people see that ? I'll have tramps on your screens every fucking week. People's tramps! Like Charlie Chaplin did. We both came from the East End slums, mate. We're one in a million.

JOHN
Two in a million.

JOHNNY
And we ain't going back. You can worship the fucking workers if you like but you haven't had to live with 'em. Eat with 'em. Go to their schools. Have lice in your hair! Be shaved bald! Wear hobnailed boots, if you're lucky! Discover Bernard Shaw by sheer fucking luck. And the Unity Theatre with Connie. Bertolt Brecht, mate. We got out. And we're not going back. Even for fucking Christmas!

JOHN
OK Johnny. I understand – but is that an excuse for creating revisionist history? Like your pal, Stalin. History is Darwinian. The strongest history survives.

JOHN
Yes, OK, but I thought we were friends.

JOHNNY
We are f… f… friends.

JOHN
While it suits your purpose.

JOHNNY
Look, John, listen – that fucking building is full of friends, right? Best mates, the directors love each other – except Spike, he fucking hates everyone so it's a level playing field – in and out of each other's offices, laughing and drinking – it's one big fucking party all day long in this agency.

JOHN
Well, what's wrong with that?

JOHNNY
I'm just saying it won't last. The best of friends make the worst of fucking enemies. Stalin was right. Move first. Purge the bastards.

JOHN
But I'm your best friend, Johnny. I mean who's safe?

JOHNNY
No-one.

JOHN
Come on. What would you do if we fell out? I mean I wouldn't even know we'd fallen out. Because you'd move first, while we were still friends. What would you do?

JOHNNY
I wouldn't fucking talk to you any more. Ever.

JOHN
Is that all?

JOHNNY
Well, what you want me to do? Fucking shoot you?

# SCENE 17

JOHN
Johnny kept telling me, forget Judy. I could have forgotten Judy – and I should have forgotten Judy – but I hadn't forgotten Judy. Yes, Speight was right in an ideal world – a Stalinist world – a beyond right and wrong Nietzschean world – but we weren't there yet... I'd heard on the grapevine that George – Judy's intended new hubby – was on a spot of sick leave from the Beeb – compulsory, some said. Between me and her it had gone quiet which was understandable, given the circumstances. Out of the blue I received an invitation from Beckett to come and have lunch at the Gay Grenadier in Soho...

*The Gay Grenadier Restaurant.*
*Dance and music.*
*Enter GEORGE. The MD takes his dressing gown. GEORGE is clad in pyjamas and wearing slippers.*
*Enter GILBERT and young man dressed as woman.*
*They all enter in the dance.*

GILBERT
Have you met my chauffeur ?

SOMEONE
Who does he drive ?

GILBERT
Me, darling. Mad.

*Enter JOHN.*

GEORGE
Hello young Johnno !

JOHN
Why are you wearing pyjamas, George ?

GEORGE
It's my costume. My role calls for it. I'm on sick leave. I'm playing sick. I'm having my compulsory BBC nervous breakdown. It goes on my CV. It's all

smoke and mirrors boyo, believe me. You know something about that, eh ? Now tell me – between you, me and the gatepost were you sick or playing sick when you left Sandhurst ?

JOHN
I don't know anymore, George. The miming's very good in this restaurant, isn't it ?

*WAITER mimes drawing cork from bottle and serving wine.*

GEORGE
Best in London. Very obsequious.

JOHN
How's Judy ?

GEORGE
Best not to ask... *waves.* Hello Guy! Hello Ian! *Confidentially.* Burgess and Maclean. On the firm... Judy sends her regards. No she doesn't. She was lying in bed unconscious when I left this morning.

JOHN
Not an overdose ?

GEORGE
Hard to tell. If she doesn't wake up we'll know, won't we? Don't worry, the cleaning lady knows what to do. She'll phone the ambulance if she has to. It's all manipulation and I'm not having it. I've been sold a pig in a poke, Johnno. Beverley has out-manoeuvred me. I've been out-gunned. He wanted me to have Judy. I should have seen it coming. He was looking to unload his wife. She's totally dependant and ruinously expensive. And she hates my piano playing.

JOHN
I thought she loved it.

GEORGE
For a week after she moved in.

JOHN
Oh, this is bad news.

GEORGE
Well it's news. It's a game. You've got to think about the next move, not worry about the last one.

JOHN
It will blow over. Change is always difficult.

GEORGE
It's either her or loneliness. Judy fills the vacuum. Don't think I don't worry about her. In fact if I didn't worry about her I wouldn't have anyone to worry about. And that could be fatal... My mother, a widow for many years, did not enjoy the best of health, no – several suicide attempts – now she's gone to Heaven. So I'm obviously looking for a replacement. Judy's ideal. I've discussed it all with my psychoanalyst. In the best Freudian tradition he's helped me turn total misery into everyday unhappiness.

JOHN
So you got what you wanted with Judy?

GEORGE
That's being blunt. Talking of Blunt... *he waves.* Hello Anthony !

*As GILBERT'S COMPANION passes near the table to exit from the restaurant, he waves back to George.*

GEORGE
You're not Anthony! We know who you are.

*GILBERT'S COMPANION exits.*

JOHN
Is Anthony Blunt on the firm?

GEORGE
He's on something.

JOHN
George, why are we here?

GEORGE
As opposed to anywhere else? You're looking for motive? Motivation? You're the writer eh? What is the purpose of this scene? Is that it?

JOHN
Well...

GEORGE
You still miss her, don't you? And I hold the key. Not Beverley. She's my woman, cash down and paid up. You're talking to me now. So if your balls ache...

JOHN
I don't have to take this, George.

GEORGE
You do. Sit down, you young buckeroo... The arrangement stands. She's yours weekends. *He hands John an envelope.* You're booked in the Savoy next Friday as Mr and Mrs Dubleck – can you do a Russian accent? And two tickets for a West End show, Saturday night. Plus spending money.

JOHN
*Looks at the tickets.* The Pyjama Game.

GEORGE
It's all on the firm, boyo. Judy is an asset. And I am the asset manager.

JOHN
*Puts envelope down.* You really are sick, George. You think everything is for sale?

GEORGE
If it's not nailed down, yes.

JOHN
Judy is not pass the parcel. So politely, fuck off, will you?

GEORGE
Everything must serve the cause. Everyone. It's all hands to the pump now. Colonel Nasser will nationalise the Suez Canal. If we move into Egypt the Ruskies will deal with Hungary.

*FADE IN RUSSIAN CHOIR AND RED LIGHT FX as before.*

GEORGE
It's tricky. It's a fine balance. H bombs are pointing both ways. There are Reds. Reds under the beds. Troublemakers. Trot's. It's the ideal time for them to strike. Those who would destabilise the Realm. Do you think I give a fuck about Judy when we could be living in a nuclear wasteland tomorrow. Give me a name, Johnno.

*Enter JUDY. The nightmare FX continues.*

JOHN
Give me a life.
*Picks up the envelope.* Gilbert Harding.

*GILBERT calls from across the restaurant.*

GILBERT
Can I have the pleasure of this dance, Tavorich?

*Russian music and ensemble Russian dance.*
*One of the actors carries the Red Flag, or it flies in.*

*As GEORGE's nightmare deepens.*

*A COSSACK joins the dance and eventually GEORGE is caught in the middle of a circle of dancers.*
*The music breaks as GEORGE is cast from the circle onto his knees. As RUSSIANS the actors torment him one by one with the following couplets.*

The Reds are coming, if you've a pal in
The BBC he should mention Stalin

The Reds are coming / The Radio Times
Will list the names / And all class crimes

The Reds are coming / Be sure they can
Check licence in detector Ivan

The Reds are coming Trafalgar Square
Kaput Lord Nelson hello White Bear

The Reds are coming, spare a rouble
Bread queues are back, prices double.

The Reds are coming, nightmare true
Tavarish we're human, just like you.

OMNES
The Reds are coming for you and me
We love Frankie Howerd on the BBC!

GEORGE
*Cries out.* Frankie!


*BLACKOUT*

## SCENE 18

JOHN
Gilbert Harding was never the same after. Call it coincidence but he broke down on that John Freeman, Face to Face, programme and cried. Was he reaching out for help? What were the pressures on him? He died in circumstances normal, but then that South American poison leaves no trace. I don't feel guilty about it. We were writing for the Beeb during the Cold War, there were bound to be repercussions, even in Light Ent. There were bound to be casualties. George Beckett went for a walk in the wood and put a gun to his head. Without making it back to the Beeb. War-time trauma or did someone turn the tables on him? You couldn't tell in those days. Can you now? Judy took the dosh from Beckett's estate – he left her everything – and took off with some ex-RAF bod to Rhodesia. Everything changes. Beverley married Betty, the village woman who's first husband fell into a threshing machine. How much of that he planned we will never know. I mean basically, the rest of us lived happily ever after. Well we lived. We survived. Surviving's not a bad deal when you see what happened to the others...

The Frankie Howerd series was finished. So was our partnership. I was given, or rented my own office down the corridor. Was it a Monday, or a Tuesday, or a Wednesday, I collected up my things to move out...

*JOHN enters office.*
*JOHNNY is reading a newspaper (mime).*
*JOHN packs some scripts (mime).*

JOHNNY
They don't need to fucking repress the workers in this country because they're so fucking docile. As long as they've got their fucking News Of The World, football pools, and a fucking murder and a good fucking hanging every now and again, everybody's happy.

JOHN
We are known for our tolerance, Johnny, throughout the world. And our system of law.

JOHNNY
Don't make me fucking laugh, will you? There's one law for the fucking rich

and another for the poor. A judge, this week – cunt – he said to an Old Etonian up before him for GBH – you've suffered enough having your name dragged into the courts and put him on six month's probation. He'd assaulted a policeman and broken his arm. Even the policeman said 'It was very slippery underfoot that night. I might have gone down anyway'.

JOHN
I nearly got duffed up in the cinema when I walked out during the National Anthem. It's not against the law, is it? I told this bloke I'm a Republican. You stand there if you like, I said.

JOHNNY
How long have you been a fucking Republican?

JOHN
Since last week. And I think we should abolish the House of Lords. It's not democratic, is it?

JOHNNY
It's the only fucking thing going for it. Of course they're twots. Upper class gits…

JOHN
Chinless wonders.

JOHNNY
But the Commons is worse. They're time serving, lick-spittling, pygmies – running around like headless chickens wondering what the population thinks. The population doesn't fucking think. It drinks! And it goes to church. Even worse!

JOHN
Religion is the opiate of the masses.

JOHNNY
You're better off with a drunk. You're better off with Churchill, mate. Him drunk is more fucking lucid than half those bishops sober.

JOHN
I've never seen a sober bishop.

*JOHNNY scratches his right leg, down near the ankle.*

JOHN
Why do you keep scratching your leg?

JOHNNY
What? What? I've told you it's my neurotic safety valve. Connie gave me some ointment to cure it, it made my stammer worse. I'd rather have a sore on my leg and not f-fucking stammer…

JOHN
I'll be just down the corridor then.

JOHNNY
What ?

JOHN
In my office. If you need me.

JOHNNY
I never needed you, John. I never needed fucking anybody, right ?

JOHN
Right.

*JOHN exits.*

JOHNNY
Except Connie… and George Bernard Fucking Shaw !

*BLACKOUT*

*THE END*

Note : In The White Bear production four chairs made up the set, and this fluidity of movement – use of space – should be kept. The actors re-arrange the chairs as required but not in blackout. Mime is constantly used. There is no typewriter, no glasses or other objects... except the skull, an umbrella, Beverley's cane, the Red Flag, the gun. The sound FX are made by the cast, except thunder. The cast of eight made their own music, except for the Russian music. In other words use the variety of talents available in the company.

*(TESSA was also played by young man as woman).*

*Enter FRANKIE HOWERD, silver suit, into spotlight.*

FRANKIE
So this lady came up to me and she said she said hold this baby a moment will you? I said is it yours? She said no a man gave it to me when the music stopped. I said what music missus? And she jumped on a bus. Well you can imagine, what was I going to do with a baby? I couldn't hear any music, and even if I could and it stopped there was no-one to hand the baby on to. I was on me tod. The street was empty. I was alone. I was speechless. I was clueless. But I wasn't baby-less. Oh, no...

*It's as if he goes FREEZE FRAME.*

BLACKOUT

THE END

# LACK OF MORAL FIBRE

## by

# JOHN ANTROBUS

Radio adaptation for BBC Radio 4, The Saturday Play, 20th February, 1999, Director: John Tydeman.

Richard Briers played WING COMMANDER TEDDY WILMOT (Skipper), retired. Now running a pub on the moors.
Brian Murphy played DENNIS, his barman.

The Skipper is trying to cope with a failing business and with his wife ill in hospital using the same character traits that saw him win through at Bomber Command. But civilian life is a different game. Dennis tries to save his friend from decline but it's doubtful this time the Skipper will get home on a wing and a prayer.

This is the THEATRE version.

# LACK OF MORAL FIBRE

*SCENE: An old country pub / hotel on the moors, isolated. The action takes place in the bar.*

*TIME: Immaterial.*

*CAST:*

    *TEDDY, (Skipper) Wing Commander Teddy Wilmot, retired*

    *DENNIS, his barman*

    *MOLLY, Flarepath Molly, wife to Teddy*

    *SERGEANT McCRINDLE, RAF, rear gunner*

    *CAPTAIN DONNELLEY*

    *MOURNERS, as available*

## ACT I

## SCENE 1

*TEDDY is listening to an old radio set.*

RADIO NEWS ANNOUNCER
*Crackly effect behind.*
… And early this morning seventeen bombers returned from the Ruhr… three are missing, believed shot down… one is missing, believed stolen… Any person who has seen a brown Wellington, with RAF markings, should report this immediately to the Air Ministry…

*Fading. Crackle:*

And as the battle for Stalingrad continues, the Red Army tightens its iron grip on General Paulus and the German 6th Army. It is reported that Field Marshall Goering's Luftwaffe has managed to parachute in three tons of contraceptives to their beleaguered troops … Happy Christmas Fritz!

*More atmospheric crackling.*

*DENNIS (he has a slight limp) has entered during radio broadcast. TEDDY becomes aware of his presence and switches off the radio.*

TEDDY
Well?

DENNIS
Well what?

TEDDY
What do you think, Dennis?

DENNIS
You want to know what I think?

TEDDY
I do. For once.

DENNIS
Or how I think, perhaps? Are we a product of our genes and is thought an electrical phenomenon that plays across the neurological circuits, giving an illusion of consciousness? An illusion of decision making? When all the time it is the body running the show.

TEDDY
Put a sock in it, Dennis. What do you think of this radio set?

DENNIS
It's incredible, Skipper. That news broadcast must have been made years ago. During the war.

TEDDY
It's a very old wireless.

DENNIS
That wouldn't explain it. In the normal course of events you would still be getting today's programmes on an old radio set.

TEDDY
Well I know that.

DENNIS
Do you?

TEDDY
Of course I do. I'm not a bloody fool.

DENNIS
Let me put it another way – do you get today's programmes on this set?

TEDDY
I don't know. I've never tried. I just turned it on, for God's sake. I dug it up from an old country sale for ten bob.

DENNIS
There's a lot of it about.

TEDDY
What?

DENNIS
Pardon?

TEDDY
What is there a lot of? About, Dennis?

DENNIS
About Dennis? There's nothing about Dennis. What I do know is , you don't read about it in the papers. Not the full story.

TEDDY
The subject is exhausted. Get off the air.

DENNIS
Wilco Sunray.

TEDDY
Roger and out.

*TEDDY opens the hotel register.*

TEDDY
Have you checked the guests' rooms?

DENNIS
Yes. There aren't any. I looked under the beds.

TEDDY
That tallies with the register. No guests…
*Closes the register.* I have to keep the paperwork in order. The bumph.

DENNIS
We haven't had any guests all winter, you don't need to look in the register.

TEDDY
And you don't need to look under the beds, Dennis.

DENNIS
True. Well, we play games and we keep going. Out here on the moors one begins to doubt one's own existence. It's very cut off. A good place to write a book. My novel...

TEDDY
Now, Dennis, this is the first day of the season – the summer season...

DENNIS
I now declare this hotel open. Shall I cut a ribbon?

TEDDY
All guests...

DENNIS
Yes?

TEDDY
All guests – when they arrive – will get an issue of soap – which they will sign for.

DENNIS
In triplicate.

TEDDY
No, they won't get three bars of soap.

DENNIS
Good. They don't need them. I'm not in favour of too much hand washing, unless you're Lady Macbeth. And she is not expected.

TEDDY
Morning tea will be at seven fifteen, for those so inclined.

DENNIS
Most of them will be inclined horizontally.

TEDDY
Breakfast will be between eight and nine a.m. No late comers will be served, is that clear?

DENNIS
These people are on holiday, Skipper. Assuming any turn up.

TEDDY
We're not running a rest home, are we?

DENNIS
It's not a boot camp either, is it?

TEDDY
Guests need a firm hand. They need a structure, believe me, or they become frightened. Anxious. They start milling around like sheep, looking for packed lunches, bus timetables and spare wellington boots. They start to get on top. There's always one of them emerges as the leader. That's the bastard you have to trip on the stairs.

DENNIS
Guests do need a framework of discipline, yes, in the form of some simple rules of the establishment. Written down and publicly displayed.

TEDDY
Squadron orders, yes. They need responsibilities, guests. They need tasks.

DENNIS
You had that man from Tidworth on the roof last season – mending tiles, remember?

TEDDY
The one who fell off? Yes...he'd have hurt himself badly if he hadn't fallen on his wife. They left in a huff, didn't they?

DENNIS
No, in an ambulance.

TEDDY
Very funny. Glad to get rid of the buggers. No conversation, do you remember? Never heard from them again, did we?

DENNIS
No, we heard from their solicitors. I don't think anybody's coming back from last year. It was a particularly nerve-racking season. You wouldn't let anyone sign in if they had long hair.

TEDDY
Men, you mean? I let a few in on the understanding that they pop into Penzance the next morning for a short back and sides.

DENNIS
They thought you were joking, and went along with it for a holiday with a difference, I suppose. Look, chum, your behaviour has become increasingly erratic. Your regulars will not be coming back. They had to make their own beds last year, then stand by them for inspection… Alright , it's a lark! But you didn't know where to stop. You can't lock people in the coal cellar because of dust under the bed…

TEDDY
That man agreed.

DENNIS
He thought it was fun and that you would let him out soon after… He wasn't that kinky!

TEDDY
I let him out after dark to watch Bridge Over The River Kwai.

DENNIS
By the time he got out he thought he was in Bridge Over The River Kwai! You've got to ease up, Skipper. That is if anybody comes off the road this year.

TEDDY
Off the road? I don't like strangers, Dennis.

DENNIS
That's what a hotel is for, it's the whole object of the enterprise. To take in strangers.

TEDDY
Strangers aren't family. You don't know what riffraff are driving around these days. Looking for trouble. Murderers, rapists... I didn't fight in the last war, Dennis, to see the whole country going to the dogs. Someone has got to maintain standards...

*They are tidying up the bar, prior to opening time.*

DENNIS
About that radio? Do you think we should report it?

TEDDY
Report it? To whom?

DENNIS
To whom it may concern. Perhaps the Defence Ministry.

TEDDY
What's it to do with those wingless wonders? The Ministry of Defence? What's my radio set got to do with them?

DENNIS
We could let them decide that. After all it is war broadcasts we're hearing. Yes. I should think the first thing they would do is to give us a psychological test.

TEDDY
Do you? Well I don't believe in psychology so it wouldn't work with me.

DENNIS
You don't have to believe in psychology for it to work, Skipper. It's like biology. You might not believe you have a liver but it works.

TEDDY
Yours hardly does. You're looking distinctly Chinese these days. The point is, Dennis, the Menace, it is the radio that is wonky. Not us.

DENNIS
I hope you're right. I hope that proves to be the case. *Pause*. Anyway...

TEDDY
Go on.

DENNIS
As long as we haven't been hearing voices.

TEDDY
I've been hearing voices. Yours particularly. And it's very disturbing.

DENNIS
That's a good one.

*They continue to work.*

DENNIS
Permission to speak, Skipper.

TEDDY
Granted.

DENNIS
Do these broadcasts come in any particular sequence?

TEDDY
Sequence?

DENNIS
Of battles?

TEDDY
No. You never can tell – it's all mixed up...

DENNIS
Like a teenager in love. Heartbreak Hotel.

TEDDY
That's us. You were saying?

DENNIS
Oh, yes. You mean it's likely to be, say… say the landings at Anzio? Then Dunkirk?

TEDDY
Those were your battle honours, weren't they? Or dishonours. Your shady past in the army…

DENNIS
Don't start please, Teddy. I'm not your whipping boy. That's not what I'm paid for. If I was paid, that is. I'm not the boastful type so I won't defend myself from your insinuations. I mean, do you get a day by day account of the war? On this 'ere radio?

TEDDY
I've only been listening to it for the last twenty-four hours. As far as I am concerned it's a crock radio set. If I could find someone to complain to, I would. That's what happens when you buy a piece of second hand electrical equipment.

*DENNIS goes to the radio.*

DENNIS
May I?

*DENNIS turns on radio again. REPORTER speaks over crackle of small arms fire.*

REPORTER
*Machine gun fire ,etc.*
And here at Arnhem we're having a hell if a scrap with Jerry. We're fighting on, holding on to this side of the bridge – the huns got the other side of the bridge – and the Poles are fighting each other in the middle of the bridge. It's a bit confused… *Mortar shells exploding…*
But we're brewing up for a tea break. So keep knitting those letters from home, because we're planning to stay here awhile…

*TEDDY switches off the radio.*

DENNIS
Somebody's got a sense of humour. Could be Martians. A sign of intelligence, eh?

TEDDY
If it appeals to your sense of humour, Dennis, it's a sign of infantile regression. This radio set is out of bounds to all ranks from now on. You're not to touch it. Nor to mention the subject of that radio again. Understood?

DENNIS
Loud and clear. Wilco, Skipper.

TEDDY
Roger and out.

*TEDDY exits with crate of empty beer bottles. DENNIS dusts the radio, to find an excuse to examine it. He moves on quickly as TEDDY returns.*

TEDDY
I find it very difficult without Molly.

DENNIS
Of course you do. We all find it difficult without Molly.

TEDDY
I mean what a time to go and visit her sister. Why couldn't she have gone in February?

DENNIS
She did go in February, Skipper.

TEDDY
I know she did. That's what I meant. February, yes.

DENNIS
Time flies, eh? The darts of our mortality do not stop its flight. Would you bring this precious bird to sing upon my lovers grave? It's work in progress.

TEDDY
Danger Poets At Work. Stand well back. I haven't looked at a calendar in months. That's what this place does to you…

DENNIS
The radio doesn't help.

TEDDY
I told you not to mention that radio!

DENNIS
Sorry!

TEDDY
Bring the light ales in, there's a good chap.

*DENNIS exits.*

*TEDDY goes to radio. Examines it. DENNIS returns with crate of light ales. Starts stacking them.*

DENNIS
Where did you get these light ales? I thought the brewery had cut off our supplies.

TEDDY
I opened a new line of credit from an unsuspecting off-licence in Penzance.

DENNIS
You've got the gift of the gab, Skipper, you have, I'll give you that. You can talk people into giving you anything.

TEDDY
I could always scrounge up a couple of extra Lancaster bombers for a Big Do. A thousand bomber raid.

DENNIS
I'll say.

TEDDY
Say what?

DENNIS
Nothing. I'm tuning out some static.

TEDDY
I've always seen it through, you know.

DENNIS
We expect that of Wing Commander Wilmot, DFC and bar. Mind you…

TEDDY
Mind my what?

DENNIS
Mind my bike. It's not always a virtue, Skipper, hanging on till the last moment. There's a time to bale out.

TEDDY
Not while I've got one engine running. I'll nurse the crate home.

DENNIS
It's a different world today, Skipper. With all due respect. They're not dishing out medals in Civvy Street for heroism in the face of bankruptcy, are they? It's hell out here on the moors in winter. Cold. Damp. Mildewy patterns appearing on the wallpaper. Some of them could be of religious significance. Father O'Reilly looked at the one in room Two-O-Three and said it could be symbolic of the Risen Christ.

TEDDY
Yes, His rising cost me a bottle of Drambuie and a taxi home for a drunken priest. Another of your ruinous wheezes, Dennis.

DENNIS
It seemed a good idea at the time. Skipper, frankly your nerves are shot to pieces with business worries. Supply problems from the breweries, as mentioned. Unpaid phone bills. Electricity company threatening to cut you off…

TEDDY
I've got reserves. I've got the paraffin generator in the barn, don't worry. Oil lamps. A box of candles. And I've still got my Webley revolver. I never handed it in.

DENNIS
What's the point of that?

TEDDY
To keep you guessing, chum. Not that you know anything about it.

DENNIS
Mum's the word. I say don't so anything silly, Skipper? I'd miss you dreadfully.

TEDDY
What gave you that idea?

DENNIS
Debt does funny things to a man. Especially the Japanese.

TEDDY
Well I'm not Japanese. They won't get me out of here that easily. It's my little corner of England. I fought for this country, Dennis. I've got a right to a piece of it, by God. I didn't do fifty-nine missions over occupied Europe – over Germany, to be told by some pimply faced onanist in Penzance that my credit's not good enough for a crate of light ales.

DENNIS
Haven't you noticed, Skipper? We're not pulling together anymore in this country. It's every man for himself. I'm alright, Jack.

TEDDY
You're alright, Dennis. Helping yourself. The till's full of your IOU's.

DENNIS
Someone's got to keep you company. Or you'd hit the bottle on your own. Have you seen The Lost Weekend?

TEDDY
No, where did you put it?

DENNIS
I say, you're sharp this morning. Don't cut yourself, will you? Your trouble is, Skipper, if I may venture the opinion and risk incurring your wrath... you don't know when you're beaten.

TEDDY
I'm glad to hear you say that, Dennis. I'm not chucking in my hand, just when the season's started.

DENNIS
You're not in good shape.

TEDDY
It's the only shape I've got, and I'm content to dress it every morning and get on parade.

DENNIS
You've got the morning shakes.

TEDDY
I'm a publican. It's an occupational hazard.

DENNIS
Then change your occupation, chum. I'm talking as a friend.

TEDDY
I don't call that friendly talk, Dennis. I've always had to deal with moaners. The best thing is to get them off the station as quickly as possible. One rotten apple can spoil the barrel.

DENNIS
I'd like to think of myself as a good apple.

TEDDY
Well behave like a good apple.

DENNIS
I'll behave like a toffee apple, how's that? A lick and a promise!

TEDDY
There are some financial problems, yes, I'm aware of them. I'm not sticking my head in the sand. It's been a long winter, but we've got through it. We're out the other side. In one piece.

DENNIS
The vase is cracked and leaking, believe me.

TEDDY
You've been a nightmare to live with.

DENNIS
I only moved in recently. Since Molly went to her sisters.

TEDDY
I know when you moved in, Dennis. In March.

DENNIS
No, I moved in in April.

TEDDY
Did you? What happened to March?

DENNIS
The same as happened to Ray Milland's Lost Weekend. That's why I moved in. Even though it was four weeks before the buses started running, for the summer season. Well now they are running, and…

TEDDY
And you can come and go as you please, eh?

DENNIS
I need to come and go. I need a break now and again from this insanity.

TEDDY
You mean you can't see it through?

DENNIS
Why should I see it through? What's that supposed to mean? I came here to lift your spirits while Molly was away, not to fight World War Two all over again.

TEDDY
If you paid attention, you'd learn something Dennis. You don't see the big picture. You forget. You trivialise. You don't get it, do you? You have no sense of strategy. To lose a battle is not to lose the war.

DENNIS
Well go on then, tell me. Tell me of your Grand Strategy! I'm all ears. Like Dumbo!

TEDDY
You may not have noticed, Dennis, I have a field attached to this property. I have a vision. A dream. I can see that field covered in caravans. And that will bring in plenty of business. It's a double whammy of good fortune, renting out the caravans and boosting business at the hotel where they will doubtless retire in their hordes for fluid refreshment of an evening. Plus meals. And a little souvenir and grocery shop we'll run...

DENNIS
Except that you can't get planning permission, Skipper.

TEDDY
That's a blip on the radar screen.

DENNIS
It's a blip that's been going on for several years, as I recall.

TEDDY
Because the bastards are against me.

DENNIS
The local council. To them you're a foreigner.

TEDDY
I fought for this country and it didn't stop at Plymouth! They owe me their lives! The fact they're not under the heel of the jackboot...

DENNIS
True. All true enough. But you need friends.

TEDDY
What?

DENNIS
Locally. You haven't got any. Except me, and I don't count.

TEDDY
You don't count for anything, that is true.

DENNIS
You've alienated everyone with your…well, let's put it this way, you're a one off, Skipper. Not appreciated round these parts.

TEDDY
I've got friends, what? Good friends. Friends, as it happens, in high places. I've got favours I can call in that will change everything with these minnows in their pond.

DENNIS
You've lost contact with them, ages ago.

TEDDY
Who?

DENNIS
You name them.

TEDDY
It takes one Bomber Command Reunion Dinner, Dennis.

DENNIS
The last Bomber Command Reunion Dinner you attended, correct me if I'm wrong, you had a tiff with Bomber Harris.

TEDDY
Yes, I told him Douglas Bader got the wooden leg and that he got the wooden head. Ha! It got a few laughs.

DENNIS
And it made you a few enemies. Particularly Douglas Bader.

TEDDY
It's not my fault he hasn't got a funny bone in his body.

DENNIS
Well he didn't like the Germans much either, did he? And you're next on his list. Look, what I'm saying is, see reason, old boy. Everybody has moved on. The party's over. The piano's out of tune and the runways have been returned to the plough.

TEDDY
Yes, very nicely put. Well, Dennis my lad, as soon as Molly is back you're out of here. That will be one malingerer less.

DENNIS
Molly's done her bit, Skipper. You can't ask more of her. She's stood by you through thick and thin. This hotel! This place of spirits – various spirits – bottled and etheric – can undermine anybody. You've got to have the temperament for the moors. Because this bloody scenery can take you by the throat. Take my advice and...

TEDDY
I do not require the advice of an undischarged bankrupt, thank you.

DENNIS
I say, that's a bit below the belt.


TEDDY
I'm sorry, Dennis, if that hurt. But I'm the only person round these parts who's taken pity on you. And given you employment as a temporary barman. It's no good sulking. Look, I know you've had a lot of hard luck, old boy. But you're the type that attracts it. You're a loser with a very dodgy war record.

DENNIS
Well, one war hero round these parts is enough, wouldn't you say?

TEDDY
When I was over Germany, chummy, let me tell you, I swore I'd get back. With the help of Lady Luck and my lucky rabbit's paw! Oh yes, you can sneer…

DENNIS
I'm not sneering. It's my favourite story.

TEDDY
Well learn something from it. I kept that picture in my mind – when the flak was coming up and we were dodging the searchlights, and the Lancasters were going down in flames either side of us. With people whose names you had to forget very quickly when you got home. If you could make it home…

DENNIS
And the Messerschmitts were coming in at four o'clock…

TEDDY
No, we'd abandoned the daylight raids, Dennis. Too costly. Left it to the Yanks. Do you know how I kept going? I kept that picture of a little pub, somewhere in the country. With roses over the door, yes and a loyal, sweet wife…

DENNIS
*Sings*: "We'll build a sweet little nest, somewhere in The West – And let the rest of the world go by…" And it all came true! You did marry Flarepath Molly. Who was always waiting for you at the end of the runway, wasn't she? Well done. You made it. It's been a wizard prang. But you can't celebrate forever. The photographs are turning yellow. I can't hear the boys singing in the mess any more…

TEDDY
I know you're trying to rescue the significance of your life by writing the great novel, Dennis. I suggest you save your flowery phrases for that.

DENNIS
I don't expect to be published. It might spoil the anonymity I so cherish.

TEDDY
Your anonymity is quite safe, I assure you, Dennis. I know you avoid disappointment by having no expectations at all. And you're right.

DENNIS
Could be true, Skipper. I give you that one.

TEDDY
It's you that's full of guilt and remorse this morning, and in your weevil way you're trying to project it on to me. Yours is a regrettable philosophy. Hangdog. Hangover.

DENNIS
Who mentioned hangovers?

TEDDY
Can you remember last night?

DENNIS
No. Can you?

TEDDY
I asked you first. And I do remember how the evening started.

DENNIS
And I remember how it finished. So between us we've got it, if anyone should ask.

TEDDY
Dennis, my dear deluded friend, you are in free-fall, your parachute has not opened.

DENNIS
Well, it's not going to hurt until I hit the ground, is it?

*BLACKOUT.*

## SCENE 2

*Later. There is more light in the bar from sunshine outside.*

DENNIS
We're very low on brown ales.

TEDDY
Well recommend the light ales.

DENNIS
Who to?

TEDDY
Anyone who comes in.

DENNIS
Nobody does.

TEDDY
Then we don't have a problem, do we?

DENNIS
I like brown ales.
*He has finished stacking the bottles.*
Right, that's done.

TEDDY
Have you checked the bed linen?

DENNIS
Yes.

TEDDY
Is it damp?

DENNIS
No, but I could sprinkle it.

TEDDY
Just when music hall is dying your talent appears.

DENNIS
I wanted to be a juggler at one time. But I couldn't keep the balls in the air.

TEDDY
I didn't know you had any balls. I heard you lost your wedding tackle at Anzio.

DENNIS
That's a downright lie.

TEDDY
It's your wife that's spreading it.

DENNIS
She doesn't understand trauma. War trauma. Have you read Tennessee Williams?

TEDDY
Never mind Tennessee Williams – did you tread on that pencil mine on the Anzio beach-head? Or did you not?

DENNIS
Yes, I did. My whole life flashed before me. I knew I'd be for it as soon as I took my foot off.

TEDDY
How long were you standing on the mine?

DENNIS
About two hours.

TEDDY
Your life must have flashed before you in slow motion.

DENNIS
Yes, it was like being at the cinema. Very entertaining but no popcorn. Right, I'm off…

TEDDY
Where do you think you're going?

DENNIS
St Ives, on the bus. As I was going to St Ives, I met a man with seven wives. One of them was mine.

TEDDY
I don't remember giving you the afternoon off, Dennis.

DENNIS
No, I decided to take it off. To show some independence.

TEDDY
Oh. That's very unlike you. Very well. Leave granted. However, I'm sure nobody wants to see your miserable face in St Ives.

DENNIS
I've got to show it somewhere. I plan to take my little daughter for a walk. I do have visitation rights. Or I would do if I went to court. But Peggy is not in favour of that sort of thing. No, we'd rather settle matters amicably between us. Reasonably.

TEDDY
What's reasonable about some other bloke living in your house, sleeping with your wife?

DENNIS
I think – I think that's a temporary thing. Quite honestly. He's – he's only down for the season. Peg and I were getting on each other's nerves. I needed some space.

TEDDY
Space? Your wife kicked you out and her boyfriend's dog bit you. You call that giving yourself space? You've probably got rabies. It would explain your behaviour.

DENNIS
There have been some changes, yes. You've noticed? The ground has been moving under my feet recently. I've been having some rather acute emotional problems.

TEDDY
Emotional problems? You're not a ruddy land-girl! You're a failed restaurateur – gone broke. That's not an excuse to go emoting all over the place, and losing your hair. I'd like you to wear a hat in the kitchen.

DENNIS
I've been going through a period of adjustment.

TEDDY
You couldn't adjust your dress before leaving the lavatory, my boy!

DENNIS
I only want to finish my book, Skipper. To get it out of my system. Don't you ever have bad dreams? Don't you wake up sweating? Wondering where the hell you are?

TEDDY
Never. I've got a good conscience, that's why.

DENNIS
You think you can forget. You imagine you're set fair. That you've got your moorings at last. And you can sail on a bright untroubled sea. Well, that's when the storm clouds are brewing up, over the horizon…

TEDDY
What a loser you are, Dennis. I do recall that all was set fair for you once upon a time. All was very well when Captain Cohoun first hit town. Some years ago now, with a suspiciously large gratuity.

DENNIS
My mother had died. I received an inheritance.

TEDDY
How convenient. Wherever the money came from, Dennis, you were certainly able to buy your popularity.

DENNIS
True, true.

TEDDY
You bought your favours. You bought your friendships. You bought your restaurant. You bought your young wife – a local belle – your child bride…

DENNIS
How true. I don't dispute that. There's no need to rub it in. Live and learn, Skipper.

TEDDY
If only you would.

DENNIS
I've learnt not to put my faith in earthly things.

TEDDY
As you don't have a pot to piss in, it's just as well. The cheek of it is, after this utter fiasco and public bankruptcy, you expect to turn around and advise all and sundry. After your marriage collapsed amongst the other debris, you advise me on my marriage. The Skipper's marriage ! And my business! You presume to know exactly what Molly and I should do with our lives…

DENNIS
How about Malta, Teddy?

TEDDY
What?

DENNIS
It is the George Cross Island and with your DFC you should go well together. Sell up and go there! Molly thinks it's a good idea.

TEDDY
Does she? Does she really?

DENNIS
Yes.

TEDDY
Oh, good show. Wizard prang. Everybody's making plans for me behind my back now, are they? All the defaulters and malingerers think they know better than the Skipper, eh?

DENNIS
If you ask me...

TEDDY
Nobody is asking you!

DENNIS
I would like you to learn from my mistakes...

TEDDY
I have learnt. I've learnt that you're dead in the water, Dennis. You've gone belly up and the yellow streak is showing.

DENNIS
If you say so. Who am I to argue? I was merely explaining to you my trauma. War trauma. You have to face the past and make peace.

TEDDY
Don't come to me with your talk of traumas. I've been in the war too. I never had a trauma. Look at me, I'm trauma-less. Your war stories are as wonky as your leg. I don't believe you trod on a pencil mine for two hours.

DENNIS
Believe what you like.

TEDDY
I will. Oh I will, don't worry about that.

DENNIS
I wasn't expecting any sympathy.

TEDDY
And you won't get it from me.

DENNIS
Good. That's very bracing.

TEDDY
You think you can chat me up like some Lyons Corner House nippy looking for a knee tremble.

DENNIS
I like that…

TEDDY
In the Strand.

DENNIS
Regent's Palace Hotel, if you don't mind, old chap. Room 305. No view to speak of but the bed didn't squeak.

TEDDY
I am not impressed by your charms, old boy.

DENNIS
I'm relieved they're wasted on you. You know what, Skipper, I think we should have a couple of these light ales, don't you? If you don't think it's too early, that is.

TEDDY
Very well. If you insist, Dennis.

DENNIS
On me. If you'll take an IOU?

TEDDY
Put it with the others, yes.

*DENNIS writes out IOU. Rings up the till. Serves two light ales.*

DENNIS
I'm feeling rich today.

TEDDY
Don't trust your feelings, dearie. They're as changeable as a pair of nylons.

DENNIS
How many pairs would you like, chum? Cheers.

TEDDY
First today.

*They drink.*

TEDDY
How are you planning to pay those IOU's? May I enquire?

DENNIS
From my wages owed for the last three months.

TEDDY
It won't cover it. Not after deductions for breakages. You ran amok three weeks ago, remember? Running through the kitchen naked, and smashing a lot of crockery, shouting 'Down With Franco'.

DENNIS
I know. I was out there, you know. Spain, yes, the civil war, yes, I – I broke my leg getting off a train. Well, leaping off a train, it was being bombed…

TEDDY
I thought you were standing on a land-mine?

DENNIS
Not there, I wasn't. Not then. Well, better out than in, re the other night. Worth a few breakages. I must have been smouldering like Vesuvius. Did I ever tell you about Naples '44?

TEDDY
Not this morning, Dennis, there's a good chap. Your stories aren't consistent, old boy, and you don't remember. Well I do. Don't say I'm not forbearing of all your foibles.

DENNIS
You're a damn good friend, Skipper. You've been a port in the storm, you have.

*DENNIS serve the light ales.*

TEDDY
I'm not saying you're a bad chap. You're well intended but intentions aren't enough. You have to deliver. Sometime. Somewhere.

DENNIS
Who to? I'd like to deliver to a publisher, that'll do me.

TEDDY
Your trouble is, Dennis, and I must shoot from the hip... You lack Moral Fibre. We had a lot of that in the squadron in Forty Three. Chaps refusing to fly. Not something much known, or talked about. Good chaps most of them. Done a lot of missions. Been through hell. No excuse. If they insisted that no power on Earth would send them up again, we busted their ranks – tore off their chevrons on parade – a public humiliation – and put them on latrine duty. If they were lucky. If not they went to the glasshouse.

DENNIS
Poor buggers. It's scandalous. I've heard about this. Heroes one moment, scum the next.

TEDDY
Bomber Command was on Maximum Effort, Dennis. We were hitting Jerry where it hurt. Showing the Ruskies we were still in the war, too – that was important. By God, yes... after Coventry, Plymouth, London... As Harris put it – as Bomber Harris so aptly stated – before we fell out , that is, when he wasn't believing his own publicity... 'They have sown the wind. They will reap the whirlwind...'

DENNIS
Yes, but those chaps who couldn't go up again – who couldn't fly – they had the equivalent of shell-shock. We've come to terms with that as far as World War One is concerned. But here we are today, talking about the same thing in World War Two. Those flyers in Bomber Command did not deserve to have Lack of Moral Fibre stamped in their pay books. Their rank busted and to be shoved in the stockade. It's a bloody disgrace to have treated them like that.

TEDDY
What do they expect? An apology?

DENNIS
Yes. It's time they had one.

TEDDY
Get out.

DENNIS
What?

TEDDY
You're fired. How dare you impugn the honour of Bomber Command.

DENNIS
Can I finish my drink?

TEDDY
Certainly.

DENNIS
I'm obliged to you.

TEDDY
Don't mention it. Get your kit out of here. You're posted.

DENNIS
Where to?

TEDDY
Please yourself.

*DENNIS put his glass down and exits.*

*BLACKOUT.*

## SCENE 3

*DENNIS stands beside an old suitcase, centre stage. He is reading a letter. He puts it back in the envelope and tucks it into a pocket. He looks around as if saying 'goodbye'. He is about to pick up the suitcase, when...*

*Enter TEDDY.*

TEDDY
Where do you think you're going?

DENNIS
On my travels. Without a donkey.

TEDDY
On your travels? What are you talking about, man?

DENNIS
You fired me . Don't you remember?

TEDDY
Of course I do. I remember everything. You smashed up crockery in the kitchen.

DENNIS
That was the other night.

TEDDY
And now it's daylight. Night and day...

DENNIS
You are the one.

TEDDY
Are you suggesting I don't know what day it is? Don't write to me for a reference, Dennis.

DENNIS
I don't want one. I don't want a reference as a barman, I was helping you out. Because of your war trauma.

TEDDY
My war trauma? I thought it was yours.

DENNIS
No, I've decided your trauma is deeper than mine. Mine shows, it surfaces. It's crazy… But your trauma, Skipper, is totally repressed. Actually you're in danger.

TEDDY
Danger of what?

DENNIS
I don't know. I'm not a mind mechanic. It's a sense I get that you could go off the rails. In a moment you could press the trigger. Anyway that's my assessment. I shouldn't go off and leave you on your own. It would be irresponsible, so I'm having second thoughts.

TEDDY
This is a way you're trying to get your job back, isn't it? It's quite obvious, man. It's only me that's put a roof over your head.

DENNIS
I can get by, that's just a physical problem, a roof over my head. A plate of food. I won't starve.

TEDDY
Are you refusing to go? Must I have you ejected from the premises?

DENNIS
That's my job. Ejecting people from the premises.

TEDDY
Well as a last act kindly eject yourself.

DENNIS
OK… I've done all I can here… *Picks up case.* I can see the bus coming.

TEDDY
Don't beg for your job back by pretending to be my social worker. It's demeaning for both of us.

DENNIS
The game's up, Skipper. Toodle-pip.

TEDDY
Where do you think you're going?

DENNIS
None of your business.

TEDDY
Actually... You know what? You can't leave like this.

DENNIS
Why not?

TEDDY
What do you mean, why not? You've got to work your notice, that's why. There are labour laws. I don't want to be in trouble with the tribunal.

DENNIS
What tribunal is that?

TEDDY
There's always a tribunal Dennis, these days. You have to do it by the book. Hiring and firing is a tricky business.

DENNIS
What you're saying, though you're too proud to utter it, is that you want me to stay.

TEDDY
I didn't say that. I didn't say I wanted you to stay. I said I have to consider the consequences of letting you go.

DENNIS
Am I going out for the bus, or not? It's half way down the hill.

TEDDY
Forget the bus and have a drink. On me this time. For God's sake man, what's the matter with you? Nobody else wants you. I haven't the heart to throw you out.

DENNIS
Very well, Skipper. We'll agree to your version of events. I'll stay.
*Dennis goes behind the bar and serves them both drinks.*

TEDDY
It's a temporary arrangement.

DENNIS
Tell me in life what isn't?

TEDDY
That's settled then. You're back in the saddle, Dennis. I don't want to lose a good barman first day of the season, because he's got controversial opinions.

DENNIS
I thought you fought for the freedom of speech in this country.

TEDDY
Yes, but Don't Talk Shop In The Mess.

DENNIS
Wilco, Skipper.

TEDDY
Roger that. Chocks away!

DENNIS
Happy landings!

*They drink.*

TEDDY
You can work on your book in peace and quiet out here on the moors, Dennis.

DENNIS
That's the first time you've shown any interest in my book...

TEDDY
No one to disturb you, what?

DENNIS
Except a few ghosts.

TEDDY
How is your novel coming along, old boy? This great work of literature?

DENNIS
I'd be the last to know, Skipper.

TEDDY
What is it about? I'm longing to know.

DENNIS
You've never asked before.

TEDDY
I'm asking now.

DENNIS
Why?

TEDDY
Because I'm being pleasant.

DENNIS
It doesn't suit you. It's un-nerving to be on the receiving end of your pleasantness. It's very threatening... However, my book – my novel – the great oeuvre – It's about every-day life. It's about what we expected to come back to after the war. What dreams kept us going then – and how it's turning out. Now.

TEDDY
Well good luck with that, Dennis. I'm sure it's a colossal waste of time. But every Englishman to his own folly, what?

DENNIS
Look… I know you can't bear to be on your own. So cut it out, will you? It's alright. I won't abandon you. It's gone past that. I'm here if you need me.

TEDDY
I need you to do a good day's work.

DENNIS
I meant as a shoulder to cry on.

TEDDY
No thank you, ducky. Don't get mawkish, Dennis, it doesn't suit you.

DENNIS
Did I ever tell you about Mogadishu?

*TEDDY takes two shots of whisky from the optics and serves them.*

TEDDY
Fortunately not.

DENNIS
I wasn't there. It was a mirage. But it was the most astonishing place! The sights! The sounds! The smells! A city, yes, vibrant, speaking to every jot of my being…

TEDDY
Really?

DENNIS
No, not really! That's the point. And it was the most agonising place to leave. I've never gotten over it. You see, there was a woman involved.

TEDDY
There's always a woman involved.

DENNIS
We went everywhere together. To the souk, buying materials in extravagant colours. Drinking tiny cups of coffee as rich as velvet. We spent our nights together, it was heavenly. So much love and laughter, we were as one

body. Was I her? Was she me? Then the doctors said, okay Cohoun, there's no more we can do for you, and sent me back to the front line. So you see Teddy, I've had my nervous breakdown.

TEDDY
I'm glad you've got it behind you. Cheers!

DENNIS
Prost!

*They drink.*

DENNIS
I was thinking, Skipper...

TEDDY
Oh, yes?

DENNIS
About life. About us... Yes, a chap...

TEDDY
A chap?

DENNIS
A chap is rather like a well-stuffed sofa.

TEDDY
That's reasonable, yes. A well-stuffed sofa, yes, I see.

DENNIS
Precisely. Imagine the sofa in your front room.

TEDDY
Yes. Got it. Got it, go on...

DENNIS
It's got so much stuffing, Skipper.

TEDDY
Right, like a chap in Bomber Command perhaps.

DENNIS
Exactly. You're ahead of me there. And when the stuffing's gone out of it…

TEDDY
Yes?

DENIS
You should stop sitting on it. Because all you're left with…

TEDDY
Is a spring sticking up your arse. Thanks for that homily, Dennis.

DENNIS
My pleasure.

TEDDY
So, do you accept your new terms of employment?

DENNIS
What are they?

TEDDY
That you never mention my sofa again.

DENNIS
Be Like Dad Keep Mum

TEDDY
Keep Bomber Command out of this.

DENNIS
It's you that drew that inference.

TEDDY
You were going in that direction, sunshine.

DENNIS
Well I've turned back.

TEDDY
The Command should have got a campaign medal. To put a stop to all the innuendo, if nothing else. To stop the debate. Once and for all.

DENNIS
What debate is that?

TEDDY
The one we're not having.

DENNIS
Wilco Sunray.

*DENNIS takes out letter.*

TEDDY
What have you got there? A bill from your tailor?

DENNIS
No, it's personal.

TEDDY
Oh, personal, is it? I didn't know you had a personal life, Dennis.

DENNIS
You thought my life was a matter of public contempt?

TEDDY
More or less, yes. May I ask from whom this *billet-doux* emanates?

DENNIS
Molly.

TEDDY
Molly? My wife?

DENNIS
Yes...

TEDDY
Oh. So why, pray, is she writing to you?

DENNIS
We're very good friends, Molly and I. You know that.

TEDDY
But I'm her husband. And I haven't received a letter from her in ages.

DENNIS
She asked me to give you a message.

TEDDY
I'm glad I'm not forgotten. That's nice of her. Why can't she write to me? She's got the bloody address.

DENNIS
She thought it would be better coming from me.

TEDDY
What? What coming from you?

DENNIS
What she's written. Her news. She wrote to me deliberately so that I would be here to tell you.

TEDDY
But you were leaving me half an hour ago.

DENNIS
It's just as well I didn't then, isn't it?

TEDDY
So what is her news, Dennis? I'm agog. How is the weather at her sisters? How is her sister? How is the knitting coming on? Is the jumper three miles long? Has the cat been neutered? Like her sister's husband, who sits in the

kitchen smoking all day, doing the Daily Mail crossword and looking for a bet on the three-thirty at Newbury? What is new to be told?

DENNIS
Molly's had to go into hospital, Skipper.

TEDDY
She's done what?

DENNIS
She has been admitted into hospital.

TEDDY
You mean as a visitor?

DENNIS
No, you're not admitted as a visitor. It's nothing to worry about. It's only an exploratory op.

TEDDY
Exploring what?

DENNIS
Yes, you know, a sort of reconnaissance.

TEDDY
Reconnaissance? But that's incredible.

DENNIS
Why's that?

TEDDY
Because there's absolutely nothing wrong with Molly. They must have admitted the wrong person. An admin cockup! That's what it is! She got the wrong letter and took the bed because it was a tempting offer. Oh, my God… that's women for you.

DENNIS
Skipper, she's in good hands. The doctors will decide.

TEDDY
Decide what? There's nothing to decide except that she should come home. She's not the sort of woman that gets sick. The damn medics! They're always good for a sick note, aren't they? I had to tell my medics – on the station – you can't keep laying off my chaps – we're trying to run a war here – I've got a squadron to get up over Germany and I've got half of them creeping around the base in plimsoles with their sick notes in their pockets. I had to get rid of that MO.

DENNIS
I shouldn't worry. Let's wait till we get the results.

TEDDY
Results? What results, Dennis?

DENNIS
Of the tests.

TEDDY
Tests? What are we testing? Why couldn't she tell me all this for herself? If she was going into hospital. For tests. Testing. Testing… She could have mentioned it to me, couldn't she?

DENNIS
She knows you don't like to hear that sort of thing. Exploratory ops. Intrusive surgery.

TEDDY
Intrusive surgery? What's that?

DENNIS
They can do wonders these days, Skipper. It may not come to that.

TEDDY
Nothing may come to anything, Dennis, so what are we talking about?

DENNIS
Only that Molly decided it was better to have me around when you heard the news, in case you went into a flap.

TEDDY
I do not flap, Dennis! I am not a flapper! I'm quite able to appraise the situation and take the appropriate action. That's why I was promoted to Squadron Leader during the war. Then Wing Leader. Because of my ability to face the facts cooly, objectively, without sentiment and to issue orders. Is that clear? Any questions? Speak up at the back! So how bad is it?

DENNIS
We won't know precisely, good or bad, until we get the tests analysed.

TEDDY
She was perfectly fit when she left here. She didn't need to have anything tested. That's the trouble with women, they're always finding more things to test. They'd be better off if they didn't know they had so many organs in their bodies. Because once they know it's there, they want it looked at.

DENNIS
Molly was exhausted. This place is deceptive. You lose your moorings if you stay here too long. They make sure of that.

TEDDY
Who?

DENNIS
Oh you'll meet them. If you hang around long enough. Get out into the fog.

TEDDY
Now you listen to me, Dennis, and I'll tell you something. This hotel, this very spot, is where Molly and I came during the war. Our first liaison...

DENNIS
You've told me this before, by the way.

TEDDY
From that first moment I knew I'd come back here. That we both would. We both knew it. I knew I'd buy this hotel out on the moors one day. Like I know a lot of other things... That we'd see it through, together! And that's what we've done, Molly and I. We have realised our dream. How many people can say that?

DENNIS
Things can change.

TEDDY
Nothing changes! Except for the better! Because I won't have it any other way. Never have done. Nothing that a little holiday for Molly won't put right. At her sister's, if she likes… though personally, going to her sister's would have made me ill. Everything around her is dying. Flowers wilt as soon as you give them to her… Look, you must have some idea what's going on?

DENNIS
That's what the tests are for, Skipper.

TEDDY
I don't know what I'd do without her.

DENNIS
Now you're jumping to conclusions. You'd better have another drink – on me.

TEDDY
On you? It must be serious.

*DENNIS goes behind the bar and serves two whiskies.*

DENNIS
Look at it this way, old chap. Everything has to go in for a service now and again.

TEDDY
Yes, an old kite's got to be turned round and patched up for the next mission, eh? It's amazing what we got off the ground and back into the sky in twenty-four hours, working round the clock.

DENNIS
Bung-ho.

TEDDY
Happy landings.

*They drink. DENNIS rings up till. Writes IOU. Puts it in and closes till.*

TEDDY
So Molly's on sick parade. Full kit.

DENNIS
Excused boots.

TEDDY
I won't go and see her. The only cases I go and see are bad cases. Burns mainly. I find hospitals depressing places. Chaps swathed in bandages, I've had enough of it, I tell you. Truth to tell half the time you don't know who they are unless you read the chart at the bottom of the bed. You're looking for a hole somewhere, in the bandages, to shove in a Players Full Strength. You can still smell the burning flesh. Basically you have to get off that ward as soon as you can and get on with the job with the lucky ones. Lucky this week, that is.

DENNIS
It's over, Skipper.

TEDDY
Yes.

DENNIS
It's alright. You don't have to go to the hospital.

TEDDY
What?

DENNIS
Molly doesn't expect you to visit her.

TEDDY
Then I won't. I'll hold the fort here until she gets back. The sooner the better and we can get back to normal. Normal service will be resumed.

DENNIS
Yes, we won't assume anything. We'll wait for the telephone call from the hospital.

TEDDY
They're going to call us?

DENNIS
Yes. Or… or Molly's sister will call.

TEDDY
I'm not talking to her. I might catch something. When her and her husband came to our wedding, do you know what present they gave us? A burial plot!

DENNIS
I suppose it was to keep family continuity. So you could all be buried on the same patch.

TEDDY
Perish the thought. I don't want her diseased worms devouring my body. Or her nails growing out of her coffin and clawing at mine. Oh God, where were we?

DENNIS
Don't worry, I'll answer the phone. All you need do is relax.

TEDDY
I am totally at ease, thank you. I know that M for Molly will get home. Okay, there might be a bit of flak on the way. But she'll make it back… on a wing and a prayer, if necessary. Yes, my lucky rabbit's paw has never let me down. It's not going to let me down now. I've still got it. Here it is…

DENNIS
That's the spirit. Only you're the one standing at the end of the run-way this time, Skipper. Waiting for M for Molly to get home, from her mission.

TEDDY
How true. Waiting. The waiting was always worse…

*Lights fade to the bar in the evening.*
*MOLLY enters – WAAF uniform, gas mask over her shoulder. She is unaware of TEDDY and DENNIS.*

*TEDDY and DENNIS, unaware of MOLLY, exit – DENNIS taking his suitcase.*
*MOLLY crosses to radio. Switches it on, song from Vera Lynn.*
*MOLLY takes out compact and applies lipstick, trying to catch her reflection in a mirror behind the bar.*
*TEDDY enters – RAF uniform, gas mask and haversack. But casual, with a silk scarf round his neck. Possibly fur lined leather flying jacket.*

MOLLY
I think we've picked the ideal spot for a dirty weekend, Skipper.

TEDDY
Roger that.

MOLLY
I expect you will. I feel I've been here before.

TEDDY
Do you really?

MOLLY
Yes. Or I wouldn't have said it, would I? I'm not really into silly conversations, Skipper.

TEDDY
Comment noted. Stay on message. It's déjà vu, old girl. I had it once over Nuremberg.

MOLLY
What, on a bombing trip?

TEDDY
No, on a bicycle trip.

MOLLY
Well, how were you 'over' Nuremberg?

TEDDY
No, that's how I felt 'over' Nuremberg.

MOLLY
I didn't know you had any feelings, Skipper?

TEDDY
No, can't afford them. Well, until I met you, that is.

MOLLY
Come off it, Skipper. Everybody's at it. 'Don't you know there's a war on?' They all want the same thing, poor lambs. It could be their last. It might be their first, and last. A shag is their bid for immortality, darling.

*TEDDY fiddles with his pipe.*

TEDDY
Possibly, yes… Well good luck, I say. So would you describe yourself as an angel of mercy?

MOLLY
You mean am I in the habit of providing squadron comforts? You wouldn't expect me to do it for my own pleasure, would you? Never mind… Running the show keeps you far too busy, Skipper. I'm surprised you found time for me, frankly.

TEDDY
I've had my eye on you for some time.

MOLLY
Seeing as how I work in your ops room, that's not too difficult.

TEDDY
I'm surprised you found time for an old codger like me.

MOLLY
You must be all of twenty-nine.

TEDDY
And the rest.

MOLLY
To tell you the truth…

TEDDY
Because you're in the habit of lying?

MOLLY
It's second nature, darling, I'm a woman. It's a form of camouflage.

TEDDY
Camouflage and deception are essential in wartime, Molly. It's a matter of survival.

MOLLY
Then you know how I feel, Skipper.

*MOLLY takes out a cigarette case, and a cigarette. TEDDY lights it for her with his lighter.*

MOLLY
Actually, I'm tired of boys.

TEDDY
The Brylcream boys. We love them all.

MOLLY
One at a time, please.

TEDDY
I would have asked you out for a drink earlier. It took a while to get round to it because you always seemed, well… otherwise engaged.

MOLLY
I did have other…

TEDDY
I was willing to wait my turn in the queue.

MOLLY
Gorblimey, you don't 'alf make me sound like an old tart!

TEDDY
That's the way I like 'em, ducky.

MOLLY
Do you, dearie?

TEDDY
Yers, just like Mum.

MOLLY
Was she an old tart?

TEDDY
She was a bolter. I was left with a wet nurse.

MOLLY
What happened to your father?

TEDDY
He was left with the wet nurse as well. He didn't seem to mind so much.

MOLLY
Is he still alive?

TEDDY
I haven't asked him recently. We don't talk much. I get postcards from Mummy sometimes. She likes to keep in touch. She was in Nuremberg at one time.

MOLLY
Oh you visited her on your bicycle, didn't you?

TEDDY
Yes, that's right. You remember?

MOLLY
Yes, you only told me five minutes ago.

TEDDY
So I did. Yes, back to my mother… she did manage to get out of Germany before the war.

MOLLY
Just as well. You might have bombed her.

TEDDY
That would have been a good idea. Actually Mummy's living with an actor in Brighton these days. He does propaganda films. Same as Doctor Goebbels, only for the other side. She used to know Goebbels.

MOLLY
That's a coincidence.

TEDDY
What do you mean?

MOLLY
Them both doing propaganda.

TEDDY
Mind you, she could be lying.

MOLLY
Well that's what propaganda is, isn't it?

TEDDY
Exactly.

MOLLY
How can you tell when people are lying?

TEDDY
They stare at you when they're talking. They look you in the face, frankly. And don't blink.

MOLLY
I hope I don't do that. It sounds very ageing. Why are we talking about lying again, Skipper?

TEDDY
We want to get off on the right foot, don't we? I feel I can tell you anything.

MOLLY
But you don't know much.

TEDDY
True, I can't talk shop, old girl. That's off limits, sorry. Anything else, apart from the war.

MOLLY
What else is there?

*TEDDY has gone behind the bar and fixed more drinks.*

TEDDY
Bung-ho!

MOLLY
Chocks away, darling.

TEDDY
Happy landings!

*They drink.*

MOLLY
Do you have any plans for this weekend, Skipper?

TEDDY
What, apart from getting sloshed?

MOLLY
I wasn't at the briefing for this do.

TEDDY
There wasn't one.

MOLLY
So where do I fit in?

TEDDY
I'm better on overall strategy, Molly. I don't know where I fit in, either. As far as this mission is concerned, I thought I'd keep driving... as long as we didn't go beyond the Point Of No Return.

MOLLY
We might already have done that, darling.

TEDDY
Yes. Do you think so? That might be a jolly good thing. I told you I don't get much time for this sort of thing, so I... I don't know the routine. I'm sorry.

MOLLY
And you think I do?

TEDDY
What?

MOLLY
Know the routine?

TEDDY
I didn't say that, old girl.

MOLLY
You hardly know me.

TEDDY
It's not my fault. This is as good a way as any, what? Look, we'll drive back tonight if you like...

MOLLY
No, I did want to come away for the weekend, Teddy. Or I'd have said I'm washing my hair.

TEDDY
Didn't you wash your hair?

MOLLY
Yes I did.

TEDDY
Oh good. I don't want to rush you.

MOLLY
Not at all. Everything's in a hurry these days. Nobody knows how much time they've got, do they?

TEDDY
I… no, I suppose not. Do you find me slightly annoying?

MOLLY
Of course I do. You're a man. Don't worry about it.

TEDDY
Why…?

MOLLY
Because I find them necessary. Like cleaning your teeth, darling.

TEDDY
Oh, that's good news. I could become a good habit, like oral hygiene. Look, I'll start a tab until the landlord shows up. He's probably on coastguard duty. Doing his bit looking for German spies landing by submarine on this wild coastline.

*TEDDY puts the bottle on the bar. He tops up the drinks.*

TEDDY
Cheers.

MOLLY
Prost.

TEDDY
Here's to the Second Front.

MOLLY
Here's to Uncle Joe !

*They drink.*

MOLLY
It's an awful muck-up, isn't it, Skipper? On the Station. I mean if I'm not lowering your moral to mention it.

TEDDY
Go ahead, old girl. We are off duty.

MOLLY
I mean recently it's been getting worse.

TEDDY
It is a pretty bad show, yes.

MOLLY
Losses. Can I say that?

TEDDY
It's a war of attrition really. You see, between us and the hun. I think I can put it that way.

MOLLY
It's nice of you not to censor our conversation, Skipper.

TEDDY
Strictly entrée nous.

MOLLY
Like you censor our letters.

TEDDY
I let the padre look after that. He cuts out all the sexual innuendo and keeps in the war news. He's hopeless.

MOLLY
He's a religious maniac.

TEDDY
Being religious is being a maniac. In my book.

MOLLY
Don't you believe in anything, darling?

TEDDY
I believe in doing the decent thing, Molly. That's why I'm wearing this uniform.

MOLLY
If you weren't wearing it you'd be in your underwear, Teddy.

TEDDY
That's true. Well said.

MOLLY
I never know what to say, so I pretend I'm in a film.

TEDDY
What film are we in?

MOLLY
The Lady Vanishes.

TEDDY
I say, I hope not.

MOLLY
I haven't decided. It might be my own film that I make up in my head. I often do that. Don't get drawn in, will you? My films always have an unhappy ending, Teddy.

TEDDY
Well they like a good cry in the one and nines. That's a chance I'm willing to take.

MOLLY
Don't say you haven't been warned, darling. I won't say anything that's not in character.

TEDDY
Do you have a character?

MOLLY
Oh yes. I always make myself up. Or else I wouldn't know what I'm doing here, or anywhere else for that matter. When I was a child – an only child – much on my own – I always invented a role for myself.

TEDDY
Did you talk to the fairies?

MOLLY
Yes, only they were real.

TEDDY
So, what is your role today? Have you decided yet? Have you invented yourself?

MOLLY
You'll find out if you don't go away.

TEDDY
How could I with a star like you? I'm lucky to be in a supporting role.

MOLLY
The supporting cast has not been very supporting recently. People move through your life so quickly these days, have you noticed?

TEDDY
Fickle.

MOLLY
Dead mostly.

TEDDY
Isn't that easier? Better than Missing In Action. At least you know. It's over.

MOLLY
Can it ever be over? One of my Brylcream boys wrote me a poem. Johnny.

TEDDY
I remember Johnny, yes. Canadian Johnny?

MOLLY
Yes. Would you like to hear it?

TEDDY
No thank you. I don't like airmen's poetry. I find a lot of it cleaning out their lockers. It's dreadful stuff. Except Yeats, of course… How's it go then? Johnny's poem? Let's hear it. It will pass the time.

MOLLY
The end.

TEDDY
Yes, but how does it begin?

MOLLY
That is the beginning…
In the beginning is the end
Let that be the basis for our friendship.
In the end is the beginning.
So let love start here, and end here,
And be all here…

TEDDY
Yes, I do like that. Pity about Johnny. Bought it over Berlin. Put an end to a literary career, it seems. Let's be grateful for small mercies.

MOLLY
Then there was Alex Morton.

TEDDY
Pardon? Oh, you were friendly with Alex, were you?

MOLLY
You could put it like that, yes. Very friendly.

TEDDY
Did he write poetry?

MOLLY
No.

TEDDY
Thank God.

MOLLY
You do remember him?

TEDDY
Of course I do. I remember all of them. Every man jack. Every face. Every smile. Every thumbs up...

MOLLY
Alex went for a burton over Northern France.

TEDDY
Yes, I remember writing to his next of kin. His parents. What can one say at such a time? Standard stuff. Alex was irreplaceable. No-one kept wicket better than Alex, I wrote. He played from the centre of his bat. A woody sound...

MOLLY
Did you mention the war, darling?

TEDDY
I might have forgotten.

MOLLY
He wasn't killed in a cricket match, was he? By a ball hit for six?

TEDDY
No. I would have told them what happened to Alex, in a general way.

MOLLY
The others saw him bale out but his chute didn't open. He was raspberry jam.

TEDDY
I wouldn't have put it like that. It's not help to anyone. To the war effort.

MOLLY
It was no help to my war effort. I decided to be a nun after Alex. Or nun-like.

TEDDY
That would be a terrible waste.

MOLLY
That's what Graham Bell thought.

TEDDY
Flight Sergeant Ring My Bell and ask for Gladys. Yes. This is becoming quite a list. You don't have to tell me.

MOLLY
I hated Graham. He was so good-looking and full of himself. I went out with him to spite him. I was curious what would happen. I'd get him to fall for me and then jilt the twerp. He'd already played fast and loose with two of my pals.

TEDDY
So what happened?

MOLLY
The first part happened. he did fall for me.

TEDDY
Right. And then?

MOLLY
And then… You know what happened next, Skipper.

TEDDY
Graham bought it over Cologne. Damn good pilot. Rotten luck. Apparently he was caught in a searchlight cone and couldn't get out of it.

MOLLY
Yes, I read the report. He tried a dive to the right as B for Berty was taking evasive action.

TEDDY
To the left. Which resulted in a mid-air collision. We lost two splendid crews that night. Nobody's fault.

MOLLY
It was my bloody fault.

TEDDY
Don't follow?

MOLLY
Isn't it obvious? Haven't you heard?

TEDDY
Heard what?

MOLLY
I'm the squadron Jonah, darling.

TEDDY
Oh come on. How do you make that out? You've had some bad luck, yes, Molly. Three chaps handing in their locker room key.

MOLLY
I'm the bad luck.

TEDDY
Steady on, old girl. That's… that's just not true.

MOLLY
So you hadn't heard the news?

TEDDY
I don't listen to station gossip. I occasionally start a rumour to see how quickly it will come back. And trace the trail.

MOLLY
You don't mind then?

TEDDY
What?

MOLLY
My reputation? As a femme fatale .

TEDDY
It's nonsense. It's sheer superstition, Molly. There's too much of it in the squadron. On the base. Okay, so we've all got our lucky lighters, scarves, knickers... I've got a lucky rabbit's paw! But if I lost it, it wouldn't stop me flying.

MOLLY
Are you sure?

TEDDY
I did lose it once for a couple of days. Fortunately we were fogged in. So it wasn't an issue.

MOLLY
Skipper, I should have told you before we started off on this escapade – this mission – but there didn't seem to be the opportunity, and ... and I assumed...well...

TEDDY
It makes no difference.

MOLLY
It bloody well does. I can see it in your demeanour. You're put off, aren't you?

TEDDY
No, I'm bloody well not put off! I stand by my lecture to the squadron. I had to call everybody in and tell them. Superstition cannot rule us. It was getting out of hand, Molly. I mean you know that. I told one and all. Soon they wouldn't be flying if there was an *r* in the month! And one crew – I quoted this – were physically involved in fisticuffs on the tarmac – on the runway – because the navigator wouldn't piss on the landing wheels before boarding. He couldn't. They had to give him water... the delay could have ruined the holding pattern upstairs and led to planes colliding before they even got en route for Hamburg. Superstition was running the show! I had to put everybody straight, and put a stop to it. And I jolly well did.

MOLLY
I know. I was there, Skipper. Attendance was compulsory.

TEDDY
Good.

MOLLY
It was a good lecture, you told everyone to get on with it.

TEDDY
Yes, and we are going to get on with it. Our weekend, Molly, we're going to get on with that too. I'll say we are! Your peccadilloes, well... I didn't know and I don't need to know. And if I do know now, because you've told me, so what? You're a lovely girl, and that's it. That's good enough for me.

MOLLY
Are you sure?

TEDDY
I'm quite sure.

MOLLY
It won't make any difference to our... Whatever it is we're doing?

TEDDY
Absolutely not. I propose we get pleasantly tight this evening, and... and let the rest of the world go by! As the song goes. Is that alright by you, Molly?

MOLLY
Ideal, darling.

TEDDY
Jolly good. Bang on...

*Teddy pours more drinks.*

MOLLY
Oh there was one more , Skipper...

TEDDY
One more what?

MOLLY
Another flyer, darling. I should mention.

TEDDY
My God, not another one? We should have brought the Catholic padre along with us for a weekend of confession. I hope this is the last one?

MOLLY
Yes, it is. The latest, actually.

TEDDY
Good. This airman, did he prang? Like all the others?

MOLLY
Yes, he bought the farm, Skipper.

TEDDY
Went for a Burton, did he?

MOLLY
How many ways are there of saying he's dead? He's an ex rear gunner. He was my fiancée. We were going to get married.

TEDDY
Oh, it was serious?

MOLLY
I didn't say that. I said we were going to get married. Of course it was bloody serious! And you know who I'm talking about. Because you, as good as, signed his death warrant, didn't you?

TEDDY
I thought we might get round to this. I hoped not. I didn't sign anything.

MOLLY
You could have done. You could have posted him to a training unit.

TEDDY
Is this a weekend for your revenge, Molly? Is that what it's all about? Is that what we're playing at? Is that why you agreed to come away with me? With

the Skipper? Tell me what I've got to pay, will you? And I'll tell you whether I think it's worth it.

*BLACKOUT*

# ACT II

## SCENE 1

*Night. The bar lights are on.*
*DENNIS enters. He crosses to front door – which may be offstage – opens it. Wisps of fog drift in. Sound of mournful ship's siren, off. He closes the door, re-enters the room. He crosses to the radio. He listens in case TEDDY is nearby. Satisfied, he turns on the radio.*

RADIO REPORTER
*Crackle.* And here at Alamein...
*Explosions, Artillery barrage:*
... the barrage is terrific. The Eighth Army is here, ready to advance. Or retreat. The whole sky is lit up. The ground is trembling. It's an awesome spectacle, fascinating to behold, defying the Heavens. Monty's on the job, Rommel's on the run. Nothing he can throw back at us seems to be doing much damage...

*Big explosion. Radio shakes. Wisp of smoke from back of the set. Silence.*

*TEDDY enters, behind bar. DENNIS does not notice. TEDDY switches off the radio.*

TEDDY
I told you to leave that blasted radio alone, Dennis. It's out of bounds.

DENNIS
What, for officers?

TEDDY
For all ranks! And what your rank was, I'm still not convinced about.

DENNIS
I was conducting some private research. We're in a pretty pickle here, Skipper. If this radio is anything to go by, essentially we don't know what year it is. And even if we do, it could still be several years at the same time. It could be a time collision...

TEDDY
Like two Lancasters that collide in a holding pattern.

DENNIS
We could be in two places, or more, at the same time. Like the Philadelphia Experiment.

TEDDY
I don't want to hear about the Philadelphia Experiment.

DENNIS
Forget the Martians. We don't need Martians to explain this radio set, that's a – a red herring, Skipper! We must look to the quantum theory...

*TEDDY has served drinks.*

TEDDY
Put a sock in it, Dennis! How many more times? Just forget about it, will you? And it might go away... Down the hatch!

DENNIS
Bung-ho!

*They drink.*

DENNIS
You can't bury this thing, you know.

TEDDY
Any news on M for Molly?

DENNIS
Nobody's rung in Skipper. We're all standing by. The fire tenders are at the end of the runway in case of a forced landing.

TEDDY
I had a nap. I dreamt I was down here in the bar with Molly. It seemed so real.

DENNIS
It's when the dreams and reality start sliding into each other that it gets quite hairy. How do you know it was a dream? That could have been real and this could be the dream.

TEDDY
It felt like that, yes.

*Sound of distant fog horn.*

TEDDY
What's happened to the first day of the summer season. Where's it gone?

DENNIS
It's vanished. Out here on the moors, the times o'clock and days run amok. Who knows when it is? The clocks and calendars give us an illusion of control, they are simply constructs to convince us that we have been somewhere and that we are headed somewhere else. It's never what's staring us in the face. We can't take that.

TEDDY
Always assume there's a rational explanation for everything, Dennis. If I didn't know better I'd say you've been on drugs.

DENNIS
I have been experimented upon. It times past, that is.

TEDDY
That's obvious.

DENNIS
I, well… I volunteered…

TEDDY
What, to get out of the front line?

DENNIS
That's not worthy of you. I volunteered for some government trials. I was in a tight spot, yes, not what you think… and it seemed the easy way out. I finished up in a worse state than before. That's why I wondered about this

wireless? Is it a plant? Have they finished with me? Will they come again?... I had you there, for a moment, didn't I? You thought I was serious?

TEDDY
You've never been serious, Dennis. I don't expect it of you. You're the flippant type.

DENNIS
True. Yet something did happen back then, under rather amazing circumstances. And it's my guess it's not finished. They never let go, you know.

TEDDY
Who are <u>they</u>?

DENNIS
Them.

TEDDY
Oh, them!

DENNIS
We know a lot more than – than we care to admit Skipper, consciously, and... yes, we won't let it come to the surface. So the pressure builds up...

TEDDY
I can take some of that. Pressure? My God, I can take pressure. I've had to, it goes with the job, pal!

DENNIS
You're not getting the message, Skipper. We all have our demons.

TEDDY
Ones that drift in off the moors, eh? The occasional drowned sailor with bulging eyes and wet hair! Gliding through the door, spewing fish...

DENNIS
Go easy on the scotch, man.

TEDDY
Why? It's my scotch.

DENNIS
'My' is how we own things by the use of language. Well my ghost has not arrived. Has not glided through the door yet, spewing curses. You know who I mean, don't you?

TEDDY
No idea.

DENNIS
I think you do. I'm expecting him.

TEDDY
Never heard of the chap.

DENNIS
Yes you have. You have heard of the chap.

TEDDY
What's his name?

DENNIS
Captain Donnelley.

TEDDY
Never heard of the bounder.

DENNIS
Yes, you have.

TEDDY
Doesn't ring a bell.

DENNIS
It does ring a bell. *He rings the bar bell.* He always arrives first day of the season, Skipper. Captain bloomin' Donnelley! We've done this a thousand times. It's always the same. There are minor changes of dialogue, I agree, but the outcome is always the same. Inevitable. Like a train hitting the

buffers... Then suddenly, for no reason at all that I can discern, there's a major change to the script and Captain Donnelley does not arrive.

TEDDY
What did they do to your head? You poor blighter, you have been interfered with, that's for sure. And it's landed on my doorstep.

DENNIS
Well where the hell is he?

TEDDY
Ah, you talking about your book! A character in your book, Dennis.

DENNIS
Am I? I wouldn't be so sure.

TEDDY
When does he arrive? This chap?

DENNIS
In 1944, in a time slip.

TEDDY
Better than a pink slip.

DENNIS
You always say that as well.

TEDDY
Who knows how the script's been changed Dennis, by the Great Author, who has seen fit to spare us so far. You see I can match your imagination. I know why you didn't get on that bus chum, there's nowhere else you can drink. You're banned from all the pubs in St Ives, you're the wild man. With the staring eyes. You're the ghost Dennis, you could empty a cemetery by just opening the gate. So you stay put here, pretending to be an eccentric literary genius.

DENNIS
Oh yes I'm the Great Pretender! *Sings:* Pretending that I'm not afraid!

TEDDY
Pretending you're on an errand of mercy to look after me? That's ripe! You're a complete fraud. You're the one needs twenty four hour watch, my old son, because you can never tell when an attack is imminent.

DENNIS
It is imminent. You can see right through me, can't you?

TEDDY
I can see for miles and miles and miles…

*Fog drifts through the front door and, in a strange light, enter CAPTAIN DONNELLEY.*
*TEDDY is not aware of this arrival.*

TEDDY
I'm going to feed the chickens, Dennis.

DENNIS
At this time of night? Are you sure?

TEDDY
Yes, they've got used to it. Don't do anything silly while I'm away, will you? I can't watch you all the time.

*TEDDY exits.*
*DENNIS pours himself another whisky and downs it.*
*DONNELLEY bangs the bar bell.*

*Lights fade up to bright sunlight.*

DONNELLEY
Top of the morning to you.

DENNIS
You're late, Captain Donnelley.

DONNELLEY
Delays. Interminable. And for the worst possible reasons. I've been heavily edited, I have.

DENNIS
Oh dear. I suspected as much.

DONNELLEY
Almost obliterated. Red pencil slashing. You're lucky to see me at all. All my earlier scenes are gone. Cut to blazes!

DENNIS
That's dreadful. They were such good scenes.

DONNELLEY
Don't tell me about it! Don't I know that? And only because I am an interesting person that foreshadows all others. Or was! Ah well now, we might as well make the most of what's left. A pathetic mess, if you ask me. Wartime restriction, I suppose. We must all expect to suffer cuts.

DENNIS
But your original arrival showed off your character to great effect. Enhancing everything.

DONNELLEY
I don't have any character left now. I'm a device. Like that bloomin' radio set, a catalyst. Set them up, will you? I'm really distraught. All that stuff about me signing in, offering my ration book coupons, so that nobody knows whether it's 1944 or today.

DENNIS
It's always today. It's the key to eternity.

DONNELLEY
Then we must make the best of it. I don't quarrel with that. Damn shame. All character is subject to edit. Nobody's safe. What can you believe any more? I'll be glad when it's all over.

DENNIS
Do you think things will ever get back to normal?

DONNELLEY
Never. Oh no. Character is finished. You'll never find a well rounded cameo in a play again. There'll be no call for it. They'll have forgotten what it's like.

*DENNIS has served drinks.*

DONNELLEY
Cheers.

DENNIS
Bung-ho.

DONNELLEY
Down the hatch.

*They drink.*

DENNIS
It's on the house.

DONNELLEY
Most kind.

DENNIS
We must all make sacrifices. In wartime, as you say.

DONNELLEY
I haven't established the war. Do you think I have? I tried to put it in context. They might as well have left me with what I had before. Lovely scenes… Oh, don't go on about it. Now where were we?

DENNIS
Well you don't fool me. You've got military policeman written all over you.

DONNELLEY
I used to have three scenes to get that point across. But we'll take your word for it. OK, let's get on with it.

DENNIS
Yes, let's get on with it.

DONNELLEY
A wartime expression. Right, you may be able to help me. I'm sniffing around. Following a few leads. Not trying to get anyone into trouble but to

help them back on the straight and narrow. To avoid the agony…

DENNIS
And get them back to the front line.

DONNELLEY
Minus their stripes, yes.

DENNIS
You're looking for a deserter.

DONNELLEY
*He takes out a snapshot photograph.* I am looking for a fella, you're right. You might have set eyes on him. Rumoured to have fetched up in this neck of the woods. I've a picture of him here in uniform but God knows what he looks like now.

DENNIS
Where was this taken?

DONNELLEY
Italy. Monte Casino. He's the one standing by the big gun.

DENNIS
What about the rest of them? Standing by the big gun.

DONNELLEY
Oh, they're still with the battery. This bugger's on the run. Had a high old time in Naples, made a pile on the black market, like a few of them.

DENNIS
A few thousand of them, I heard.

DONNELLEY
You heard right.

DENNIS
*Looks at photo…*
No. I don't know him from Adam.

DONNELLEY
About your height.

DENNIS
I'm not my height. Sorry.

DONNELLEY
*Puts photo away.* Not to worry, I am sorry to trouble you, sir. If anything comes to mind, let me know, won't you? We're all on the same side. And making the best of what scenes are left to us. Lucky to have a shred of credibility remaining…

DENNIS
You've done very well.

DONNELLEY
Thanks for that vote of confidence. It seems some people are doing alright. You wouldn't know… Never mind! We can be expecting the Big Push. Any day now. Bear that in mind. I'll be shoving off then. Pity that. I could have stayed here a few days, at the hotel, and most welcome. In a previous version… Well maybe not. Who knows? Another time. Time, that's what they're playing with. You can't change what's done. Or can you? Can you go back and change the past? Some say yes. Some circles are challenging conventional thought. Experiments are in progress. Light bulbs are popping.

DENNIS
Mine are. Frequently.

DONNELLEY
It's no coincidence. Force fields are being manipulated, believe me.

DENNIS
Einstein's Theory has opened up a can of worms.

DONNELLEY
You've been thinking about it too. We are stepping into the unknown every day. Why do we cling to the familiar? Odours? Sensations? To old scripts? Identity, that's why. Don't rob a man of his identity. Though he may seek to change it himself – for devious reasons.

DENNIS
Look, Donnelley, let's not beat about the bush. We both know that photo is of me. That's why you're here. So, what do you want?

DONNELLEY
You know what I want. Respect. Somebody's got to do my job, Bombardier. Hunt down the deserters. And that's what you are, aren't you? Cohoun? A man on the run. How romantic! You have more respect for the enemy than you have for your own Red Caps. How do you think that makes me feel? You hate us worse than the Nazi's, don't you? But I'm only doing a job and if you'd give me a chance I'd come over far more human. If you prick me, do I not bleed? How was that? Did it establish my character? On the last gasp?

DENNIS
Oh yes. With great sufficiency.

DONNELLEY
I praise Saint Jude, the patron saint of lost causes.

DENNIS
But let's keep in mind what you are... A literary illusion. A theatrical device...

DONNELLEY
That I am. Farewell!

*There is an explosion, and DONNELLEY disappears in a puff of smoke, a la pantomime!*

*DENNIS returns to bar and takes a swig of whisky from the bottle.*

*BLACKOUT.*

# ACT II

## SCENE 2

*Night. DENNIS and TEDDY are drinking.*

TEDDY
… the Chief Of The Imperial General Staff is known to me. He attended the Bomber Command Reunion Dinner at which I was invited to be the guest speaker.

DENNIS
You didn't show up for that dinner.

TEDDY
Didn't I?

DENNIS
You got pissed in Penzance and missed the train.

TEDDY
Well you were seeing me off, that was your fault. I sent them a telegram, Apologies For Absence.

DENNIS
The next year you sent them a telegram Apologies For Presence. You mistook the lift for a public urinal.

TEDDY
Yes, because I saw Air Marshall Harris using it the same way. It was a natural mistake. How many people round here have been invited to the Palace? To Buck House? The King himself gave me my DFC. Before he died…

DENNIS
He couldn't do it after he died, could he?

TEDDY
She was there. Elizabeth. I met her, the future Queen.

DENNIS
Write to the Queen and remind her. Of your meeting.

TEDDY
She wouldn't remember me. I was just one war hero amongst many.

DENNIS
It's only the cost of a stamp, man. Start at the top! Ask Her Majesty to intercede on your behalf. For this caravan planning permission you're so keen on. She'll shake the locals up, issue a Royal Warrant. Then you can flood Cornwall with caravans and little holiday shops. She may even ask you to develop a caravan park in Balmoral. Think of that! Or a corgi theme park! Selling greetings cards that bark when you open them...

TEDDY
Shut up Dennis! Concentrate. What do you think of my Master Plan? Seriously.

DENNIS
Seriously? As you say, it depends on what real influence you've got left, Teddy. You haven't had any invitations from the Air Ministry for the last three years. Not since you sent that parcel bomb to Bomber Harris.

TEDDY
It wasn't a parcel bomb, it was an exploding cigar. It was a joke, for heaven's sake!

DENNIS
Yes, after Dresden he could have taken the point.

TEDDY
I wasn't making a point.

DENNIS
It comes across like that.

TEDDY
Why do you mention Dresden?

DENNIS
Did I?

TEDDY
Dresden was necessary, Dennis.

DENNIS
Look, we don't have to talk about it…

TEDDY
I've got nothing to be ashamed of.

DENNIS
Oh, that's good.

TEDDY
Dennis, it gave us no pleasure to destroy a beautiful city. All those historic buildings. Dresden was on everybody's Baedeker Tour list before the war. Not to be missed.

DENNIS
It's a damn shame, yes. And of course all that Dresden porcelain got smashed with all the bombing.

TEDDY
It couldn't be helped. I do think of it, yes.

DENNIS
And then, it's worth mentioning, there were the people to consider.

TEDDY
What?

DENNIS
In the buildings, people. People. All the lonely people… Did it cross your mind? As the bombs rained down creating a firestorm. People in the streets of molten tarmac. Refugees fleeing the Russian horde. Including many women and children who were incinerated or suffocated in cellars. All those people, yes… of course it was a deliberate tactic. A policy brought to a fine art in other Jerry cities. But don't call it terror bombing, will you? No, good

heavens, no. We don't use the word terror. We de-house the population, that's all. It's a technical matter. Yes... of course. Of course, the way we did it – killing ten of thousands of inhabitants – would make the Germans a little anxious. Let's call it anxiety bombing, shall we?

TEDDY
What is your point, Dennis? I assume that you are making one?

DENNIS
I should have thought it was obvious. The point is... could you have done it if you'd been on the ground? Using a flame-thrower perhaps? Blasting into their shelters. Setting light to people? But you dropped your stuff from the heavens. You were above it all. You must have had some idea what was going on down below.

TEDDY
We weren't paid to think about it. We had to win a war.

DENNIS
It was already won, at that stage. 1945.

TEDDY
We were supporting the Russians.

DENNIS
What, by giving them an above ground cemetery to occupy? It was all so impersonal for you, wasn't it? You never stopped being good chaps, did you? Seeing it through.

TEDDY
We didn't start it, Dennis.

DENNIS
You didn't start it, Skipper. What I'm saying is you didn't know when to stop.

TEDDY
We were obeying orders.

DENNIS
Which it was established at Nuremberg to be no excuse.

TEDDY
I don't need an excuse. Everything I've done has been honourable.

DENNIS
Do you think so?

TEDDY
I know so.

DENNIS
Then you've nothing to worry about, have you?

TEDDY
I'm not worried about anything I did during the war. I've never missed a wink of sleep over it.

DENNIS
Your conscience is clear?

TEDDY
Absolutely. It was cricket. We played on a sticky wicket and lost a lot of men. But we dug in and…

DENNIS
Hit 'em for six.

TEDDY
Yes, that's right.

DENNIS
Forgive them Lord, they know not what they do.

TEDDY
We don't need forgiveness. Don't bring the Lord into this Dennis. He was on our side.

DENNIS
A sort of bent umpire. This Lord is not only a Lord of justice, but of mercy. Where was that in your bombing of German cities in the last year of the war?

TEDDY
My bombing? We were part of the machine chum. It wasn't my bombing. The orders came from Churchill down...

DENNIS
Yes, and he pretty well disowned Bomber Command when it suited him. You never got a campaign medal, did you? Your lot?

TEDDY
What's that supposed to mean?

DENNIS
It speaks volumes. Why can't you give things a proper name? You annihilated the population with a scourge of fire and brimstone. It was revenge, pure and simple, and you were the instruments of it on behalf of a vengeful nation. I'm not blaming you Teddy. However righteous the cause, war eventually corrupts everyone. So less of the toffee about being a hero, please. You killed, as you were ordered to do, indiscriminately. And you had your egg for breakfast.

TEDDY
I'm warning you, your employment hangs by a thread. We'll have no more of this talk. I've thrown you off the premises for less.

DENNIS
You started it, chum. Not me, tonight.

TEDDY
I fought to give you the privilege, Dennis. The privilege to abuse free speech. And tonight...

DENNIS
For 'one night only'.

TEDDY
I decided I would let you... let you push the boat out. With your fetid, wretched and corrupt anti-patriotic ranting.

DENNIS
Let's concentrate on what you want to say then, shall we?

TEDDY
I have nothing further to say.

DENNIS
I think you have Skipper. Or you would not have brought the subject up. What haven't you told me? Yet? I'll listen.

TEDDY
You don't understand. What it was like. We were all in the sausage machine. Obeying orders. Carrying out orders. Passing on policy. Do you think after the hell of 1943 we had any thoughts but to flatten Germany? When at last we were coming out on top. We'd lost so many good men by then. Billy McCrindle! Do you think I had any choice in that matter? For example? I was The Skipper. I couldn't crack…

DENNIS
Why does Billy McCrindle play on your mind so much?

TEDDY
What?

DENNIS
It was years ago. Why does he stick out of the crowd?

TEDDY
Did I mention him?

DENNIS
You did. Why him?

TEDDY
Sergeant McCrindle. Rear gunner. On his third tour of ops. He was a legend. We all loved Billy, boys and girls alike. He was a stunner really but the quiet type. If I'd been a WAAF the ground would have trembled beneath my feet, believe me. When he came into my office and slapped an application on my desk, to be grounded, I was shocked… He looked at me with those startling blue eyes. I can see them now. You don't often see eyes like that…

DENNIS
Claire's got them.

*Enter SERGEANT BILLY McCRINDLE.*

BILLY
My luck's run out, Skipper. I can't go up again. It's as simple as that.

TEDDY
As simple as what, Sergeant McCrindle?

BILLY
As simple as processing my posting, sir. I've done eighty-five ops. Nearly three tours.

TEDDY
Five to go, Billy-boy, then we get the Daily Mirror man down. With a photographer. Your photograph in the paper, front page, guarantee it. Think of that. You'll be a hero. Ninety ops! Three tours! You'll be everybody's pinup!

BILLY
I don't want to be a pin-up, sir. I want to get off this station to a training unit.

TEDDY
There's plenty of accidents in training units. If your number's on it, it could as easily be there. Five more ops, Billy, and we'll send you on a national tour. Better still, send you to the United States of America to sign autographs and have lots of sexual intercourse with the Southern Belles! How's that?

BILLY
Can't do five more ops, sir. Sorry about that. You'll have to find another hero for the Daily Mirror.

TEDDY
But you're so photogenic, Billy. Have you considered that?

BILLY
I don't photograph well dead.

TEDDY
That's not for you to say. You belong to the RAF and we will use you as we see fit.

BILLY
I know it in my water, Skipper. The next op would be my last.

TEDDY
We've all felt like that sometimes, Billy. That we can't deliver. That we won't come back. That we'll prang.

BILLY
Some have known it, sir.

TEDDY
Who?

BILLY
The ones who didn't come back. And told us they wouldn't be coming back. Next time. The ones who knew that with the next mission they were going for a Burton. Do you want some names?

TEDDY
They were defeatist. They put a hoodoo on themselves. Confidentially there has been definite signs of voodoo black magic going around the stations of Bomber Command. We should never have recruited that Jamaican squadron. I have a confidential report that a Trinidadian ground crew were ritually slaughtering chickens behind the Sergeants' Mess at Biggin Hill.

BILLY
I've heard that one sir, going the rounds. They were having a barbecue, I heard. The ground crews don't get the same quality food as the air crews. You don't have to believe all the rumours, you told us that, sir. Anyway, with all due respect, you're a dab hand yourself at ritual slaughter.

TEDDY
Don't follow.

BILLY
Burnt offerings to the Gods of War.

TEDDY
That's not worthy of you, Billy. I'll overlook that remark. Look, man, I am relying on you... You are going to help me prove the witch doctors, spell makers, lucky charm and potent potion vendors and you must never wear purple socks when you go up merchants... All the black magic wizards lurking in Bomber Command, wrong! There is no luck Billy. There is only training, training... and statistics!

BILLY
I'm glad to hear it, sir. Cos statistics have done for me. Statistically I'm cooked, and I'm not going up again.

TEDDY
You've had your say. That's what I'm here for. Now you listen to me... I cannot afford to let you go, Sergeant. You're already a legend on this station. With morale at an all time low, that would be an awful blow to us, to see you sidestep into a training unit. You're destined for glory, one way or the other, is that clear?

BILLY
It would cost you the whole crew, the next one I go up. I've had the vision. I've seen the Lancaster go down in flames with the ammunition exploding and all of us inside being roasted. I've seen it. I know it. You'll lose the whole crew of F for Freddie if I stay as Rear End Charlie.

TEDDY
We don't calculate like that in Bomber Command. The private visions of men. This superstition must stop! Nothing is foretold. Get a grip man. Have a long weekend, how's that? Give me five more ops and you're done. Is that clear, Sergeant McCrindle? This application for a posting? Well I never received it, so I can't turn it down.

BILLY
You're a bastard, sir.

TEDDY
That's better. Fall out, Sergeant...

BILLY
I won't fly.

TEDDY
The alternative isn't a posting. We'll bust your rank, on parade, and shove you in the glasshouse.

BILLY
As a way of saying thank you for eighty-five ops completed?

TEDDY
Billy. I won't send you up in that state of mind, I'm not a monster. As of now you pick up your 72 hour pass in the orderly room, I'll phone it through. We'll run in a replacement Rear End Charlie while you're away. Better to start them with an experienced crew. There, it's all sorted out. I know how you feel, Billy, and I'm going to make room for your feelings. Because you are going to feel like a different man in a couple of days time.

BILLY
It won't change anything.

TEDDY
You'll bounce back, Billy. I've complete confidence in you.

BILLY
Don't count on that. Permission to fall out, sir!

TEDDY
Fall out, sergeant.

*SERGEANT McCRINDLE salutes and exits.*

TEDDY
Billy, yes. He flew again. Good man. I knew he would, once I'd put the ginger back into him. He bought it over Hamburg on his next op. They all went down, I'm afraid, in F for Freddie. No survivors. Well, what can you say?

DENNIS
They had their egg for breakfast. You could have posted him.

TEDDY
If I'd posted him I would have had to post half the squadron. In the event Billy McCrindle did us proud.

DENNIS
Yes, you kept your hero, didn't you? Dead or alive. That was the important thing.

TEDDY
We kept what we needed. What the country needed. We were on Maximum Effort.

DENNIS
It still doesn't explain a few things.

TEDDY
Oh. Like what?

DENNIS
Well I was hoping you'd tell me.

TEDDY
What? What are you implying?

DENNIS
Nothing. If you're not ready to blab.

TEDDY
Blab? It's you that has the secrets, Dennis.

DENNIS
Secrets as silent as a sale at Selfridges.

*They are drinking steadily*

DENNIS
Prost.

TEDDY
Up periscope.

DENNIS
You're like a cat on hot bricks tonight. What's the matter with you?

TEDDY
It's the waiting gets to me. Always did. M for Molly. Come in M for Molly… Come in M for Molly… Well who's going to bloody well phone us? What are we waiting for? Why can't we phone?

DENNIS
Of course we can.

TEDDY
Well I won't. No, I won't crack…

DENNIS
Then I'll phone…

TEDDY
You stay away from that phone, Dennis. Another expense that you don't care about. And you stay away from that radio as per company orders. And while you're about it, stay away from my whisky! Do you hear?

DENNIS
Roger that. In that case, Skipper, you can drink on your own. I'll go to bed. Goodnight.

TEDDY
Where the hell are you going?

DENNIS
Upstairs. Unless that's out of bounds to all ranks. In which case you'd better put it on company orders with all the other restrictions.

TEDDY
What? What are you talking about?

DENNIS
What is allowed in this dump? That makes life worth living? I fought for the right to sponge off whoever would let me, don't forget that. While I write! What does your money and your bourgeoise damn bloody caravan shit site

mean to me? Leave the field green, man, as it is. It's a lovely meadow full of summer flowers and buzzing insects, where one can lie and chew a blade of grass and feel the earth moving... My poor earth, ever recovering from the bombardments of man, and their exploitations. Listen, I don't give a monkey's about your petty bourgeois business worries. Go ahead and cover the world with caravans! I'll live in my mind, it's the only safe place. You can't cover that with caravans!

TEDDY
Calm down, Dennis. There's a good chap. Have a nightcap before you go up.

DENNIS
Oh very well.

*DENNIS serves more drinks for both of them. And sets out one more measure of scotch.*

TEDDY
What's that for?

DENNIS
The next ghost that turns up.

TEDDY
My daughter? Claire? Is she...

DENNIS
Claire. Yes, she's there. She'll phone the results. From the hospital, as soon as they come through. She's staying at Midge's. Your sister-in-law...

TEDDY
How do you know that? How do you know everything about my family? How do you know about Midge?

DENNIS
You've been too preoccupied on overall strategy Skipper. So I stepped in. Everyone's doing their best. Best foot forward, what?

TEDDY
So you say. About Claire…?

DENNIS
Claire is with the buttercups
Claire is with the dandy clocks
Claire is where Claire should be
Claire is busy as a bee
Hear her whisper, come and find me.

TEDDY
You entranced my daughter with your rhymes, Dennis. But now she's all grown up and gone. It's as if my youth went with her. And I never… ah well, never mind…

DENNIS
What?

TEDDY
There was something between us. A distance I could not bridge, with Claire. I always had her best interests at heart.

DENNIS
Claire is doing her bit. Staying with her aunt. They come and go to Molly's bedside at the hospital. Molly's got plenty of company, don't worry, Skipper. Let the women handle it. They'll be in touch. All in good time.

TEDDY
I suppose you're right. M for Molly will get home. On a wing and a prayer. My lucky rabbit's paw has never let me down. It's not going to now. I've still got it… *Brings out the paw.*

DENNIS
That's the spirit. Only you're standing at the end of the run-way this time, Skipper. Waiting for M for Molly to get home. She could be the last to get back, and you're praying that a bomb's not stuck in the loading bay and that she gets her landing gear down.

TEDDY
You're not helping, Dennis. Did you feed the chickens today?

DENNIS
No, you did.

TEDDY
Did I? Yes, you're right. You're not to. Not any more. Not after the other night. When you slept in the coop.

DENNIS
Because you locked me out.

TEDDY
I don't want you getting familiar with my chickens.

DENNIS
How does one get familiar with a chicken? I confess I don't know.

TEDDY
Dennis, I came across it during the war.

DENNIS
What?

TEDDY
Superstition. Blood sacrifice. Attempts at black magic to sway the fates. I had to put a stop to it...

DENNIS
I have not been sacrificing your bloody chickens. Whatever gave you that idea?

TEDDY
Dennis, I counted the chickens and there are three missing.

DENNIS
*Three Of Our Chickens Are Missing*! Now showing at your local cinema! Well you can't count, chum. We'll go out and count them now if you like. You are a paranoiac piss pot Skipper! I am not smuggling your wretched chickens up to my room and with them engaging in erotic rites! I've had enough...

TEDDY
And I've had enough of you, Dennis my lad. If you want sex with an animal, leave my chickens alone. Get a dog!

DENNIS
You're bloody crazy, you are!

TEDDY
I don't come home in the morning covered in chicken shit and feathers.

DENNIS
I've already explained that. You locked me out!

TEDDY
You could have slept in the coal shed, couldn't you?

DENNIS
And come in looking like a Kentucky Minstrel? With your racial prejudice? I'd rather be strung up by the Ku Klux Klan, thank you very much.

*The phone rings.*

TEDDY
Dennis, no. No, don't answer it. I have a bad feeling about it.

DENNIS
I should take the call. Look, if M for Molly has crashed in Belgium, we should know.

TEDDY
I don't want to know. Missing In Action is worse than confirmed killed while in action over enemy territory.

DENNIS
We should take the call, Skipper.

TEDDY
No. That's enough, damn it. That's quite enough. Don't put any more on my shoulders! I've carried the lot of you through and I'm telling you it's enough! I can't take one more damn statistic…

DENNIS
It's time you were relieved of your command, Skipper.

*The phone stops ringing.*

*BLACKOUT.*

## ACT II

## SCENE 3

*Later that night. DENNIS is on his own, cleanIng the ashtrays, washing a few glasses.*

*DONNELLEY appears on a wire, flying in, dressed as a Military Police Captain, with side arm, white Blancoed webbing, red band round his cap. Except that he wears a tutu and has a pair of wings.*

DONNELLEY
I'm re-inventing myself, yet again, as a figment of your imagination. Or an hallucination. I had a perfectly good part, conventional, ruined by cuts, so I'm going for broke. You've been absent without leave for seven months now, Cohoun. I've followed your trail of nylons, Johnny Walker and Lucky Strikes from Naples to Nancledra. I just want to know why? Why you left your unit in Italy? Just for the crack, if you'll humour me.

DENNIS
Why the hell should I?

DONNELLEY
I could make life easier for you, soldier.

DENNIS
Off the record?

DONNELLEY
I'll promise you the moon, Cohoun. Just spill the beans. Spew it out. You'll feel better, I promise you. I care about how you feel. I don't want you to feel bad. It's my job to make you feel good about yourself. That's my job-description, by the way. Not theirs. The brass-hats. They don't care about feelings. But I am willing to let my hair down – to express my feminine side, which we've all got – and to listen to you. To lend an ear…

DENNIS
Very well. That day – in Italy – there was a lull in the fighting – all along the front – it was hot in the valley. A river lay between us and the Jerry positions. One day a hun, stark naked, jumped out of his trench, ran to the

river and dived in. He splashed about a bit and waved to us... Next thing one of our blokes hops out of his trench and into the river. Soon there was a swimming party – both sides splashing each other – a truce, if you like. We did it daily when the heat was at it's worst. Until a new officer came up to our line. Jerry jumps into the river – as per usual – but our new Sandhurst Issue Officer ordered rapid fire. There was blood in the water. Corpses floating everywhere. I rather lost interest in the war after that and slipped away as soon as possible.

DONNELLEY
You became a pacifist?

DENNIS
No, a black-marketeer.

DONNELLEY
That's in your favour. I'm sorry about the disrupted swimming party, Bombardier. It's the sort of thing gives world wars a bad name. Never mind. I've a proposition for you. It's official. Take it from me. From further up. They want you back in Italy.

DENNIS
You're not shipping me back to the front. I'd only go AWOL again.

*DONNELLEY is lowered to the ground.*

DONNELLEY
It's nothing like that. It's jammy, don't worry. They want you back in Naples. There are certain gentlemen they want kept an eye on – black-marketeers – you know them already so that's good. That's why you get the job. They're very keen on you, Cohoun.

DENNIS
They?

DONNELLEY
Army Intelligence. Though it's a contradiction in terms, I know. We've got to fit you up with a story that convinces. Now say you tried to make an escape – I winged you, not too badly – made you unfit for active service. Then you'd really be useful to us. A bitter man, ready to betray his country for a

small fortune. We've got you a good story. It's watertight. Or you can go to the stockade where my pals will beat the shit out of you. Not that I want it. I can't stop it.

DENNIS
I'll go for the small fortune, ta very much.

DONNELLEY
You've made the right call there, believe me. Very good. You'll be commissioned, bombardier. You'll be one of us, think of that. You'll no longer be the prey – you'll be the hunter. *He takes out revolver.* Now let's fix you up with the story, shall we? Best foot forward…

*DONNELLEY shoots DENNIS in the foot.*

*DONNELLEY exits, ascending.*
*Enter TEDDY. He is wearing pyjamas. He goes behind bar and fixes drinks.*

TEDDY
Cheers!

DENNIS
Down the hatch!

*They drink.*

TEDDY
Dennis…Earlier you witnessed that I… that I had a bad moment. Well I do admit Dennis, that I'm only human. But I'm alright now, I'm back in command.

DENNIS
Only human, eh? The Skipper is only human. I've been waiting to hear that for a long time. Never thought the day would come.

TEDDY
You see, Dennis, you've got to play the cards you're dealt. The hand life gives you. It's Kismet. That's not superstition, by the way.

DENNIS
What about your lucky rabbit's paw?

TEDDY
Molly hated it. My rabbit's paw. She tried to burn it once. Molly hated Lady Luck, you see. She said the bitch had ruined her life. I was welcome to her, she said. She was my mistress – Lady Luck – she said. My true love.

DENNIS
You were always faithful to Molly.

TEDDY
Yes, I married Flare-path Molly, didn't I? I did the decent thing by her, didn't I? A white wedding. Squadron turn out. Arch of swords. Did morale no end of good. The Skipper had married the station Jonah, what? Well known… And he kept flying. That made a hell of an impression. Four fiancees gone down in flames. One to go. But I wedded the bitch. I – I grappled with superstition and restored station morale in one go. Marrying Molly was a coup, if I say so myself. It couldn't have come at a better time. We were on Maximum Effort.

DENNIS
Yes, well done. But surely, Skipper, you didn't marry Molly just to restore station morale?

TEDDY
No. No, not at all. She was a beauty. She was the pick of the bunch, Dennis. But I'd killed two birds with one stone, if you see what I mean? If I say so myself.

DENNIS
What I don't understand is – fill me in on this one – why was it decent of you to marry her? Molly? Why was it doing the decent thing?

TEDDY
Did I say that?

DENNIS
Your own words.

TEDDY
Because I always do the decent thing, Dennis. Even if it means picking up someone else's dirty laundry. Let's leave it at that, shall we? I was there for her when it counted. You can count on the Skipper. They all used to say that. My door was open to anyone, night or day. They all counted on me, yes.

DENNIS
But you couldn't marry every WAAF that turned up in your office in distress.

TEDDY
That's true, Dennis. Fortunately.

DENNIS
So, Molly came to you with a problem?

TEDDY
No, she didn't. We got together through working together. She was in the ops room and suddenly we found, out of nothing really, that we hit it off. I do admit I put the stuffing back into Molly when her morale was low, that was my job. I married her, yes, and fixed her up good and proper, if you see what I mean?

DENNIS
No, I don't. There is some confusion…

TEDDY
Not in my mind.

DENNIS
Good! Splendid! It is a remarkable story. As you tell it, that is… You were the hard man of the outfit, eh? You were Robert Shaw to her Mary Ure… a marvellous story that! A wartime wedding that hit the headlines, eh? Photo in the Daily Mirror! How's that? *He taps a framed photograph on the wall.*

TEDDY
Yes, for a moment we lifted a Nation's spirit! That wedding, reported nationally! Yes… not that I sought celebrity, Dennis. And it was far too soon, nose back to the grindstone.

DENNIS
Maximum Effort in the bedroom, eh, Skipper?

TEDDY
Can't pull the wool over your eyes, eh?

DENNIS
We'll drink on that. Oh, I forgot, my credit's run out.

TEDDY
I'll back you for one more round Dennis. As you're in such a congenial mood. But go easy on the scotch, will you? I don't want another case of delirium tremens. I don't want my kitchen smashed up again.

DENNIS
I'm off duty, aren't I? You'll get paid out of my book advance, don't worry. Including for any breakages.

TEDDY
Oh yes? Yesterday you had doubts you would even be published.

DENNIS
Yes, well, after a few drinks I admit everything looks rosy. You know, Skipper, now you've admitted you're human – how human you are – referring to your earlier message... I'm going to let you into a little secret as well. I'm human too. I'm bloody human, yes. Did I mention that Captain Donnelley has arrived?

TEDDY
Where?

DENNIS
He's very edited this time. You'd hardly notice him.

TEDDY
Has the bounder booked in?

DENNIS
He doesn't need to.

TEDDY
Is he here, or not?

DENNIS
That's a good question, Skipper. It depends what year we're in. Like when we're listening to the radio. That bloomin' radio set over there.

TEDDY
It's the wireless that's in the wrong year, not us.

DENNIS
I admire your confidence. I'll tell you why he's come here, Captain Edited Truncated Re-invented Donnelley. He's looking for a deserter…

TEDDY
I don't want to hear your sordid tale. It's all pretence. What's true with you one day is a house of fallen cards the next.

DENNIS
I was spinning you a line, I confess, about standing on a pencil-mine on the Anzio Beach-head, remember that one?

TEDDY
It's all line-spinning with you Dennis. Cut it out.

DENNIS
You see, Captain Bloomin' Donnelley decided to shoot me in the foot to keep me out of the front line. Yes, that's the right version Skipper. Print that. The trouble is… The trouble is – here's the punchline – he keeps shooting me in the foot. You see we're trapped in serial time. He keeps turning up and shooting me in the foot…

*DENNIS grabs whisky bottle. TEDDY grabs it back.*

TEDDY
No. No more whisky.

DENNIS
It's damn painful. Can't you see? I'm putting the record straight between us. Man to man. For the record I was recruited for Army Intelligence. Hanging

around the black market in Naples…
*Sings:*
"He loves to hang around,
The Roma underground,
Living off the earnings of the signorinas…"
You see the Yanks had decided it was better to have the Mafia on our side – after the war – rather than the Reds. It was a temporary arrangement that had got out of hand. So I was roped in to liaise with the mafia…

TEDDY
So now you're not a deserter? You're a spy ! You're the Scarlet Pimpernel! No, better than that… disgraced for a purpose!

*DENNIS grabs bottle. Drinks directly from it.*

DENNIS
That's it! Keep it under your hat, won't you, Skipper?

TEDDY
Why? Did you sign the Official Secrets Act?

DENNIS
I signed everything they put in front of me. Including my mess bill. Cheers.

*DENNIS drinks from bottle again. Then gives it up to TEDDY*

TEDDY
The war was wasted on you. A great opportunity for character building and all you could do was betray your country.

DENNIS
Perhaps we should have another war. I'm sure there'll be one along in a minute. They always come in threes. When you've been waiting for a war, to produce another crop of heroes, what? And to find out who's got the yellow streak this time.

TEDDY
Calm down, Dennis. I'm not judging you for not putting up a good show.

DENNIS
My ghosts do that.

DENNIS
It's all decided, old boy, isn't it? It's Kismet, that's what you said. It's Kismet. It is already written in the firmament. While we're pissing around, trying to improve our characters.

TEDDY
What have you got there?

DENNIS
Your lucky rabbit's paw, Skipper.

TEDDY
How did you get hold of that? Give it to me.

DENNIS
You don't need it. After all it's you that held the squadron together against a sea of superstition. You married the squadron Jonah, didn't you? And you kept flying, didn't you? You showed them. You led by example …

TEDDY
Give me that…

DENNIS
This bauble? It won't make a jot of difference. Never has. Never will…

*DENNIS drops the paw into the log fire, which is burning.*

DENNIS
There, my dear fellow, now there's nothing. Nothing between you and Molly. Nothing for Molly to be jealous of, is there? Lady Luck and her symbols have gone up in smoke. That's it. You're right, it's over. I reckon I've done you a big favour there.

TEDDY
Thank you, Dennis. I've been meaning to do that. For some time now, yes. You're absolutely right. You have done me a favour, it is character that counts, you're right. Thank you for reminding me.

DENNIS
Why can't we re-invent ourselves, like Captain Donnelley?

TEDDY
If you've got a good story, Dennis, stick to it. Don't keep changing it.

DENNIS
Which story are you referring to?

TEDDY
Well, how about this one? Molly writing to you because you're just good friends.

DENNIS
We are good friends, Have been for years.

TEDDY
I know. Stick to that. Stick to it like shit to a blanket! Always bear the Greater Good in mind, what? That's what I've had to do. It might make me feel good for five minutes to spill my guts, but it's not going to help anyone else. You're the family friend Dennis, aren't you? Now that's a bloody good story, that is. Stick to that one…

*The phone starts to ring.*

BLACKOUT.

## ACT II

## SCENE 4

*A church bell tolls. Effect of rain. Mourners enter, black umbrellas, crossing the stage. Exit.*

*Amongst the black umbrellas, one of them is a smaller red tartan.*

# ACT II

## SCENE 5

*TEDDY and DENNIS, wearing black suits, enter. TEDDY first, hurrying in out of the rain. Followed by DENNIS. He has the tartan umbrella. They close the umbrellas, put them in a stand. Take off coats, if they are wearing them.*
*DENNIS goes behind the bar and fixes the drinks, spirits to warm them.*

**DENNIS**
Mao Tse-Tung!

**TEDDY**
Ah so!

**DENNIS**
I think that went very well. The vicar handled the ceremony with sensitivity and even a certain good humour, don't you think?

**TEDDY**
Yes, I was grateful he wasn't wearing a red nose.

**DENNIS**
A funeral doesn't have to be a sombre affair Skipper.

**TEDDY**
Obviously not.

**DENNIS**
He was sharing his faith with us that death is only a transition.

**TEDDY**
To the Palace Of Varieties in his case. I fail to see the relevance to Molly.

**DENNIS**
You must agree the vicar's eulogy went down well, that's what I'm saying.

**TEDDY**
It did, yes. A treat. Yes…

DENNIS
Reflecting Molly's sense of humour.

TEDDY
She was a manic depressive, Dennis.

DENNIS
Oh, come on. We all have our moods. Did you like the bit about wiping M for Molly off the operations blackboard? Because she'd bought the farm...

TEDDY
The vicar didn't know what he was talking about. Who put him up to that?

DENNIS
I did clue him in. With jargon that I thought would appeal to you... and a few others. Making it a memorable event. After all she was Flare-path Molly.

TEDDY
The bit about Molly handing in her locker room key, was that your idea as well? The vicar made it sound like she was a piece of left luggage at Waterloo Station. Quite frankly, Dennis, as far as I'm concerned the whole funeral service was a complete fiasco.

DENNIS
Well... okay, we'll dig her up and bury her again next week! If you're such a perfectionist.

TEDDY
Don't get humpty now. I know you meant well, Dennis.

DENNIS
Don't leave things to me if you don't trust me. I only wanted to put up a good show for Molly. As a family friend...

TEDDY
You're certainly that.

DENNIS
And you weren't up to organising anything. So we just got on with it.

TEDDY
Thank you very much for making all the arrangements Dennis. You're right, I – I couldn't have done it.

DENNIS
The flowers will go to the local hospital.

TEDDY
I thought they'd come from the local hospital.

DENNIS
Did you like the wreath? With the anchor?

TEDDY
Was that from us?

DENNIS
Yes.

TEDDY
Molly wasn't in the navy.

DENNIS
No. The florist got a bit mixed up. They were burying a fisherman today. He fell overboard in a storm apparently.

TEDDY
I hope that they didn't notice he had an RAF wreath with They Sewed The Wind, They Will Reap The Whirlwind , written on it.

DENNIS
It was a bit of a mixup, yes. Though, Teddy, after all, Molly was casting anchor wasn't she? In a manner of speaking.

TEDDY
Yes, you don't have to justify it, Dennis. It was a complete cock-up, let's leave it at that, shall we?

DENNIS
Ah well. Such is life. Her relations have gone back to Wiltshire. They live quite near Stonehenge.

TEDDY
I thought they lived under Stonehenge. Especially that one gnawing a bone.

DENNIS
Did you talk to any of them much?

TEDDY
It was grunting mainly. Their means of communication.

DENNIS
Did you speak to her brother? He's some sort of engineer.

TEDDY
Yes, he's still working on the wheel. He's late delivering.

DENNIS
You don't seem to like Molly's relatives.

TEDDY
I don't even like my relatives, why should I like her relatives? I didn't marry her relatives.

DENNIS
You don't like relatives full stop. Okay... when we met – you and I – we were strangers. That's how we got off to such a good start.

TEDDY
Yes, if you'd been my mother it wouldn't have gone so well.

*DENNIS has served drinks. He rings up the till. Puts money in.*

TEDDY
Are you putting money in the till? At last?

DENNIS
Yes, I've sold an article.

TEDDY
What, an item of clothing?

DENNIS
No, literature Teddy.

TEDDY
What size?

DENNIS
36 round the waist. To *The Spectator*. Mud in your eye!

TEDDY
May all your troubles be little ones! Then you can watch them grow...

*They drink.*

DENNIS
I had a chat with Claire.

TEDDY
Did you now?

DENNIS
Yes. She was sorry she couldn't stay the night. She had to push off.

TEDDY
That's alright by me. I adore Claire, but... she and I didn't get round to saying much to each other. What did she have to say for herself? Any gossip?

DENNIS
Oh, she's enjoying being at university. Her TV Journalism course.

TEDDY
Investigative TV Journalism, yes. She couldn't have chosen something else?

DENNIS
I'm sure she'll be good at it.

TEDDY
I fear so.

DENNIS
Yes, she was always asking questions, Claire. She has a great curiosity about life.

TEDDY
Like Miss Marples, yes. She'll uncover the crime. She'll find where the bodies are hidden.

DENNIS
She went off with that chap. I don't know who he was.

TEDDY
Don't you?

DENNIS
No idea. We weren't introduced.

TEDDY
I'm sure you do know who he is.

DENNIS
No...

TEDDY
That was a chap called Billy McCrindle.

DENNIS
Billy McCrindle? That's the bloke who bought it over Hamburg, surely?

TEDDY
Obviously not.

DENNIS
You said...

TEDDY
I was following the official handout, Dennis.

DENNIS
Oh. You mean it was propaganda?

TEDDY
What do you think I bloody well mean? Claire dug him up from somewhere? As she was bound to, given time. Given that investigative journalism is her line of country. I think McCrindle runs a tobacconists in Bristol. She looked him up. She found him. She's very obstinate, Claire. Very perseverant. She'll find out what she wants to find out. Eventually. She'll make a good TV journalist, yes. Practises on her own family first. But then she's every right to know, to get to know her... her father. Now are you satisfied, Dennis?

DENNIS
You didn't need to tell me that. I mean, Skipper, you didn't have to say it out loud.

TEDDY
Not that she ever wanted for anything from us.

DENNIS
I know that. You gave Claire everything, you and Molly.

TEDDY
Except the full story. But who needs that? You've got to be selective in what you tell people. It's a matter of keeping up morale, Dennis. It's a matter of being responsible. You don't broadcast to the entire nation the next morning that you've lost 23 bombers over the Ruhr the night before, do you?

DENNIS
That's the job of being Skipper. The habit of lying to keep everyone going. You have to decide the truth. Your version. For everyone to digest.

TEDDY
The truth? What is the truth, Dennis?

DENNIS
Whatever you decide, Skipper. For the Greater Good. Of the country. Or of the family, come to that. You decide what yarn to spin.

TEDDY
Do I really?

DENNIS
You decide why Billy McCrindle came back from the dead, turning up at Molly's funeral.

TEDDY
It wasn't my idea. He could have done the decent thing and stayed away. I didn't rake him up. He was better off dead. Dead and buried in Wales. But Claire had to find him, didn't she? She wouldn't rest until she got the full story.

DENNIS
The full story? There can be half a dozen different stories, all of them serving a purpose, if only to pass the time. How many stories does a child consume in a lifetime? We have an appetite to know who we are. The more stories the healthier they grow up to be. Claire loved stories.

TEDDY
Molly and I agreed, well… that if it ever came out… or the moment came, when we decided it was better for Claire to know her true parentage, we wanted her to be proud of her absent father. So one day Molly told her.

DENNIS
The hero version?

TEDDY
Who wants a coward for a father? Sergeant McCrindle was the best rear gunner in the business. But he got the notion I could stop the war for him. That I could ask Hitler to call off the whole thing.

DENNIS
I've got the general picture. Just join up the dots for me, will you? Let's get through the flak and get home, shall we?

TEDDY
Billy. Billy had got emotionally involved with a woman. Well lots of women. But eventually he met his match with…

DENNIS
Molly. Flare path Molly. The squadron Jonah. New readers join here. Go on…

TEDDY
McCrindle waded in. He wasn't aware of the superstitious rumours. Or he didn't care. She was such a good-looker herself. What a couple they made, Billy and Molly. The best of the bunch, they were. Then the worst thing happened. He made her pregnant. That's when he came to my office and asked to be grounded.

DENNIS
But you sent him up again?

TEDDY
The bugger wouldn't go. He opted for the court martial. They packed him off to the glasshouse for two years and that's the last I saw of him. Until today. It's funny the effect a woman can have on a man.

DENNIS
Why didn't Molly wait for him?

TEDDY
What?

DENNIS
To come out of the glasshouse?

TEDDY
Oh, come on. She fell in love with a flyer, not a coward clearing out the latrines. She couldn't bear the shame of being associated with him.

DENNIS
That doesn't say much for her.

TEDDY
She put her country first.

DENNIS
And broke off the engagement. That's where you came in, Skipper.

TEDDY
I couldn't leave her in the lurch with a brat coming, could I?

DENNIS
So you did do the decent thing. You married her. You married Flare-path Molly. Well done, Skipper. All the hard work was done.

TEDDY
Yes, wasn't I lucky?

DENNIS
Jammy.

TEDDY
You don't blame me then?

DENNIS
I could blame Molly for being so crass. It's hardly Terence Rattigan, is it? It's not The Flare-path.

TEDDY
To be fair, Molly would not have deserted Billy if I'd posted him away as an instructor. The fault was mine, really. I could have accommodated him.

DENNIS
But you were jealous of Billy. You wanted Molly for yourself. So you sent him back to the war.

TEDDY
Hang on, that's good for a Greek tragedy, Dennis. It wasn't the case. I wasn't aware of, well Molly's condition. It was only later, when Claire came early, that I suspected that my daughter…

DENNIS
She is your daughter in all but one act of progeny. You brought that girl up. You loved her. And Molly. You did all you could for both of them. You don't need to rewrite the script, as far as I'm concerned. Is that all?

TEDDY
What do you mean, is that all? I've spilled my guts, haven't I?

DENNIS
Did you have a word with him at the funeral? Ex-Sergeant McCrindle? After all those years? After being instrumental in his downfall and the ruin of his personal life? From which you profited handsomely.

TEDDY
McCrindle? Yes, I thanked him for coming. We shook hands actually, and I… well, I apologised.

DENNIS
For what?

TEDDY
I didn't say for what. For the whole damn mess, I suppose. I left it hanging. Like my goolies. In the wind. I was not in a position to issue a Royal pardon. There was a war on, you know. You might not have noticed, but we did win.

DENNIS
I don't think all of us won.

*DENNIS exits.*

*LIGHTS CHANGE TO FAVOUR MOLLY – as she enters, young as ever, in a forties Summer dress.*

TEDDY
I knew you'd get home Molly. I never gave up hope.

MOLLY
Hello, Skipper. I can't stay long.

TEDDY
That's a pity. We could lay on a party.

MOLLY
I wanted you to know everything's alright.

TEDDY
Topnotch.

MOLLY
Tickety-boo.

TEDDY
Any complaints?

MOLLY
Report them to the duty officer.

TEDDY
Good show. I kept our little fib going as long as I could, old girl.

MOLLY
We don't need to lie any more, Skipper.

TEDDY
No, we don't.

MOLLY
I never seemed to find time to tell you.

TEDDY
What's that, old girl?

MOLLY
Never mind. Something about love I suppose. You'll find it in the lyrics of a cheap song.

TEDDY
Run Rabbit.

MOLLY
That's the one. You were always there when it counted, Skipper.

TEDDY
My job description.

MOLLY
And you were always there when it didn't count. You were a bloody nuisance most of the time. Come to think of it.

TEDDY
We did what we had to do, Molly.

MOLLY
We didn't have to do most of it, quite frankly, darling. I've come to realise.

TEDDY
That's what I'm saying.

MOLLY
You're saying the complete opposite.

TEDDY
I suppose I am. Does it matter? Surely we agree on something .

MOLLY
Yes. We turned Billy back into a hero, didn't we, Teddy? Just the two of us. It made it easier. Through the years. Our version. It seemed more British. That you'd married the pregnant fiancée of a hero. Just like the movies.

TEDDY
It was a good story, Molly. We kept it shining bright. It was something we could have told Claire. If need be. A twenty-first birthday present perhaps. But things got beyond that point…

MOLLY
The story's over Skipper. We've come out of the cinema into the light. We blink and we're dazzled and we wonder what's real for a moment…

TEDDY
I always knew the difference. I never for a moment thought I was Gregory Peck.

MOLLY
Do be happy, darling. There's no point otherwise. The whole show will have been an entire waste of time.

TEDDY
There's something I wanted to ask you…

MOLLY
Must fly, darling.

*She kisses him lightly.*

TEDDY
I just wanted to say…

MOLLY
Oh, what?

TEDDY
That I don't understand why we never… you know… why we never consummated the nuptials?

MOLLY
It's you that refused to have intercourse, Teddy.

TEDDY
It was meant to be a temporary arrangement. I said let's wait until after the war. Or at least while I was still flying, because…

MOLLY
Because I was the station Jonah, Skipper! By the time the war was over, darling, I'd gone off the whole idea. I'd lost interest.

TEDDY
You never had any interest, Molly.

MOLLY
I did on that first weekend! Fuck you, darling! You should have taken what was on offer. They all said you wouldn't sleep with me. And they were right.

TEDDY
Oh everyone knew, did they?

MOLLY
They were taking bets on it, darling.

TEDDY
Well they lost their bets, didn't they? Because the whole station thought we did consummate the nuptials. That's the point! We pulled it off, Molly. We fooled the lot of them. We confronted their superstitions and kept them flying.

MOLLY
We saw it through.

TEDDY
Yes we did.

MOLLY
Is that all it meant to you?

TEDDY
We were on Maximum Effort.

MOLLY
Not in the bedroom. Why did I bother to come back? To say goodbye to a man who made a respectable woman of me, is that it?

TEDDY
I thought you wanted that.

MOLLY
I needed it. I didn't want it.

TEDDY
There was much more as far as I was concerned.

MOLLY
Well we didn't get round to it, did we?

TEDDY
I suppose not.

MOLLY
Never mind. It's done now, Teddy. We did the best we could.

TEDDY
We got on with it, Molly.

MOLLY
Yes. We got on with it, Teddy. It was only because you were bleating on about M for Molly coming home on a wing and a prayer that I got permission.

TEDDY
What?

MOLLY
To materialise, darling. It involves a tremendous amount of bumph. I rather wish I hadn't come.

TEDDY
Don't say that. It means the world to me.

MOLLY
It means the next world to me. It's not easy to get a pass, Skipper. You know, to visit. Bags of Red Tape up here.

TEDDY
We always managed to cut through that, old girl. I could always scrounge up the extra Wellington for a thousand bomber raid.

MOLLY
Not again, Teddy. I've got to go. I've got to report to… You remember *A Matter Of Life And Death*?

TEDDY
Yes. Very good. David Niven as the pilot who should have died but there was an admin cock-up in Heaven.

MOLLY
It's a bit like that on the other side.

TEDDY
What, with that huge ascending staircase…? And Marius Goring played the French aristocrat – the fop – the guide from heaven who had lost Peter in the fog – our pilot … And there was a court case because they wanted Peter up there, but meanwhile he had fallen in love on Earth… It's a bit like our story, Molly. Only it's reversed, because I want to be with you, and…

MOLLY
Don't take matters into your own hands, Teddy, please. The administration is awful up here. Napoleonic! I promise you… They have a schedule for everybody and they don't like people just turning up. It only means an endless wait, darling, until your number's called. So you might as well let nature take it's course.

TEDDY
Oh. That's worth knowing.

MOLLY
Goodbye, Teddy. Do look after yourself. Try not to drink so much.

*MOLLY exits.*

TEDDY
Molly? Molly? Wait… Oh God, she's gone…

*LIGHTS UP ON BAR. DENNIS serves whisky. They drink.*

TEDDY
You know our favourite film?

DENNIS
I didn't know we had a favourite film, Skipper.

TEDDY
Molly and I. Not you and I. We never had a favourite anything.

DENNIS
You know how to wound.

TEDDY
It was *A Matter Of Life And Death*.

DENNIS
Yes, I liked that film too. With Roger Livesey. He was the doctor who died and pleaded the case of the Squadron Leader in the celestial court, and love won the day. We saw it together.

TEDDY
No we didn't.

DENNIS
Look, Teddy, I'm quite willing for it to be our favourite film, now Molly's gone.

TEDDY
But that's the whole point. She hasn't gone. Not far.

DENNIS
I see.

TEDDY
No, you don't.

DENNIS
How can I be of help, Skipper?

TEDDY
I suspect you've been helping yourself.

DENNIS
As far I'm concerned you had a good marriage. You and Molly, I envied you. You had something that lasted through the years. You had a silver anniversary.

TEDDY
Tarnished silver, yes.

DENNIS
It's got to count for something. All those years of companionship.

TEDDY
Just listen, will you? Pay attention! Now it's too late you might as well know… I never had intimate relations with Molly. Alright? No jig-a-jig, got it? No sex, please, we're British! Now do you hear me?

DENNIS
Loud and clear. Tell me something I don't know.

TEDDY
Was it that obvious? Or did she tell you? Did Molly confide in you, the family friend? Pillow talk, was it?

DENNIS
That's all we were, best friends. For God's sake… that's all I was to her. Look, it doesn't matter…

TEDDY
What matters is that I lacked Moral Fibre, Dennis. That's what matters. When it counted. I couldn't climb into bed with her that first night we went away together. I was like an unstuffed sofa – and that's where I slept. On the sofa. I was terrified to touch her. I knew I'd prang if I did. Next mission. It should have been me put on latrine duty and sent to the glasshouse for cowardice.

DENNIS
Yes, well don't send your DFC back. They won't understand.

TEDDY
I'm selling up, Dennis. I'm giving up this damn place. I've had enough. It's bad luck. The previous owner hung himself, I should have paid attention to that.

DENNIS
Nonsense.

TEDDY
It's not nonsense Dennis. You're right, I should have bailed out a long time ago... But I...I tried to keep the kite flying. Now Molly's gone, and my parachute's shot to buggery. Like David Niven in A Matter Of Life and Death...

DENNIS
Put a sock in it, Skipper. We'll carry on, for her sake. Molly, it's what she would have wanted. We'll regroup – with the insurance money. Take what's on offer. It's enough to get us operational.

*DENNIS takes two more whiskies from the optics.*

DENNIS
We are little lost sheep who have gone astray.

TEDDY
Baa, baa, baa.

DENNIS
God bless Molly.

*They drink.*

TEDDY
We're going to Malta.

DENNIS
Who?

TEDDY
The two of us. Who else, you blithering fool? It is the George Cross Island. We'll open a small bar there. Call it Molly's Bar. What do you think of that?

DENNIS
I don't know who put that idea in your head. It would be a fitting memorial to Molly, however... I'm not at all sure...

TEDDY
When it comes to action Dennis, you're never sure. I can see it now. I'll put up some old squadron photographs for atmosphere. Maybe a propellor.

DENNIS
I didn't know you had one.

TEDDY
I can scrounge up anything. I've still got influence. Of course I'll need a barman. And as nobody gives a monkey's where you are you've got the job. Congratulations.

DENNIS
Someone's got to be your tail-end Charlie.

TEDDY
I'll post it on squadron orders. Oh, by the way, Dennis.

DENNIS
Was there something?

TEDDY
From now on this is the Official Version.

DENNIS
For the Greater Good of all. What do you mean?

TEDDY
Make sure you toe the line, there's a good chap. Pay no attention to rumours and don't walk round with your hands in your pockets.

DENNIS
I say you're on song! Skipper? Are you… well are sure you're okay?

TEDDY
Never better. The only way out is through, what? Carry on, Dennis.

DENNIS
Wilco Sunray.

TEDDY
Roger that.

*DENNIS exits.*
*TEDDY waits until DENNIS is out of the way, then takes a service revolver from under the bar counter, using a key to unlock a hidden drawer. He goes to the radio. Tunes it. Crackle, then...*

PILOT'S VOICE OVER STATIC

Hello. Hello, how do you hear me? How do you hear me? G for Georgy calling base. G for Georgy... I can see the coastline. Coming in over the Humber... But we're not going to make it. Sorry. We're going down into the drink. It looks damn cold down there. Whoever's on duty, give my love to Molly. Goodbye...

*More static.*

TEDDY
G for Georgy? She didn't mention him. That bugger didn't come to the squadron until after we were married!

*TEDDY fires a shot at the wireless, destroying it.*

TEDDY
I've had enough of that wireless. Nothing but trouble since I bought it, spreading demoralising scandal. Molly's right, yes. It's time we got on with it. The move to Malta is the Official Line to keep morale up, station morale. The story will hold. That's the Official Line, that's the version we're putting out. When a decision's called for, ask the Skipper. He won't let you down. It might be a tough call, but he'll make it, by God he will. You don't get a DSO for pissing around...

*TEDDY exits by door to interior. Enter DENNIS, hurriedly.*

DENNIS
Skipper?! He's shot the damn radio to pieces. I thought he'd topped himself. There are too many ghosts holding sway here, we've got to get out while the going's good...

*Sound of revolver shot, OFF.*

DENNIS
Christ! Is he shooting the chickens because we can't take them with us?

*DENNIS exits, interior door. Pause. He comes back . Goes to phone. Dials.*

DENNIS
Police. Ambulance. Both… I don't know… Send the lot. A shooting… Yes… Soon as you can yes, but it won't change anything… I can't describe it, just come… It's an – it's an awful story…

*He puts the phone down.*

*DENNIS exits.*
*Enter from opposite sides of the stage, TEDDY in his flying kit, and FRENCH FOP, period French revolution costume.*
*Effect fog.*

FRENCH FOP
Always fog en Angleterre. Il fait mon emploi impossible! I cannot see my foot in front of my mouth…
*He sees TEDDY and waves*
… Ah, hello! Hello! Ici! Oui…Over here…Oui! Voila! Merci beaucoup… Je suis votre guide. Are you ready, Monsieur?

TEDDY
Hello. Where are we going?

FRENCH FOP
Upstairs. Escalier! Monter. Faire l'ascension d'escalier

TEDDY
Oui, oui, je comprende… Pardoner moi… What is my category? Classification?

FRENCH FOP
Victime de la guerre. War casualty. What else?

TEDDY
But... the way it happened?

FRENCH FOP
Pardon?

TEDDY
It was a self-inflicted wound... He mimes shooting himself in the head. That is a court martial offence.

FRENCH FOP
Non, non. C'est la Guerre! It is the result of the war. You are un autre victime... A casualty, oui... Comme les autres, tout les autres... Come, come...
Avance mon brave! Follow me... Allez, allez... Peur rein... Allez...

*They exit.*

**THE END**

# THE LOONEYS

## by

## JOHN ANTROBUS

First produced at Traverse Theatre, Edinburgh, December, 1971. Director: Michael Rudman.

A revised production of the play was directed again by Michael Rudman at the Hampstead Theatre Club, London. October 1974. Leonard Rossiter and Colin Welland played the two looneys, BRIAN and ERIC. Also with Jane Wymark as 'Twenty-One Today!' KATEY

Re-titled as LOONEYS for BBC Radio 4, Saturday Play, 30th August, 1986. Director: Gerry Jones. Robert Stephens played the father, ARNOLD GOSPORT, ruminating amidst the ashes of a once dazzling film career.

As KATEY celebrates her twenty-first birthday in rather desperate mode – for where is her alcoholic father, fallen film star, absent again? Another broken promise. Only the jaundiced sarcasm of her younger brother, ROGER, and the enabling encouragement of MOTHER make up the party until two looneys, who have escaped from a local mental hospital, break in to bring more company. When Daddy, ARNOLD GOSPORT, eventually arrives home he brings his own agenda and preoccupations to the scene. He is more concerned in relaunching his career with a film sequel of his once-upon-a-time success as 'Elephant Bill' and wonders whether the gangster brother of BRIAN would be interested in investing in his film.

# THE LOONEYS

SCENE: *the lounge of a cottage in the country, surrounded by trees*

TIME: *maybe needed*

CAST:

    ROGER: *younger brother to Katy*

    KATEY: *'twenty-one today!'*

    MOTHER: *Vera Gosport*

    ARNOLD: *'Daddy!' Arnold Gosport*

    DIGBY: *agent to Arnold Gosport*

    BRIAN: *a looney*

    ERIC: *a looney*

    HELEN: *mistress to Arnold Gosport*

    SHERIFF

    POLICE SERGEANT

## ACT I

*LOUNGE – Evening. MOTHER, ROGER, KATEY.*
*ROGER is seated at the piano. He plays and sings.*

ROGER
She's twenty one today
Twenty one today
She's got the key of the door
We've changed the lock,
The silly old whore…
*He bashes the keyboard, discordantly.*
Well, where is he?

KATEY
Who?

ROGER
You know who! Who? Fuck, like… who else is there?

KATEY
Daddy is hardly likely to forget my twenty-first birthday party, is he? So you can shut the fuck up, Roger. I don't know where he is.

MOTHER
Your father knows where he is, that's the main thing.

ROGER
He didn't last year when he woke up in Dublin.

MOTHER
That's Irish hospitality for you. He was with Peter O'Toole.

ROGER
Not on the window ledge he wasn't. Peeing into Grafton Street.

MOTHER
He couldn't find the bathroom, and you've only got the hotel manager's word for that story.

KATEY
I like having a famous father. It's more fun. It's not boring.

ROGER
A man who wet himself while seated on Aer Lingus.

MOTHER
Didn't he pay a supplement for that?

ROGER
Yes, Excess Urine. But that's enough about dad's bladder problem, the scourge of five continents. You're right Katey, God save us from being boring. It's the ultimate sin in this family. We must always be witty and eccentric. Like we're in some endless sitcom, yeah? Playing to an audience we cannot see.

MOTHER
OK, your father does have the occasional – binge. Let's face it, it comes with the territory folks. It was the same with John Barrymore. Eugene O'Neil, Tennessee Williams. He's in there with the heavyweights. Richard Burton. And, of course, his close friend, Peter O'Toole.
Boys must have fun.

ROGER
You read all the show business biographies, don't you? You know what makes a great actor tick. But none of them were making elephant pictures, like Arnold Gosport.

KATEY
Eco-friendly movies.

ROGER
Yes, me Tarzan, you health and safety officer. This is all so fucking pathetic. Dad's not famous. Not any more. We're not a famous family. We're nothing. We're forgotten. It was never worth remembering. If we don't draw attention to ourselves we don't have to be ashamed, that's all.

MOTHER
Ashamed? What's he talking about? Ashamed? What of?

ROGER
Arnold Gosport hasn't made a film for twelve years.

KATEY
Thirteen.

MOTHER
We go from twelve to fourteen, Katey. Touch wood. And I don't only read show business biographies, Roger, as an inspiration of what the human spirit can overcome.

KATEY
Winston Churchill.

MOTHER
That's a good example, Katey, but a very common one. It doesn't stretch your mind.

ROGER
Yes, every idiot says Winston Churchill. *(Mimics her)* Winston Churchill…

KATEY
What?

MOTHER
Charles de Gaulle! He spent thirteen years in the wilderness before he returned to save France.

ROGER
He didn't save France from the ivory hunters. He wasn't hanging from plastic creepers in his back garden to keep himself in trim, beating his chest saying I will take the army out of Algeria.

KATEY
So you could study history at Oxford? You know, go!

ROGER
No. Not unless you come with me. I am your carer.

KATEY
No you're not. You're my fucking creepy brother with fucking spiders for fingers...

ROGER
All I'm saying is – if anyone's interested – that Our Father, as the prayer goes – that Dad, right? is just a run-of-the-mill alcoholic and we are a family in trauma. OK? I can live with it. I can live with it if you can. We can tick the box.

MOTHER
Your father is not an alcoholic, Roger.

ROGER
Then why did he go to AA?

MOTHER
He visited them to see if they could teach him to drink moderately. But they had no idea about that. Very nice people, he said, but they were all losers. None of them could drink, they'd just given up on it. No will power at all...

KATEY
The point is – everyone, hello? We... right?

ROGER
What?

KATEY
Eh?

ROGER
We what?

KATEY
I'm coming to that, aren't I? What the fuck's the matter with you, Roger? We... You're fucking getting on my tits you are!

MOTHER
That's quite enough, Katey…

KATEY
He won't let me say…

ROGER
What?

KATEY
That we all have to make sacrifices! So that Daddy…

ROGER
The Dadda, yes?

KATEY
Can go to town and network. That's the movie business, isn't it? You've got to be seen coming and going. I mean just hanging out really. Being there is it.

ROGER
Being there is it?

KATEY
That's why Arnold Gosport is staying at the Savoy this week.

MOTHER
Yes Katey, you're right, and damn the expense. Alexander Korda used to book in at Claridge's. Stayed there for months, during the war, and never paid the bill. And now they've named a suite after him, think of that? The Alexander Korda suite.

ROGER
Yes, maybe they'll have an Arnold Gosport broom cupboard at the Savoy one day. He did sleep in one.

KATEY
Jesus slept in a stable.

ROGER
He didn't have any choice, did he? He was a baby.

KATEY
He was also the son of God.

ROGER
He didn't know it then.

KATEY
He might have done.

MOTHER
Do you have to be so cynical, Roger.

KATEY
Yes, do you have to be, Roger? On my birthday?

ROGER
There's not room in your pink bubble for anyone else Kate. It's all so predictable, isn't it? Dad will hole up in his expensive room at the Savoy – while we eat potatoes round a candle at home – that is, assuming he ever gets to the Savoy.

KATEY
Of course he'll get there, Stupid.

ROGER
And then what? He won't be seen coming and going from the hotel, like you say. Chatting up the doorman? Not a chance! He's frightened, Arnold Gosport. Demoralised. Feeling like shit. Like he's broken somewhere inside and it can't be fixed. Dad will stay in his room until he is asked to leave. He'll get no further than the fridge minibar. The curtains will be drawn tight, with only the flickering light from the TV set to show him where the bed ends.

KATEY
Very poetic. I'll use that... *Writes in her notebook.*

ROGER
Where are you going to use it?

KATEY
I don't know, Roger. Will you stop being so anally retentive? About your phrases? Like, OK? Words are out on the air like bumblebees and I am a beehive, alright? It's my honey, OK? Any fucking problem with that?

MOTHER
Roger, your father still has that spark of ambition. The pilot light that glows in the darkness at noon.

ROGER
It's <u>your</u> ambition, not his. This is Eugene O'Neil. Isn't it? We're there. I mean this is Act One of Long Days Journey For The Fucking Iceman…

KATEY
I thought we were in a sitcom?

ROGER
I bet Dad got no further than Exeter this time.

MOTHER
Stop that, Roger. Perish the thought.

KATEY
We can't just give up, can we? And become ordinary. The world is full of ordinary people.

MOTHER
Remember, Katey, it's the little people who pay the pennies. We must not despise ordinary. We never give up, Roger. Not this family. I want nothing from my life but what's good for your father. I want a great acting talent to be vindicated. I was there when it started. With his Hamlet at the Old Vic. Arnold Gosport brought method acting to the London stage.

ROGER
The night he pissed in the skull.

MOTHER
It had nothing to do with a weak bladder. Rod Steiger was in the stalls that night and he was very…

ROGER
Splashed.

KATEY
Dads is still in demand, isn't he? He opened a supermarket in North London last April, didn't he?

MOTHER
And a garage on the M1 last July.

ROGER
He's scared to open his mail these days.

MOTHER
It's easy to criticise your father.

ROGER
It takes an effort. Of imagination.

MOTHER
Why don't you get a life, Roger? You're not half the man he is.

ROGER
No, I'm crippled inside, living in the overpowering shadow of his genius. *He plays John Lennon song – few bars – on piano…* Thank you John Lennon.

KATEY
They showed Elephant Bill on television last week. A lot of people saw that. The demand for a sequel will be overwhelming.

ROGER
It wasn't the last half dozen times they showed it.

KATEY
As nobody's coming to my party I might as well get sloshed.

MOTHER
Aren't you forgetting Digby? He's never let us down. He'll show up.

KATEY
Good old reliable Digby.

ROGER
Dad's agent.

MOTHER
And a true family friend.

KATEY
The only one we've got. We must treasure Digby.

MOTHER
He's loyal. Digby will never stab Arnold in the back like some I could mention.

ROGER
He's a useless agent though. Everyone's left him over the years. Who else has he got on his books these days apart from Arnold Gosport? A couple of Irish boy dancers he's trying to date, and a dog act he's hired out to a security firm.

KATEY
We're isolated. That's it. Aren't we? I mean living out here in the country. Why did Dad buy a house away from it all, like this?

MOTHER
It's a wise investment, Katey, to have a weekend place.

ROGER
Weekend? We've been living here three years.

MOTHER
I mean a second house.

ROGER
We sold the first house. In town. Or the bank did, for us.

MOTHER
We bought this place second, Roger, that's what I'm saying.

ROGER
Well it should be promoted to first. As it's all we've got now.

KATEY
What? What are you staring at?

ROGER
Twenty-one? You're an old woman, aren't you? All your dreams are behind you now. They've turned into a bucketful of regrets. You'll never get to drama school.

KATEY
That's true.

MOTHER
Typical Roger, negative propaganda.

KATEY
I am living in a world of smashed mirrors, it's true. There are pieces of me everywhere I look, reflected bits of disconnected experience. I shall write about it.

MOTHER
Bravo! Bravo!

ROGER
Bravo... *He claps.*

*SOUND OFF – SIREN*

KATEY
Listen. It's the mental home siren.

ROGER
The old tunes are the best.

MOTHER
It's probably only a practise. The first Wednesday of every month they sound it.

ROGER
This is Friday.

MOTHER
Then they've got the wrong day, Roger.

ROGER
How can you break out on the wrong day?

KATEY
Who said anybody's broken out? You mean escaped?

MOTHER
What are you trying to do? Scare Katey?

KATEY
I'm not scared Mum, I am concerned though. That there are people out there in the dark. Bumping into trees. Some disadvantaged people looking for a life.

MOTHER
Who are we to judge? There are always people less fortunate than ourselves, Katey.

ROGER
That's becoming less true every day. Unfortunately. It's a poor comparison. I mean look at Katey. Rescued from a life of glue sniffing.

MOTHER
She was trying to launch a show business career.

ROGER
Pole dancing in King's Cross?

KATEY
It's only a couple of stops on the Northern Line to the West End, Roger.

**ROGER**
Two stops from stardom!

**KATEY**
I did not sniff glue.

**ROGER**
You sniffed everything else. More went up your nose than goes through the Blackwall Tunnel. Ha, ha, let's keep it going. Lots of funny lines and occasional bursts of blazing sincerity.

**KATEY**
It's you that's doing it.

**ROGER**
I know, I can't stop. So, Daddy found her in The Blue Pussy Cat.

**MOTHER**
I don't want to be reminded. It was an agonising search for his daughter.

**ROGER**
That was his excuse for trawling the sex clubs.

**MOTHER**
Arnold brought her home, that's what's important. And there are no recriminations.

**ROGER**
Try again when you're forty.

**KATEY**
Why don't you leave home?

**ROGER**
Because I'm waiting for it to collapse under me, that's why.

**KATEY**
You haven't the confidence to go to Oxford, have you?

ROGER
True, but they can wait, can't they?

KATEY
To read history.

ROGER
Well, there'll be more history to read the longer I wait.

KATEY
That's funny.

MOTHER
Don't listen to Roger. He's scared to fail, so if he doesn't do anything, he can't.

ROGER
True. Very perceptive.

KATEY
As long as I get *The Stage* once a week, to read the ads. I should have stayed in London. They're doing a lot of musicals in town. But you have to be there to get the auditions.

MOTHER
Emotionally you weren't ready. Katey, concentrate on being an author. You've written a lovely screenplay for your father, The Last Elephant.

ROGER
How can The Last Elephant be the prequel? Shouldn't it be The First Elephant?

KATEY
Do you think I've got talent, Mum?

MOTHER
Yes, yes. Believe, daughter, believe! You have a writing talent. Look in the mirror every morning and say twelve times, I have a great writing talent and I am expressing it now.

ROGER
Yes, do it while you're shaving.

KATEY
I do not shave.

ROGER
Your legs.

KATEY
I do not shave my legs in the mirror.

ROGER
Listen, if you want to feel better pop a few more Prozac. They always work.

MOTHER
What she has, Roger – our Katey – when you've finished undermining her – what she has is enthusiasm. Something completely lacking in your case. Theos, God. Enthuse, to be filled. To be filled with God.

ROGER
Is it alright to be ordinary for a few moments in this household? Instead of being filled with God? Or supporting absent genius?

*FX Sound off, branch breaking.*

KATEY
Listen? I hate those trees so near the house.

ROGER
Well move them. Faith can move mountains, so why not move a few trees?

MOTHER
Faith. Faith is all we need, children. Faith is the substance of things hoped for. The evidence of things not yet seen. St Paul. Though I'm an atheist.

ROGER
God is Dad. 'Our Dad… '

*PHONE RINGS.*

MOTHER
That'll be your father. He always phones when he's delayed.

KATEY
It might be Digby…

*MOTHERS picks up phone.*
*ROGER and KATEY converse aside.*

ROGER
Can't you see it coming?

KATEY
What? It? What?

ROGER
The pregnancy of a new world is in The Invisible, Katey. And it's mutating.

KATEY
Don't be spooky, Roger.

ROGER
Do you have to drink so much?

KATEY
I'm celebrating. I'm twenty one.

ROGER
You love the bottle more than the boys.

KATEY
You love the boys more than the bottle.

ROGER
Maybe.

KATEY
Meaning?

ROGER
I haven't decided, OK?

KATEY
You can't decide. It's what you are. You're a fucking faggot.

ROGER
That is not a politically correct remark. You're infringing my human rights.

KATEY
You're not fucking human either!

ROGER
I do have animal rights.

KATEY
Yes, you are an animal, Roger, I grant you that. Leave me alone, OK?

ROGER
I haven't touched you.

KATEY
You're sexually ambiguous, aren't you?

ROGER
I hope so. I want different things at different times. Like when you go to a supermarket.

KATEY
Well I'm not a packet of cornflakes, right?

ROGER
I know.

*MOTHER has been listening on phone. She puts it down.*

MOTHER
We were cut off. I assume it was your father. He must have leant on the instrument with his elbow.

ROGER
Or foot. Did it sound like a foot?

MOTHER
How could it sound like a foot? The line went dead.

ROGER
'Dead, dead, and never called me mother!'

KATEY
Maybe the looneys' cut us off.

MOTHER
What looneys?

KATEY
They could have escaped. We heard the siren, right?

ROGER
Right.

KATEY
They could be out there. In the trees.

ROGER
Nesting.

*SOUND OF BRANCH SNAPPING – OFF*

KATEY
There is someone outside. I'm frightened.

ROGER
There is someone inside. It's terrifying.

KATEY
Who?

ROGER
You!

MOTHER
Oh Katey, he's trying to upset you on your birthday.

KATEY
He tries to upset me every day. It doesn't matter. I'm stronger than him because I have the courage to be vulnerable, right?

ROGER
I'm going down the lane to the phone box. I'm going to have our line tested.

*ROGER exits.*

KATEY
Roger, don't leave us…

MOTHER
I think he should leave us. He's becoming impossible.

*ROGER comes back, putting on cycle clips.*

ROGER
I hope these cycle clips are the right size. Oh, and one thing before I go Kate, I am willing to go to Oxford but I'm waiting for Dennis.

KATEY
There'll be lots of Dennises at Oxford. That's where they go. Dennises. And Clives go to Cambridge. All the Clives I know. And Harrys go to Afghanistan, so…

ROGER
Shut up, Kate. I don't want a new Dennis. I want the Dennis I know.

KATEY
You're so scared of being hurt, aren't you?

ROGER
I expect to be hurt. That's what relationships are about, in case you didn't know. I reserve the right to choose who's going to hurt me, that's all.

MOTHER
It's sad, isn't it? I never planned to have a brood like this. My God, what's the world coming to?

ROGER
It's come. It's arrived. It's here, mother! Hello… Goodbye.

KATEY
Don't go Roger. We need a man about the house and you're the best we've got.

ROGER
Then you're in trouble.

*ROGER exits.*

*SOUND OF FRONT DOOR SLAMMING – OFF*

MOTHER
I've got to cut the apron strings, Katey. It's no good Roger hanging around the house waiting to be cast as Sabu in Arnold's next jungle feature.

KATEY
Is that it?

MOTHER
Of course. He's not a boy anymore, he's grown up, he's too tall. I can't see Roger on an elephant, can you?

KATEY
I can see him inside an elephant.

MOTHER
I can cope with you at home, darling, writing, revising *The Last Elephant*. I smell film rights. I smell a deal.

KATEY
You're psychic.

MOTHER
I'm never wrong. Something's in the wind. We'll lay down our own conditions. Our own price for the screenplay, sweetheart.

KATEY
We're talking telephone numbers here.

MOTHER
You better believe it. Hang on to that dream, Katey, and hitch a ride to Hollywood. They're rolling out the red carpet for you, baby girl!

KATEY
I couldn't ask for a nicer birthday present...

*French windows burst open.*
*BRIAN DAREY and ERIC DEWITT enter.*
*ERIC wears hospital pyjamas and slippers. BRIAN wears a long macintosh, and carries several plastic bags.*

BRIAN
We hoped you might have a new attitude to mental illness.

MOTHER
What are you doing in our house?

BRIAN
That's a good question. I have prepared a statement.. *Takes out paper from his bag.*

KATEY
Daddy, where are you?

*BLACKOUT*

*LIGHTS UP – Bar*
*ARNOLD on a barstool, drinking.*

ARNOLD
I am in Exeter. Of that I am reasonably sure. I have looked from my hotel window and seen the cathedral spire. Although it could be Salisbury

cathedral, that is true, I am not minded not to ask anyone if that be the case. It is not York. I know York Cathedral well. Did I not play Becket there? And well, with sober notices.
I am not in York, and will not torture myself with that thought. I would be far off route to be there. Far from home...
Shall I call it home? Where resides my blessed Katey on her twenty-first birthday...
*(Sings)* She's twenty-one today, twenty-one today... Or was it yesterday? Or is it tomorrow? Who knows? What o'clock?
One is as sure as one can be. About anything. These days...
Take paternity, for example. August Strinberg's *The Father* is hardly encouraging on that score – a part that I have played, times since – and recently I have had mine own doubts about paternity...
Yes, indeed, any sensible man would have doubts about paternity. Yet stupidly, in the vanity of paternalism, a happy family life is usually centred upon the male line. What vanity lies in that! And all deceptions follow, as they must. For a man's seed, he decrees, shall fall into the ground he owns – the woman. You get my drift? It's all to do with property. Property!That's where it starts...
Don't count upon the stratagems of men, their laws, religions, customs, reeking of domination. To be a man is to be a cuckold in waiting. I'm glad 'tis so. It is deserved. Nature is stronger than fidelity, and lust in it's season will overcome the fondest hearth and home. A woman's sexuality is a storm when released, a biological necessity to mate with the strongest genes, while at the same time securing the nest. There's the rub! The two don't always go together, do they? No, indeed not...

*Enter DIGBY*

Who goes there? Halt! What manner of spectre be you? Clothed as one with whom I am familiar. Digby? What do you here? What does Digby in Exeter? What is your business in Exeter? Do you come to communicate with me? Have you cast off shrouds to assume a common aspect? Digby? Speak!

DIGBY
What brings you to London, Arnold? This is a surprise. Come in, come in...

*LIGHTS UP. DIGBY'S OFFICE.*

*DIGBY leads ARNOLD to his desk. He sits down and beckons for ARNOLD to sit.*

DIGBY
I was not expecting you. By the way, how did you get into the office? I didn't buzz you in.

ARNOLD
Credit card. Slipped the lock. Trick I picked up in a police series, long time since.

DIGBY
You don't need to break in to see your agent.

ARNOLD
I've lost confidence in our relationship Digby.

DIGBY
For Heaven's sake! Things aren't that bad between us. Please don't do it again.
Well…? So…? What have you been up to recently?

ARNOLD
My God, when your own agent has to ask you that.

DIGBY
It's a difficult time of year, Arnold.

ARNOLD
I've never known a time of year with you when it's not been difficult.

DIGBY
What does bring you to town, Arnold? To what do I owe the pleasure of this visit?

ARNOLD
You really want to know?

DIGBY
I do indeed. That's why I'm asking.

ARNOLD
You have time to hear me out then?

DIGBY
I am making time, Arnold. State your case.

ARNOLD
I intend to produce, direct and star in a prequel of *Elephant Bill*. What do you think of that?

DIGBY
Complete rubbish. Count me out. I want nothing to do with it.

ARNOLD
Right.

DIGBY
That subject is well past it's sell-by date. They're not making movies like that anymore.

ARNOLD
Thank you. Let's move on.

DIGBY
My advice, Arnold, is to forget all about *Elephant Bill*. like everyone else has.

ARNOLD
I've already forgotten. Thank you for straightening me out on that one, Digby. I won't mention it again. You see how reasonable is your favourite client. How open to persuasion. What have you to offer me?

**DIGBY**
Look… they are doing *Macbeth* at Chichester next season.

ARNOLD
I'd love to play Macbeth at Chichester!

DIGBY
They're offering you Banquo's ghost.

ARNOLD
Banquo's ghost? That's a piddling little part. Didn't they see my Wild Duck at the Globe?

DIGBY
Yes, unfortunately. It was the night you kicked the rabbit into the audience.

ARNOLD
It was Peter Hall's fault for using live rabbits.

DIGBY
It was Peter Hall's fault for using live actors.

ARNOLD
Tell Chichester to get stuffed.

DIGBY
I already have done. In more polite terms.

ARNOLD
Good.

DIGBY
So I'll see you at Katey's party tomorrow, shall I?

ARNOLD
Tomorrow? Is it tomorrow?

DIGBY
Yes. Katey's twenty-First.

ARNOLD
Yes, I know how old she is. My own daughter. I do know she's twenty-one, Katey, I'm aware of that. Are you coming then?

DIGBY
Yes, as an old family friend. I have been invited by Vera. I am a favoured guest. Unless you have any objections, that is?

ARNOLD
Why should I have any objections?

DIGBY
I can't imagine, old boy.

ARNOLD
You've known us for ever. You knew Vera even before I appeared on the scene. You represented her.

DIGBY
Indeed I did. A beautiful talent. A wondrous dancer. She could have been the next Pavlova.

ARNOLD
More like the last Tessie O'Shea after you'd finished with her.

DIGBY
It's not my fault she put on weight. Arnold, why are we raking up the past?

ARNOLD
You introduced us – Vera and I – you pawned her off on me, didn't you? I married her quick, and the baby came prematurely, or did it? Follow?

DIGBY
No. I don't. Sorry... Where are you going with this?

ARNOLD
Think Gregers Werle, The Wild Duck. Employer gets girl pregnant, marries her off to needy employee.

DIGBY
The role you played. Some time ago. The rabbit incident...

ARNOLD
It was my last leading role.

DIGBY
Don't take it to heart. I would say the trouble began before then.

ARNOLD
What trouble?

DIGBY
Well, mental really. You've never been the same since you came back from the Edinburgh Festival, where you were playing in *Six Characters In Search Of An Author*.

ARNOLD
Pirandello. The master. Yes, I seek my author, I do not deny it.

DIGBY
My opinion is, which you may not welcome but I'll give it to you anyway. You have been suffering from a – a sort of submerged nervous breakdown , for some time. You need a rest.

ARNOLD
Well I'm getting that with you as my agent. Plenty of rest, aren't I? Pirandello – your Pirandello – my Pirandello... might pose this question. What is the difference between playing mad, and being mad?

DIGBY
Ah!

ARNOLD
Awareness, Digby.

DIGBY
I am glad we've cleared that up.

ARNOLD
What we haven't cleared up is the matter of paternity.

DIGBY
You're being quite absurd.

ARNOLD
I love absurd theatre.

DIGBY
Why did you wait until Katey's twenty-first birthday to bring this up?

ARNOLD
Because it suited both of us. To have an arrangement. Over the years. An unspoken silent agreement.

DIGBY
I am not aware of any such thing. Silence does not constitute an agreement.

ARNOLD
You cancelled a five hundred pound debt I owed you, as a wedding present. Why would you do that?

DIGBY
I wanted to see you and Vera – both dear friends – get off to a splendid start.

ARNOLD
You got us off to a splendid start alright. With a nice little present, wasn't it? All wrapped up in pink and smiles.

DIGBY
Oh this is preposterous! Stop this nonsense, Arnold, please… Are you doing it to torture me?

ARNOLD
You'd like that.

DIGBY
I don't appreciate this form of humour. Stop it, I say.

ARNOLD
It all fits together, luvvy. Sorry. The money you've given me over the years. The cottage you lent us – we're still in it. You've kept the family going, haven't you? Without you we'd have fallen apart.

DIGBY
I haven't got a family of my own. I've adopted your family, Arnold.

ARNOLD
Adopted? That's a good word.

DIGBY
I'm a dyed in the wool, set in my ways, old bachelor. I'm gay, isn't it obvious? There's nothing to hide, these days, and nothing to spell out.

ARNOLD
Gay? That's a convenient excuse. Gets you out of a tight corner. We could all say we're gay. We've all been there, ducky. We've all lived a bit. Experimented. You can't make films in Rome with Zeffirelli without some of that.

DIGBY
It's a life choice.

ARNOLD
Maybe it wasn't, back then. Maybe it was an economic choice. Which brings me to the purpose of my visit...

*LOUNGE – MOTHER, KATEY, BRIAN and ERIC – as before.*

*BRIAN holding the gun, reads from the paper.*

BRIAN
I went into hospital voluntary as a patient, on the strict understanding I could work my way up to doctor. But as soon as I got in there, they had me locked up compulsory, breaking our agreement, I got off to a bad start, you could say.

ERIC
They put him in the rubber room. That's where the right nutters go. To bounce around.

BRIAN
It was persecution, Eric. *Confidentially*: I was looking for my mother you see. She is in the National Health Service somewhere.

KATEY
What, as a patient?

BRIAN
That's right.

KATEY
What's wrong with your mother?

BRIAN
Who said there's anything wrong with her? They took her away in an ambulance, that's for sure. And put us in care. I don't know who looked after the cows.

ERIC
They might have put them in care. Cow care.

BRIAN
I doubt it.

ERIC
Doubt is for the doubtful.

BRIAN
He ain't had his medicine tonight.

ERIC
Right, doctor.

BRIAN
You see, I been treating the sick on the ward, cos of the neglect, we never saw doctors, 'bout once a week. So I followed my vocation.

ERIC
Where to?

BRIAN
How can you treat others 'less you been sick yourself? 'Tis from the ranks of the sick they should promote you to doctor, because of our experience of being sick. But they brings in this lot from the universities – boys most of 'em – healthy as pigs, never had more than whooping cough. They didn't know you had to treat the mind.

ERIC
Like Jesus.

BRIAN
That's right Eric. It was me that was devoted to the ministering of others, picking herbs and berries from the hospital grounds to make medicines.

ERIC
Matron banned you from the 'ospital grounds. On the grounds that you – you shouldn't be out on the grounds.

BRIAN
Those accusations were groundless, Eric.

ERIC
So was you.

BRIAN
Yes, and she broke my thermometer, Eric. What I paid over the odds for. I face constant persecution. Goodness gracious I was the only one doing good on that ward. While they was giving 'em electric shock treatments.

ERIC
So was you, mate. With a hairdryer.

BRIAN
I had to improvise Eric, to test my own theories. Anyway I abandoned the trials when Dick's hair caught fire.

ERIC
He looked good bald with crayoned eyebrows.

BRIAN
It was all for the sake of medical advance. I shall demand rest – rest... what is it Eric?

ERIC
Resuscitation.

BRIAN
No it's not. It's restitution. In summation I demand restitution, compensation and promotion. In support of my claim to the court I submit case histories of my work on the ward, complete recoveries and miracle cures… *Looks up from paper.* That is the basis of my case. Plus I am bringing out Eric for outpatient treatment.

KATEY
That's a great story, trust me.

BRIAN
Thank you, Miss.

KATEY
We must have a serious talk about it. It's got feature film written all over it.

MOTHER
Katey, don't encourage them.

BRIAN
We are determined to defend our human rights in the European Court at Strasbourg. Right Eric?

ERIC
That's a goose ain't it? Strasbourg? I want to talk to you.

BRIAN
Why are you shivering? You're shivering ain't you?

ERIC
I want a – a private interview, Mr Darey. Can you arrange it?

BRIAN
I shall have to look in my engagement book, Mr Dewitt. Sorry about this… *He rummages in bag. Brings out book :* When did you want to see me?

ERIC
Now.

BRIAN
Oh, that's different. Go ahead.

ERIC
Well it's like this see. These pyjamas – these pyjamas is hospital property. And I am – hospital property see – and I am asking for trouble from Matron coming out in these pyjamas, off limits, so to speak. I should not be seen about town in hospital pyjamas. And these slippers, they're hospital too. Property what? The only size eights in the place. They've got to go back. It's a matter of trust see, Matron see, she can withdraw all me privileges, if I'm off limits in her property. It could be an end to me watching Blind Date.

BRIAN
You're not going back in, Eric, so don't worry about that. And stop shivering. Can he sit down?

*Eric goes to sit down.*
*Stands up.*

ERIC
You said…

BRIAN
You haven't had permission yet. This isn't your house, Eric.

MOTHER
Of course he can sit down.

BRIAN
You hear the lady Eric. You may be seated now. Nicely. Don't put your feet on the cushions, this ain't public transport.

*Eric sits down.*

BRIAN
Thank you.

MOTHER
Relax boys.

ERIC
One false move, Missus, you're history. Tombstone City, right?

BRIAN
Don't mind Eric. He's excitable. Influenced by television the curse of the modern age. He don't know what is the difference between the news and a movie.

ERIC
It's all moving image. Pixels! Thousands of 'em!

BRIAN
Right Eric.

MOTHER
I'm sure we can help you.

BRIAN
We been helped. We don't want no more help, Missus. Now we's helping ourselves. Where's the phone?

KATEY
It's cut off. Possibly because we're behind with our account.

BRIAN
Account of what?

KATEY
The bills.

BRIAN
You're not paying your bills? Pay them. A man who earns a pound and spends nineteen shillings and sixpence is a happy man.

ERIC
Hey, we cut the phone wire son, remember? To isolate the property. According to plan A.

BRIAN
That's as may be, Eric. But a household economy must be run on proper

lines. Bless this house and all therein. Home sweet home. Stitch it on a cushion, Missus.

MOTHER
When we have time.

BRIAN
No time like the present. And bake your own bread.

KATEY
Mum, they cut our phone.

MOTHER
Leave it to me, Katey. Now listen here, you boys, I'm going to recommend that I speak to whoever has been upsetting you at the hospital.

BRIAN
Thank you, Missus, but we's not going back to the hospital. I'll issue you with an affidavit to come to the court. In Strasbourg to support our Human Rights...

ERIC
Which have been violined!

BRIAN
Violated.

ERIC
Right.

BRIAN
Shut the window Eric.

*Eric shuts the windows.*

BRIAN
Anyone else live here?

MOTHER
No.

**BRIAN**
*Calls* : Anyone at home? Anyone at home?

**ERIC**
*Joins in calling* : Anyone at home? Anyone at home?

**BRIAN**
Anyone at home?

**MOTHER**
We are at home, and you are intruding. Now this is not good behaviour, I expect better of you. I must ask you boys, very nicely, to run along. You came in by the window. Now you're welcome to leave by the front door…

**KATEY**
Yes, you're interrupting a private party actually. It's my birthday. I'm twenty one today.

**BRIAN**
Oh congratulations Miss.

**KATEY**
And as you didn't get an invitation that makes you gate crashers. However, if you promise to go immediately afterwards you may have a glass of champagne.

**MOTHER**
Katey…

**KATEY**
Oh, come on Moms. They're alright. At least someone's turned up.

**MOTHER**
Katey, don't get in the way, I'll deal with it.

*KATEY fills two glasses of champagne, and offers them to BRIAN and ERIC.*

**BRIAN**
Stand up Eric.

*Starts singing : Happy Birthday to you.*

*ERIC joins in – as they sing the 'Happy Birthday' song. They are interrupted by the sound of a bicycle bell outside.*

BRIAN
Who's that?

KATEY
Roger.

BRIAN
Who's Roger?

*BLACKOUT*

*LIGHT UP – Bar*
*ARNOLD, drinking.*
*Enter HELEN, pulling a smart overnight suitcase.*

ARNOLD
Helen? Fancy meeting you here of all places! What a coincidence! Are you en route? In transit? It looks like it. Off on your hols? Benidorm?

HELEN
You asked me to come here, Arnold. You said you were in direst need.

ARNOLD
Did I? That's interesting.

HELEN
You don't remember?

ARNOLD
Can't say I do.

HELEN
Another of your blackouts, darling? It's a sure sign of...

ARNOLD
Don't tell me.

HELEN
You could do anything in an alcoholic blackout and not know you've done it. Even murder someone.

ARNOLD
I'm not that bad.

HELEN
How would you know? You read about it all the time.

ARNOLD
Do you? I don't.

HELEN
Yes, people kill people and don't know they've done it. They wake up in the morning wondering what happened the night before. One alcoholic, I read, always checked the bumpers on his car for blood, in case he had run somebody down.

ARNOLD
Did he really?

HELEN
Yes, and one morning he found blood on his front fender. He trailed back over his route looking for a body but couldn't find it.

ARNOLD
That's a relief.

HELEN
A week later they found the body.

ARNOLD
Where?

HELEN
In the boot of his car. It was a roadkill, like he had suspected. He hadn't

known what to do with the body and then had forgotten where he put it. Until the awful…

ARNOLD
That's enough. Helen, for God's sake! You're being very dramatic. It's because your life is basically boring so you read the papers for ghoulish items which are one in a million but feed the vacuity of the masses.

HELEN
My life is not boring with you, Arnold. I don't get a chance to be bored. A woman will put up with most things from a man, except boredom.

ARNOLD
It is the original sin, yes.

HELEN
It's why I divorced my husband. You could not have met anybody nicer.

ARNOLD
So it was self-interest that led you to come to my rescue, was it?

HELEN
I suppose it was.

ARNOLD
Typical. At least you are not dressing it up as an act of altruism. Your need to…

HELEN
To drop everything and drive across the moors in this foul weather to you.

ARNOLD
*Fair is foul and foul is fair,*
*Hover through the fog and filthy air…*
Portents. Omens. Hallucinations.

HELEN
Aren't you going to offer me a drink?

ARNOLD

Of course. Of course, darling. Actually I've been running a tab. It all goes on my room number… *(He lifts up room key which is on the bar counter)*

HELEN

It's alright. I've brought my credit cards.

ARNOLD

Oh, that's handy. I was counting on something turning up. It usually does.

HELEN

I'm not something that turns up. Arnold, couldn't you admit for once that you wanted to see me?

ARNOLD

Of course! Of course I do, darling…

HELEN

Are you sure?

ARNOLD

Yes, yes, yes…

HELEN

Because I can bail you out and drive home, I suppose. If you didn't want to see me you could have asked me to settle your hotel bill over the phone.

ARNOLD

No, no, no! The very idea! What ideas you get in your head. They're humiliating for both of us. Now you're here you might as well stay. You brought your things…

HELEN

An overnight bag.

ARNOLD

Good, good…

HELEN

In case I needed it.

ARNOLD
Of course you do

HELEN
A girl never knows. I don't know Arnold, whether I'm coming or going with you. I thought our affair was over. I should have known better – that you would drag me back – into your vortex.

ARNOLD
You were very good in The Vortex, with the Exeter City Council Players.

HELEN
It's a hobby, Arnold. I'm an enthusiastic amateur.

ARNOLD
In more ways than one, sweetheart.

HELEN
You don't have to flatter me. I'm quite ordinary. I realise that.

ARNOLD
Have it your own way. You reflect my light, I expect that's why I find you so dazzling.

HELEN
You could contradict me.

ARNOLD
Was I expected to?

HELEN
If I did get involved in all that razzmatazz that makes up your life, Arnold – media crossovers, as I prefer to call it – I'd definitely rather work on the production side. I did take an external degree in media affairs, darling.

ARNOLD
I know. Most people I meet have done. That's why I so urgently needed to see you, Helen. It won't wait. I have a new concept to discuss with you.

HELEN
Does it cross over, Arnold? Media-wise?

ARNOLD
You will decide. My future is in your hands.

HELEN
Meanwhile, have you forgotten Katey's birthday?

ARNOLD
No. I can still get home in time. It's today, isn't it? In which case I can't. You see I have to get to London to see a few people. Unless, that is, I have already been there – in which case I don't.

HELEN
What?

ARNOLD
Need to go. To London.

HELEN
You don't know whether you've been to London or not?

ARNOLD
Exactly. Sometimes I think I have. You know, been there. To London. I get that feeling… I have memories. But I cannot be sure that they are truly memories of events. They may be manufactured scenes that mollify my emotions.

HELEN
Hallucinations?

ARNOLD
Is that possible?

HELEN
You've had them before. How long have you been in Exeter?

ARNOLD
Well that's easily solved. I can ask the front desk. But I didn't want to make

waves. Draw attention to myself. Not until I was sure I could pay the hotel bill.

HELEN
You're not going to get home for Katey's birthday. Let's face it. It's too late, and the weather's awful. And you're loaded. You'll have to sleep it off and make some excuses when you get home tomorrow. It's totally pathetic but you'll have to do it.

ARNOLD
I suppose so. You're right as usual.

HELEN
And I'm not just saying it because I happen to be available for a leg-over, Arnold.

ARNOLD
I understand. You're putting other people first, I know that. As usual.

HELEN
That poor girl. Poor, sweet, broken, Katey. It must be awful to be your daughter, in constant trauma. Keeping everyone excited is not giving them love. Giving them attention does it. Noticing that they have lives as well. As do I.

ARNOLD
Don't blame me. It's hardly my fault if you are as moths to the flame of my talent…
*For He has made us, and not we ourselves.*
Helen, each must play out their own role. Life is a psycho-drama.

HELEN
That's very convenient. For you to say that…

*ARNOLD signals for more drinks.*

HELEN
Why do I always come back? This time I was getting over you. I'd gone through the withdrawal symptoms. I'd stopped waiting for the bloody phone to ring – and then it did. And I'm hooked. Back on the treadmill, chasing the

dragon. The big bad dragon, my fallen star, Arnold Gosport.

ARNOLD
You need a challenge Helen. It could have been Thai kick-boxing.

HELEN
I have taken up Thai kick-boxing.

ARNOLD
Oh, well maybe the two go together. My agent, Digby Lloyd, thinks I'm having a nervous breakdown.

HELEN
When did he tell you that? Within the last few days? In which case you have been to London, Arnold.

ARNOLD
I can't guarantee Digby told me anything, sorry. Perhaps I invented the whole thing.

HELEN
What thing?

ARNOLD
I don't know. I have such imagination, things seem real. Words. Conversations. It's my Achilles heel. It comes with the territory of being who I am. God knows how long I've been sitting on this bar stool. Do you think I'm deteriorating, Helen? Have I become strange? Recently?

HELEN
You've always been strange, and I haven't seen you recently. It's been ninety three days, eleven hours and God knows how many minutes – I've lost count.

ARNOLD
Digby believes I can no longer discern the difference between fact and fantasy. If I saw him, that is – he would have believed it.

HELEN
So you haven't seen him. Digby is playing your doctor because he's no

bloody good as your agent. Whether you saw him or not.

ARNOLD
Thank you, Helen, for that insight. Aren't we all playing roles? Don't we wake up in the morning and remember our story? The story so far. Say I decided I needed a different story? Because I wasn't getting anywhere in the story I was living. So I decided to invent a new one. But then I panicked, yes, because it may not have been me who made that decision.

HELEN
What?

ARNOLD
As to what my story should be.

HELEN
Then who was it?

ARNOLD
What?

HELEN
Who decided? Your storyline?

ARNOLD
The author. Obviously. Authors write stories, Helen. I am an actor. Only an actor.

HELEN
You are confused, Arnold.

ARNOLD
Pirandello. The master. He wrote the story. We, the actors are seeking him. Look, that's enough about me. Tell me about your life, what's been happening to you since we last got together?

HELEN
The cat died.

ARNOLD
Good.

HELEN
Why's it good?

ARNOLD
Because it happened. To accept it is to release the blessing. You said that, last time we met.

HELEN
Don't you care about how I feel?

ARNOLD
It's not you that died, is it? It's the cat.

HELEN
A dead cat can't feel anything.

ARNOLD
So?

HELEN
That's what's so sad.

ARNOLD
You know your cat's gone back to Ancient Egypt.

HELEN
Has it?

ARNOLD
Well, that's where it came from. You said.

HELEN
Yes. I suppose.

ARNOLD
Let go, Helen. Pussy is sailing down the Nile on a golden cushion on the Royal barge. Forget the ruddy cat, we have our own future to discuss.

Without the cat, or the cat litter.

HELEN
There's no future for us while you remain with your family. I don't really care anymore, what you do. Arnold, I can't keep doing it. It's them or me. For everybody's sake.

ARNOLD
It's you, definitely. I've sacrificed everything for that family, for the last twenty-one years! Surely I deserve a night off.

HELEN
Not a night off, Arnold! That won't change anything. If you were to leave them – once and for all – the family – everyone could adjust. We could all get on with it. One way or the other. If you won't decide then I will. I'll suffer the withdrawal symptoms one more time, if I have to… And then – dear God – I won't be coming back.

ARNOLD
Your position is noted, Helen. Let's go to the room, shall we?

*BLACKOUT*

*LOUNGE – MOTHER, KATEY, BRIAN, ERIC, and ROGER enter – holding a bicycle.*
*BRIAN has papers in his hand, the plastic bag (or bags) around him.*

ROGER
Who are these characters?

BRIAN
We ain't characters, sir. We is real.

KATEY
They're from the mental hospital.

BRIAN
And we ain't going back. The paperwork is all in order, sir. Here are the certificates…
*Gives Roger a paper :* Brian Darey, absolute discharge, miracle cure…

*Gives him another paper :* And Eric Dewitt, my companion, for outpatient therapy. That will be when I get my clinic going.

MOTHER
You are starting a clinic?

BRIAN
Soon as I get my compensation, yes.

ROGER
Who filled in these certificates?

BRIAN
I did.

ROGER
You can't go signing yourself out of a locked ward.

BRIAN
There's no one else is going to do it. Who else will sign us out? There's some has been incarcerated in there years. *Takes papers back.* Well it only takes a bit of paper, signed by the right person. Who gave them the right to sign the papers? God? I can sign. It's all typed.

KATEY
*Taking her notebook.* I must write down some of their dialogue.

MOTHER
Now then, Katey, don't start blurring the edges.

ROGER
I'd like to say, I mean really, what? You guys have shown great initiative.

BRIAN
Thank you, sir.

ROGER
Thinking outside the box, that is.

BRIAN
Thinking outside the hospital, sir.

ROGER
Well done you. Are you classified as dangerous by any chance?

BRIAN
No.

ERIC
I am. High risk. Top category. Twenty-four hour watch, full moon.

MOTHER
That's a silly question Roger.

BRIAN
No we're not. Not if we're treated right. Any man would be dangerous if you take away his freedom – lock him up for years – what do you expect? Any man will fight for his freedom.

ERIC
And his country. Rule Britannia. I've been to the recruiting office. The sergeant said the army was full up.

ROGER
Look fellas there's as many barmy out as there are in – incarcerated.

BRIAN
I'm not barmy.

ROGER
I am. Hello!

MOTHER
Roger, please, this isn't helping anyone.

BRIAN
Are you against the hospital authorities, sir?

ROGER
I'm against all authorities. I know what those mental wards are like. Underfunded warehouses for redundant people.

BRIAN
That's right, sir. Worst thing since Charles Dickens.

ROGER
We agree then. All agreed. Right. The thing is we're not in a position to help you. We have our own problems.

BRIAN
Mental?

ROGER
Yes. It's a family thing and, you know – it's, it's infectious. My advice is move on. You've come to the wrong place to get well.

MOTHER
Roger, that's enough.

BRIAN
I might be able to help you, sir. The family is my speciality. I do not deal with my patient in isolation, if you get my meaning. But I place them in the context of family.

ROGER
I'm sure that's best practice.

BRIAN
Yes. I'll put you on my waiting list, priority. When I start my clinic…

ROGER
Yes, book me in.

BRIAN
I was thinking out-patient for assessment.

ROGER
I feel better already.

BRIAN
You would be very interested in my case histories. All documented. Carefully filed despite the persecution. I was like Doctor Schweitzer in Wolverhampton.

KATEY
He was in Africa.

BRIAN
That's right. That's where he started. All my patient ward notes are here – what I had to hide in my mattress, till I could bring 'em out to the light of day. When we gets before the courts and claim our Human Rights, that has been...

ERIC
Vaccinated!

BRIAN
Violated.

ERIC
I been vaccinated.

KATEY
*Taking notes*. It's another screenplay. It must be.

MOTHER
That's enough, Katey. OK, boys, all out. That's it! There's the door. Goodbye...

BRIAN
Wait a minute, Missus, we got a gun. *To Eric* . Have you got the gun?

KATEY
A gun?

ERIC
No. You had it.

BRIAN
I hope so. I hope we haven't left it at the hospital. Over the toilet cistern.
*He searches amongst the papers in his plastic bags for the gun.*

ERIC
It was in the cake.

BRIAN
You ate the cake, Eric, so it ain't in the cake now, is it?

ERIC
Oh aye. Hey my brother could smuggle in another one.

BRIAN
In where?

ERIC
What?

BRIAN
We ain't in the hospital, Eric. We's outside.

ERIC
Right. Got it. We're outside the cake! Well it's been eaten, so we must be. Tell me this – you're the clever one – how do our visitors know where to come?

BRIAN
We don't get no visitors now, Eric.

ERIC
No visitors? It's a right cock-up, son. If you ask me. No visitors?

BRIAN
Except your brother will find us, Eric. It's part of the escape plan. He knows to come to the house at the corner of the woods.

ERIC
I hope he brings another cake.

*He notices ROGER.*

ERIC
Hey, give us yer bike, son.

*ERIC and ROGER push and pull the bicycle.*

ROGER
You're not taking my bike, that's stealing.

ERIC
What?

ROGER
That's criminal behaviour.

ERIC
That's me, I'm criminal. It runs in the family.

ROGER
Congratulations. But it's still my bike.

MOTHER
Roger, give him the bicycle.

BRIAN
You don't need it, Eric. We're not going anywhere.

ERIC
My brother's bigger than yours – any of your brothers!

*ERIC and ROGER are pulling at the bicycle. BRIAN finds the revolver.*

BRIAN
Ah here it is, silly me. I knew I had it somewhere.

*BLACKOUT.*

*BEDROOM – ARNOLD is watching HELEN remove her stockings.*

ARNOLD
Surely there's a writer somewhere out there who can come up with a good comedy thriller? Has there been one, really, since Sleuth? A classic comedy thriller, but post modern. Aware of itself.

HELEN
Is that your new concept, darling? But are you thinking cross-media?

ARNOLD
What?

HELEN
Could we package both up front? Like TV and novel?

ARNOLD
I don't know what the fuck you're talking about, Helen. An external degree in media affairs has addled your brain. But everyone seems to have one... Did you ever see Arsenic And Old Lace? That was a play before it was a film. Well drawn characters. The nephew, Teddy, going down to Panama – digging graves in the basement – parody of Roosevelt. Very light stuff, alright...
I don't know what this bloke, this imagined author, could come up with? I mean if we could find him Helen, we could commission something.

HELEN
What about your commitment to Elephant Bill? The prequel?

ARNOLD
It's dead. It's in the elephants' graveyard.

HELEN
That's something else you've got to tell your family.

ARNOLD
Please don't nag. I only kept the idea going to keep up their morale. You know, until I come up with something better.

HELEN
That is not responsible behaviour. That's encouraging your family to live a lie.

ARNOLD
Well, the truth is not popular at home. I wouldn't be thanked for telling the truth.

HELEN
And Katey? Who's writing a screenplay? Into thin air? When you've no intention...

ARNOLD
I'll tell her at the right time. When I have better news to distract everyone's attention. Must learn something from politics... Which is what we are working on right now, Helen. Our project. Our baby...

HELEN
What precisely do you mean, <u>we</u> could commission something?

ARNOLD
You want to be in production, don't you? Isn't that what you're saying? Aren't I hearing you right? What else are you planning to do with your so-called life? With your savings?

HELEN
I could buy a place, Arnold. With my mother's inheritance. It's a tidy sum. I have been looking around. You know, to give me some security.

ARNOLD
Security? Helen, you don't need security! How bourgeois can you get? When the revolution comes you'll be swept away. You and your property. Don't you realise property is theft? As Proudhon puts it. You need adventure. For God's sake, make up your mind. Don't be so timid. Hiding behind your wretched media studies. The media is the massage.

HELEN
You're quite overwhelming...

ARNOLD
Jump in the deep end.

HELEN
Right. You realise, we both have decisions to make, Arnold.

ARNOLD
That's my girl. I know what the world wants. It's the next good thing, a comedy thriller. Helen, the night we open on Broadway you can remind me of this moment. My God, it's not only Americans who live the dream!

HELEN
I must be mad. I can feel the ground slipping from under my feet.

ARNOLD
It's called flying.

HELEN
Let's go to bed, darling. I'm quite exhausted.

ARNOLD
I could help the author. This author. If we could find him. When we find him. Or her…
You see, I can see it now… You have got to introduce a body before the end of Act One, that's important, very important. That's what they want. Traditional, tried and tested. But you camp it up! A body. Dragged in… Just before the interval… .

*As ARNOLD speaks, FADE UP LIGHTS ON LOUNGE. It is empty, no sign of the family.*
*BRIAN enters, followed by ERIC – dragging body of NURSE ARTHUR.*

ARNOLD
The audience will love it. Put the body in the piano…

ERIC
Where shall I put Nurse Arthur?

BRIAN
Put him in the piano.

*They move body towards the piano.*

**END OF ACT I**

## ACT II

## SCENE 1

*THE LOUNGE – Next morning. Sunny.*
*FX : Establish bird song. ERIC sits, devouring a bowl of cereals. BRIAN enters, through door from cellar. He bolts it. He has the gun in his hand.*

ERIC :
We might have to kill the lot.

BRIAN
What?

ERIC :
The whole family like. They might talk. Rabbit. They think I'm dumb, oh aye. I worked it all out, in my head…

BRIAN :
It's no good killing them for Mental Health Week, Eric.

ERIC :
Self protection.

BRIAN :
The courts wouldn't see it that way.

ERIC
Animal instinct.

BRIAN
No, we must keep killing to a minimum – so we can present a good case… after thirty days.

*ERIC folds the morning newspaper into a hat.*

ERIC
I'm the brains, son't forget that, son. The Sugar Puff Kid. Why's it me always gets the plastic toy from the box? I'm lucky, that's why. Snap, Crackle, and Pop!

BRIAN
We must try and win the trust of the family, Eric.

ERIC
Family, eh? I could do for them like I did for the others.

BRIAN
Who's that?

ERIC
Me Ma'am and Daddy.

BRIAN
The judge never fully understood how much they abused you.

ERIC
Right.

BRIAN
Now you'll have your chance to state your case again. Only this time...

ERIC
Yeah.

BRIAN
You must tell everyone how they punished you for wetting the bed.

ERIC
I didn't wet the bed.

BRIAN
You did. You don't have to lie to me. It's in your case notes. Have you seen the morning paper?

ERIC
No.

BRIAN
You're wearing it.

*BRIAN takes it from ERIC's head.*

BRIAN
You've got some irritating habits. *He straightens out the paper* : The police are making a house to house search.

ERIC
What for?

BRIAN
Eh?

ERIC
Are they looking for us?

BRIAN
Well who else do you think they're looking for?

ERIC
Well sometimes they look for other people.

BRIAN
We are the… Oh I wish you'd do your dumb act.

*Piano note « 'Ping!' » Hand flops out of piano.*

*ERIC notices the arm and pushes it back into the piano. He raises lid, feels inside piano. Finds a sweet. Closes lid. Unwraps sweet and puts it in his mouth.*

BRIAN notices that ERIC is sucking a sweet.

BRIAN
What are you eating?

ERIC
Sweetie.

BRIAN
Where'd you get it?

ERIC
Nurse Arthur.

BRIAN
Nurse Arthur's dead. He cant give you sweeties.

ERIC
He wanted me to have it.

BRIAN
Spit it out! Spit it out! I wont have you stealing from Nurse Arthur.

*BRIAN fishes sweet out of ERIC's mouth, and finds wrapper. Puts sweet in wrapper – then back into piano.*

ERIC
He always gives me sweeties! He wanted me to have it! He wanted me to have it! I never have killed him if I knew it meant no more sweeties! We shouldn't have done it… Why does it have to be different? He's still our friend ain't he?

BRIAN
Yes. Nurse Arthur is still our friend. But you mustn't take liberties, Eric.

*FX OFF : CAR HORN « Beep, Beep! »*
*BRIAN crosses the window.*

BRIAN
It's the father… *picks up framed photo.*

ERIC
Oh aye, that's a familiar face, that is.

*BRIAN and ERIC hide.*

*ARNOLD enters. He carries a birthday present, gaily wrapped.*

ARNOLD
*Sings* : Happy birthday to you…
Happy birthday to you…

Happy birthday…
*Looking around, puzzled.* Dear Katey…
Calls : Anyone at home? Anyone…? Hello…? Where has everyone got to? You can't blame them for not being indoors a day like this…
Hello? Hello?

*ARNOLD puts present down, and exits.*

*BRIAN and ERIC emerge from hiding.*
*BRIAN crosses the window.*

BRIAN
He's gone back to the car. He's getting in. He's getting out again. He's coming back…

*ARNOLD enters.*

ARNOLD
Damn car won't start up. I was running on empty the last couple of miles home. I'm not hanging round here on my own while the pubs are open. Need to sub a few quid from the family contingency fund… and take Katey's Vespa keys… They might be down the Dog And Duck, I'll go and have a decko! Surprise them all…

*ARNOLD helps himself to some cash from a tea caddy on a shelf, and finds a set of keys for the Vespa. He exits.*
*ERIC crosses back to window. BRIAN pushes him back, and peers out himself..*

BRIAN
He's taken off again. On the scooter this time.

ERIC
Who has**?**

BRIAN
The father.

ERIC
He din't have time to see us then?

BRIAN
What about?

ERIC
They never let you know, do they?

BRIAN
He is not a specialist, Eric.

ERIC
Then why was he wearing a suit? Tell me that. I'm going to give his motor the once over, while he's away.

BRIAN
He don't want to find his car is up on bricks when he gets back.

ERIC
Oh aye. Depends how good the tyres are....

*ERIC exits.*

BRIAN
It's not Eric Dewitt's criminal tendencies are my province, though I do not approve of them. I must not moralise. Only where they contribute to psychopathic outcomes, that's what I have to watch out for. I took a risk signing young Eric out of the hospital. I'd have done better to bring Graham Turner, except he was eating the ping pong balls. Not a good sign. He weren't ready for outpatient therapy...

*ERIC enters, dragging body. It is DIGBY.*

BRIAN
What have you got there, Eric?

ERIC
I found him in the boot like. The boot of the car. Your man, the gaffer.

BRIAN
That's not the gaffer.

ERIC
No, but I found him in the gaffers car. Oh aye, in the boot he was, dead as a doornail. So I thought, bring him in. Don't leave a poor soul out there, all on his own. Shall I go through his pockets?

BRIAN
No, you don't. You don't have a right to disturb someone else's body, Eric.

ERIC
I'm not disturbing it. He don't look disturbed, does he? I am befriending him. I brought him indoors for a bit of company. I mean when he's at the cemetery he'll be with a lot of other stiffs so he won't feel so alone, but I can't leave him out there. It's not human.

BRIAN
We got one to look after already, Eric. Ain't that enough for you? We got Nurse Arthur in the piano.

ERIC
Oh aye. Well it'll be company.

BRIAN
There's no room in the piano Eric, for that gentleman.

ERIC
Not without overcrowding, I agree. There's too much of that these days. I blame the council, giving immigrants our space.

BRIAN
He ain't an immigrant, Eric, and he ain't going in the piano. Put him back in the boot of the car.

ERIC
Oh no, that's not Christian. No, no… I mean we could put Nurse Arthur somewhere else and put this gent in the piano – because maybe he's more musical. That would make sense.

BRIAN
Have you gone off Nurse Arthur?

ERIC
No, no…

BRIAN
Don't play the favourites. Alright Eric, put Mr Brown in the window box. For now. And I'll think of something later.

ERIC
How do you know he's Mr Brown?

BRIAN
It's his code name.

ERIC
Oh, right. Working under cover, is he? We've got a rum 'un here, if you ask me.
Mr Brown, eh? Right. Hey…

*ERIC drags the body to the window box.*

*BLACKOUT.*

## SCENE 2

*BRIAN and ERIC in the lounge.*
*Late afternoon sunshine beams through french windows.*

*FX : VESPA HORN ' Toot – Toot! '*

*Before they can hide, ARNOLD enters through the french windows.*

ARNOLD
Who the hell are you? What are you doing in this house?

BRIAN
We represent Mental Health Week, sir.

ARNOLD :
Well I only support National Lifeboat Week. I have a fear of drowning.

BRIAN
What, this far inland?

ARNOLD
Yes, it's a morbid condition. I never take a bath, I always shower. I'm not the only one either. There's a writer I know who suffers from it… Who let you in?

BRIAN
Who let us in, Eric?

ERIC
No-one. Us come in through the window, mister. Like you just did. You want to get security locks put on them windows, mate. Where I come from you wouldn't have a stick of furniture left. They'd have your pine floorboards up and shipped out to China as well. Oh aye, there's a big demand for striped pine out there. China, aye. And uranium, but you don't come across that much when you're housebreaking. Least-wise I haven't.

ARNOLD
You're burglars?

BRIAN
Perish the thought, sir. Come, come, do we look like burglars? Common thieves?

ARNOLD
I get it! You're medical students.

BRIAN
I am a student of human nature, sir, yes.

ARNOLD
You're collecting for Mental Health Week!

*ERIC picks up a toby mug and ARNOLD drops a coin into it.*

ARNOLD
This is all very well, but… Where are my family?

BRIAN
They're safe and well sir – in the cellar.

ARNOLD
In the cellar? Carrying Rag Week a bit far aren't you? What do you mean? They're in the cellar?

*ARNOLD goes to cellar door.*

BRIAN
Don't unbolt that door, sir, please.

*ERIC produces the revolver.*

ERIC
Shall I total him? Exclude him like from future broadcasting?

BRIAN
No, Eric, he's the father.

ERIC
I hate fathers! I like uncles!

ARNOLD
I am an uncle. I have a niece in Epping. Look, here's a photo of her on a horse…

*ERIC fires the gun. An ornament near ARNOLD shatters.*

ARNOLD
You've just crossed an invisible line. I know you charity collectors are becoming more aggressive, but … I won't be buying your Christmas cards this year!
My God this is real, isn't it? You chaps are from the local mental home? I might have guessed.

BRIAN
We have escaped, sir, yes. It was the only way to get out.

ERIC
We shot our way out, Mister.

BRIAN
No we didn't, Eric.

ERIC
Aye we did.

BRIAN
No we didn't. Don't exaggerate, Eric. How many more times? You must not feed your fantasies.

ERIC
No, doctor.

ARNOLD
I think I see what's going on. You chaps are in a spot of bother. Happens to all of us. So let's calm down and look at this sensibly, shall we? Take an all round view. For instance, you know what this is going to do to property prices round here, don't you? Two goons breaking out? You've just clipped fifty grand off this place. It's gone from charming reclusive cottage in the country to dodgy residence within stone's throw of top security looney bin.

BRIAN
I'm sure the market will pick up, sir, when word gets round how well we are treating your family.

ARNOLD
What is this , a hostage situation? What are you telling me? What is going on? I demand to see my family. My God if you've harmed them...

BRIAN
They're a very nice family, sir, and it's been a pleasure to meet them. It's family life that's important, sir. It's the key to mental health. Although of course it can go the other way.

ARNOLD
Why are they in the cellar?

BRIAN
Eric, why are they in the cellar?

ERIC
Everybody's got to be somewhere.

ARNOLD
I must see them, immediately.

ERIC
Visiting day's next Thursday, mister. Can you come back?

ARNOLD
No I can't. Does he know where he is? Put that gun down, will you? It's gone off once. Are you going to pay for the breakages, are you?

BRIAN
We'll make a note of them and pay you out of our compensation.

ERIC
Watch out mister. I got me eye on you, what? The evil eye, aye. I got uncontrollable urges. It's in me notes. In my file, eh, doctor?

BRIAN
He does have a history of violence.

ERIC
All our family's villains, see. And I… like I am next in line for the succession. After Mad Charlie me brother, that is. Charlie The Chopper. Chop, chop! *Sings*. Maxwell's silver hammer goes chop chop… Chop, chop, chop, chop! Only see, they'll be ashamed to discover there's mental illness in the family. I've got to beat that rap, it's the wrong diagnosis, you know? That's why I want to see a specialist. One of the suits!

*ARNOLD is helping himself to a drink. A whisky.*

BRIAN
Confidentially, sir, and this must go no further than the consulting room – Eric, Mr Dewitt, killed his mother and his father.

ERIC
Caught 'em in the bath together. Aye! Threw the electric fire in after 'em. Just cause.

BRIAN
That's what I'm saying Eric. You was provoked. Did you tell the judge about the bath?

ERIC
I didn't see no judge.

BRIAN
You will next time.

ARNOLD
Right. I've got the picture, yes. You don't need to tell me any more. I'm on your side, be sure of that. I've got a lot of influence round these parts. With doctors. Specialists from the puzzle factory. Yes, we socialise, go to the same pub, visit each other's houses. A word from me and they won't want you back. They won't even notice you've vanished.

BRIAN
Thank you, sir. Could you be a witness for our human rights before the European court in Strasbourg?

ERIC
That's a goose, ain't it?

ARNOLD
Certainly. No problem there. Only I would need to be compensated for any loss of earnings. However, where were we? Yes, I demand to see my family. At once.

BRIAN
They shall be brought right up, sir, never fear. Have you thought what you're going to tell Katey?

ARNOLD
Katey? Tell her what?

BRIAN
Her feelings were mightily hurt that you missed her twenty-first birthday.

ARNOLD
Were they? What business is it of yours? I did phone to explain the delay – or I would have done but we were cut off.

BRIAN
We had to cut the phone, sir.

ARNOLD
Are you mad? You never cut off an actor's phone. It's the last thing to go. Gas, electricity, BUPA – but keep the bloody phone! You move in – you give me two extra mouths to feed and make my livelihood totally impossible! You must be insane. That's why you were locked up. No grip on reality, it's quite obvious.

BRIAN
It'll all come out in the wash, sir. Never fear. You can explain to Katey what happened. I'll bring her up now. Eric, you watch him like a hawk.

ERIC
Oh aye,

*BRIAN unbolts door and exits to cellar.*

ARNOLD
Do you get pocket money? Do you?

ERIC
No.

ARNOLD
That's a bit unfair, isn't it? All the others do.

ERIC
What others, like?

ARNOLD
Everyone else. Round here.

ERIC
Oh aye? What – what you mean, like? They can go to the hospital shop?

ARNOLD
That's right. Buy what they like.

ERIC
What, sweeties?

ARNOLD
Yes, and chocolates. Anything they like.

ERIC
Oh aye? Do you get pocket money?

ARNOLD
Yes. Everyone does. Except you.

ERIC
I never knew about this, I'm really – confabulated. It doesn't seem fair, you're right. What have I done done to be left out?

ARNOLD
Leave it to me, I'll fix it.

ERIC
You will? Well I'm glad of that. How long's this been going on? And I've been neglected…

ARNOLD
It's alright, you'll get your pocket money, starting next week.

ERIC
Well I owe you, Mister. You're a sport, we need more like you in the world. I won't forget this in a hurry.

ARNOLD
Don't say anything to Brian. He doesn't want you to have pocket money.

ERIC
Oh my God, the duplicity of it all. I can't believe this…

ARNOLD
Don't wave that gun around, Eric. It might go off again.

ERIC
You need a favour, you come back to me…
I seen you before Mister? Oh aye, I know that boat-race. Got It! I seen you on hospital telly. No, don't tell me, it wasn't East Enders. Strictly Come Dancing?

ARNOLD
Does this mean anything to you?
(He thumps his chest, making Tarzan call)

ERIC
Elephant Bill!

*KATEY enters from cellar, followed by BRIAN. He bolts the door.*
*KATEY runs to ARNOLD*

**KATEY**
Daddy!

**ARNOLD**
Katey! Katey, I'm so sorry – I'm sorry I was late for your birthday...

**KATEY**
Dad, oh it's been awful! Awful without you here, and this situation!

**ARNOLD**
I know. I know, darling. My poor sweet... Yes, I do understand, yes...
But you try staying in London raising film finance. Now that is an absolute horror!

*BLACKOUT*

## SCENE 3

*Later. The lounge. ERIC with gun. BRIAN studying his papers. MOTHER, KATEY, ROGER... and ARNOLD.*

ARNOLD
So I was in Langan's, or was it The Wolsey? One of the two. Just about given up on making any progress, when in walked Ralph.

MOTHER
Ralph Richardson's dead.

ARNOLD
And so are a lot of the others, Mother. No, Fiennes! Ralph Fiennes. Long and the short of it is he said I'd love to do a jungle picture! He said I'd love to play Von Block, the evil ivory hunter.

KATEY
I've updated the script, Dad. Von Block's not in it any more.

ARNOLD
Isn't he? Well put him back and we'll send the script to Ralph Fiennes agent.

MOTHER
Arnold, this is hardly the time for a script conference.

ARNOLD
Why not?

MOTHER
Because... *(She indicates Brian and Eric)*

ARNOLD
Oh, them. Don't worry, I've got everything under control. I'm building bridges. Now where was I?

ROGER
You were telling us about how you found a director. For the film.

ARNOLD
Was I? Oh, I don't remember that.

ROGER
Did someone else walk into the Wolsey? By chance?

ARNOLD
No, Roger. No such luck. Funny you should say that, a director? Yes, a director. Because that evening back at the Savoy, I was in the bar…

KATEY
Being seen. Like networking, Dad?

ARNOLD
Just hanging out, you know. When in walked Dickie…

MOTHER
Dickie's dead as well.

ARNOLD
Not that Dickie.

MOTHER
Our Dickie.

ARNOLD
I know our Dickie's dead. And we were not invited to the bloody funeral, were we?

MOTHER
It was for relatives and close friends.

ARNOLD
What's that make us? I'd prepared a eulogy for his memorial service and I wasn't asked to deliver it. God, to think, I gave him his first job…

MOTHER
Dickie?

ARNOLD
Yes, Dickie!

MOTHER
Not that Dickie! He gave <u>you</u> your first job.

ARNOLD
I knew it was one way or the other. Comes the same thing.

ROGER
Well, who did walk in? Did anyone walk in?

ARNOLD
What, Roger? Where?

ROGER
To the Savoy Bar and Grill? Supposing you ever got there in the first place.

KATEY
Of course Dad did.

ARNOLD
What?

KATEY
You went to London, didn't you?

ARNOLD
Yes.

MOTHER
Roger, what's wrong with you? Interrogating your father? Aren't we in enough trouble? Is this any time to cast aspersions?

ROGER
I just wondered – to keep the story going – who walked in to the Savoy bar?

MOTHER
Arnold will get to that. If you don't confuse him.

ARNOLD
Ken!

ROGER
Kenneth Williams?

ARNOLD
No, he's dead.

MOTHER
Yes, he's dead.

ARNOLD
No, this was a live one. Ken. Kenneth Branagh. Well he owes me one, doesn't he?

MOTHER
He certainly does. You gave him his first job.

ARNOLD
I did, yes. I said, Ken – we had a drink of course – I put them up for him and Helen…

MOTHER
Mirren? Helen Mirren?

ARNOLD
Yes, of course. I said, Ken you've been doing a lot of crap recently, haven't you? Own up. I call a spade a spade…He said, I trust you, Arnold – you're not one of the arsehole-crawlers, what do you want? I said, never mind what I want, I'm giving you an opportunity, son – to direct my jungle picture, The Last Elephant. I said, it's ecological Tarzan, you don't need to know any more.

KATEY
And Helen Mirren could play…

ARNOLD
Lady Daphne…

KATEY
The reformed alcoholic. I'll have to write that part up.

ARNOLD
I've done my bit. That's it. Send out the scripts. We've got a sexy film package there, if I say so myself. And that's what makes finance. Film finance. You think it's easy. I make it look easy.

MOTHER
With Branagh directing, and Helen Mirren and Ralph Fiennes… Arnold, someone is going to green light that, I know it. I'm sure…

ROGER
What about Rachel Weisz?

ARNOLD
What about Rachel Weisz?

ROGER
Did she walk in?

ARNOLD
Where?

ROGER
I don't mind where? The Ivy? Anywhere you like.

ARNOLD
I don't know if Rachel Weisz walked into The Ivy, because I wasn't there.

MOTHER
You didn't go to The Ivy?

ARNOLD
I couldn't cover all eventualities, no. Limited resources. Time. Money. If you wanted me to go to The Ivy, you should have said so Vera. I was on the spot, I was making the decisions…

KATEY
Dad was tracking down the game, like Elephant Bill.

ARNOLD
Yes, I had to decide which watering holes to stake out, didn't I? I bagged a few, and left other game for the other hunters.
OK, I didn't see Rachel while I was in London. We don't need her, either. Unless Helen drops out. Or you want me to give her the push? Put her back in the river? Because Rachel Weisz could be a better…

MOTHER
Catch?

KATEY
Lady Daphne?

ARNOLD
Precisely.

KATEY
Decision time.

MOTHER
No, no, stick with what we've got. Stick with Helen Mirren. A bird in the hand.

ROGER
I thought we had a fish?

KATEY
What?

ROGER
You wouldn't put a bird back in the river?

KATEY
A wading bird?

ARNOLD
A heron? Roger?

ROGER
Possibly. OK, one bonus point.

ARNOLD
Good. This calls for a little celebration. I brought a bottle of bubbly home, for your birthday, Katey…

KATEY
Great! Let's make it a double celebration, everyone. Because we are making a movie!

ARNOLD
Hang on, Katey. Look, let's be clear about this. I don't want to say it, but it could unravel…

ROGER
What could? What could unravel? You mean a sleeve? Of the magic jumper you have knitted?

ARNOLD
Yes.

ROGER
How do you feel about that, Katey?

KATEY
What?

ROGER
Dad has knitted a jumper that is unravelling.

KATY
I don't want an unravelling jumper, OK? I don't know what you're fucking talking about, right? And I am getting frightened, everyone. Are we in or are we out? I can't stand indecision. Are we making a movie or are we being fucked over? By someone?

ARNOLD
Just a cautionary note, Katey.

KATEY
I don't want fucking caution! <u>I want faith like she said it</u>. What? Like faith is being the substance of all our shit, do we get it, or not?

That's what I want to know now.

MOTHER
Close your mouth, Katey. She's gawping. She has trouble breathing when she gets nervous.

ROGER
In which case she might need to keep her mouth open.

MOTHER
Yes. Open your mouth, Katey.

ARNOLD
It's not for me to raise false hopes in the family. I'm sure Roger would agree with that. There have been many false dawns before. You know that Vera. For this family. We're all in it together. Including Katey, even on her twenty-first birthday. We have had too many bitter, bitter disappointments.

ROGER
Katey can't take another one. It would send her over the top.

ARNOLD
I would spare you more disappointment. Truly. The whole family for whom I feel totally responsible. I'm sorry. I'm deeply regretting – if I – and all that incoherent darkness that threatens to engulf even the most loving family unit. Each unit is subject to its own strains, like an IKEA trial of a wardrobe being dropped from a cliff. And we all know that raising film finance is a precarious business at the best of times. It's conjuring something out of nothing. But Dicky did say...

KATEY
Dicky's dead.

ARNOLD
I mean Ken.

ROGER
Ken Conner?

ARNOLD
No.

KATEY
He's dead. They're all dead. Frankie Howerd, Benny Hill, Sid James…

ROGER
We've got Helen Mirren!

KATEY
We don't know who's got Helen Mirren.

ROGER
It's all rubbish.

KATEY
I'm sure Kenneth Branagh will direct Elephant Bill for us. Because it's an ethnically pro jungle, anti soya crop, pro game park, save the species…

ROGER
Load of crap. Have you ever considered Katey, that a herd of elephants farting produces a tremendous amount of methane gas, contributing to the polar icecaps melting?

KATEY
Shut up Roger.

ARNOLD
Yes, shut up Roger.

ROGER
Look, if he went to the Savoy…

ARNOLD
He? Yes, I did.

ROGER
You're sure?

ARNOLD
Yes, course I'm sure, what are you suggesting? I know what the Savoy looks like. It's in the Strand.

ROGER
So where's the hotel receipt?

ARNOLD
You want to see the receipt? Bloody cheek. You've turned bolshie since I left, Roger. I've already sent it to the accountant. Hard luck. I was at the Savoy. That's how I met Ralph.

MOTHER
Didn't you meet Ralph at the Wolsey?

ROGER
Get a story and stick to it, Dad. Get your facts sorted before you walk in the door.

ARNOLD
Ralph Fiennes will play the CIA man, right? Who deliberately takes the Aids virus and releases it in San Francisco because he's homophobic. Ralph loves it. Specially the naked bath-house scene.

KATEY
We haven't got a naked bath-house scene.

ARNOLD
Well I told him about it so you'll have to write it in.

ROGER
I happen to know Ralph Fiennes is in Hollywood.

ARNOLD
What do you mean?

ROGER
I read it. In a trade paper.

ARNOLD
We don't have any trade papers.

ROGER
*The Stage*. Katey gets it.

KATEY
Right.

ARNOLD
Ah! He did say – I remember now – Ralph said that had come back for the weekend on personal business. You're right, Roger. From LA, yes...

ROGER
He's making it all up.

ARNOLD
Who, Ralph?

ROGER
No, you, Dad. You've only got to look at him. He's more inventive than any screenplay you can write, Katey. I admire that.

MOTHER
Roger, don't talk about your father that way.

ARNOLD
Yes, come off it son. Give your old Dad a break.

ROGER
Every time you come home, it's with a different story.

ARNOLD
Life's like that.

ROGER
But it never amounts to anything, does it? We don't know where you've been. All we know is you didn't meet Michael Caine this time. Or Sean Connery. So we don't have a kilt scene to write in this week.

ARNOLD
True. Roger, although in the depths of his nihilism has struck the right note. What do we actually know? Philosophically? Sitting here? Existentially?

MOTHER
We know we're a talented family who's time has surely come. We know we have been tried beyond the limits of endurance, dear God. We can sink no lower. Prayers must be answered.

ROGER
We've had an answer to prayer, haven't we? Has anyone noticed we're in a hostage situation here? I don't want to spoil the party but it's quite ludicrous to be talking about The Last Elephant when we could be on the way to becoming The Last Family.

ARNOLD
What's the point of this? Roger, I am aware of the situation. I am home and I have got everything under control.

ROGER
If you had got back last night…

ARNOLD
If? If? That's a lot of ifs, Roger. Life's full of ifs. I'm talking about the future, you're talking about the past.

ROGER
I'm talking about now.

KATEY
It's all sour grapes from Roger, because he can't play Sabu again.

ROGER
I don't want to play Sabu. I was ten, right? I was covered in tanning oil for six weeks at Pinewood studios. I kept slipping off the chair in the dining room, that's all I remember. I realise that does not add up to a film career.

MOTHER
Roger burnt out early. It can happen.

ROGER
I did not burn out early. There was nothing to burn out. Why do we all have to be so brilliant in this family? Even if we've failed, we're brilliant burnt out failures. Let's forget the crap, shall we? Like Mum? We haven't heard it today… 'She could have danced with Nureyev…'

MOTHER
I chose to retire early and have a family.

ROGER
You were only in the corps de ballet.

MOTHER
You've got to start somewhere.

ROGER
That's where you finished.

MOTHER
We are not finished. We – the family – will never know what we can accomplish together, unless we go the extra mile. We must be prepared – we must be willing – when things are as bad as they can possibly get, that's when we have all got to keep going. Cheering each other along, one step at a time…

*ROGER, who is sitting on piano stool, turns and plays.*
ROGER
*(Sings)* Dear Jesus!

KATEY
*Joins in.* One day at a time…

MOTHER
Roger, get me a cushion from the window box, there's a good boy.

ARNOLD
I'll do it, I'm nearest. You sit down, Roger…
*(to Brian, as he passes)* Excuse me.

*ARNOLD goes to window box. Opens it. Has a good look in. Reacts, letting lid drop…*

*DIGBY enters – opposite – holding cash box.*

DIGBY
No, Arnold. No. No more advances, you understand? No more cheques. No more petty cash.

ARNOLD
Look, give me two hundred pound cash and I'll walk away. It's a deal.

DIGBY
You'll never walk away, Arnold. You'll lose everything unless you stop drinking. Be warned. You've gone past all social boundaries. Listen to me…

ARNOLD
Give me my money.

DIGBY
It's not your money.

ARNOLD
It's payday, chum. Compensation for misrepresentation, shall we call it?

DIGBY
No it's not.

ARNOLD
Yes it is.

DIGBY
No it's not.

ARNOLD
Do you want the full pantomime routine? You be Widow Twankey, I'll be the villain.

DIGBY
Go now, please, while there's a vestige of friendship left between us.

ARNOLD
Not without my blood money.

DIGBY
I've killed no-one.

ARNOLD
You've destroyed me without killing me, Digby. That is a worse fate. If I die bravely I can go to the orbs of light with my mind intact and with courage to take on phantoms. But now I am as a phantom myself, and you did that to me. Without a second thought. Or did you plot it? I know not. In a thousand small ways you have reduced me, Digby. As does the sea a mighty cliff wear down to become sand for children's play. Without my even noticing, it has been done, until one day I looked in the mirror and I was no longer there. I saw a stranger, an empty vessel, with eyes staring out of a vacant property, weed grown, neglected, from which I could conjure no memory of happy days…

DIGBY
A very pretty speech, Arnold, but all is lost in the wind. You have no substance, don't blame me. I am the English oak and you are a thousand parasitic beetles.
You prey on me, I will have done with it.

ARNOLD
You will call the exterminator?

DIGBY
If necessary, yes.

ARNOLD
You fop! Give me that cash box. Don't try and match language with me, Digby, it is no remedy for my not playing the Bard. I should be upon the stage. It is not a game I want with you, it is your money. It is my money!

DIGBY
No. No, Arnold, stop! Stop it…

ARNOLD
Have at you, you churl! I will have recompense!

DIGBY
No! No... Arnold...

*They struggle. ARNOLD grabs cash box. Goes to hit DIGBY on head with it. DIGBY reels back. They exit as ARNOLD strikes DIGBY. Cry off, and crash of falling body.*

*ARNOLD enters with the cash box.*

ARNOLD
My God, I've done for him. He's gone to collect the Big Percentage in the sky, where all agents have to go, eventually, looking for clients...

*ARNOLD takes cash in notes from the cash box. He pockets the money and throws the cash box off-stage.*

MOTHER
Arnold. You look like you've seen a ghost.

ARNOLD
Perhaps I have done.

MOTHER
The cushion, please. It's in the window box.

ARNOLD
You don't need a cushion, Mother. We're not going to get too comfortable in this situation, are we?

MOTHER
I can't see that it would hurt to ease my back.

ARNOLD
There's a lot you can't see, Vera. That I can see. Please, let me handle things, I am home. No cushions.

KATEY
Oh, look! A present! Where has it come from? I didn't see it before. Dad, do you know about this?

KATEY picks up the gaily wrapped present that ARNOLD brought home.

ARNOLD
Aha! Yes, of course. What with everything going on, Katey, I forgot to give it to you. Happy Birthday, my darling girl! Of course I wouldn't forget you

KATEY
How lovely! What a surprise! But I knew you wouldn't forget your little Katey....

ARNOLD
No, no, how could I forget my precious little dumpling? My one and only daughter, on her twenty-first birthday!

KATEY
Oh. It's from Digby.

ARNOLD
Digby? Is it? Are you sure?

KATEY
It says, All my love Katey, for a happy twenty-first, your Godfather, Digby.

ARNOLD
Ah, yes, he gave it to me to bring down to the country. Digby, yes, the present. I went to see him, of course. To his office, where he was picking his nose, as usual. A useless, useless agent, why do I bother? I don't know why? Misplaced loyalty, I suppose. Yes, while I was in London I saw Digby. London, yes, that proves I was there, Roger. You wanted evidence? You've got it. The present. Examine it yourself. Read the label. How else did it get here, if not from me? I can't stand doubters. Get some backbone, son. You could do worse than believe in your father.

MOTHER
But Digby was coming to the party. He always keeps his word. He never lets us down.

ARNOLD
He's not well. Digby…

MOTHER
Not well?

ARNOLD
No, he was run over by a taxi, nothing serious. He sends apologies for absence.

MOTHER
Run over by a taxi? That sounds serious.

ARNOLD
No, it was stationary at the time.

MOTHER
Then how…

ARNOLD
He was on his bike and he bumped into it. Got a bruise on his head. A big bruise.

MOTHER
He shouldn't ride a bike in London traffic at his age.

ARNOLD
Yes, he's far too young. Nobody should be riding bikes in London traffic until they're sixty-five.

KATEY
Why?

ARNOLD
Because there are too many elderly people these days. It should be compulsory, everyone over sixty-five should be required to ride a bike in London traffic. That would solve it. We need more young people and… Digby said he would be with us in spirit. In spirit, yes, for sure. I can vouch for that. Can't you feel his spirit here, amongst us?

MOTHER
I can feel something strange. In addition to our new lodgers. Arnold, we're sitting on a powder keg.

ARNOLD
Leave it to me, mother. I'll get rid of them.

MOTHER
I don't see any sign of that.

ARNOLD
You too, is it? Another doubting Thomas.

KATEY
Christ could not perform his miracles because of a lack of faith.

ARNOLD
There. That's what I needed to hear. Where are you going, Roger?

ROGER
To fetch a cushion for Mum.

ARNOLD
I've already said, no cushions! No cushions for Mum. Sit down, Roger.

*BRIAN is near the window box. He opens it and takes out a cushion. Gives it to MOTHER.*

BRIAN
Here, y'are, Missus.

*ARNOLD goes to window box. Opens it. Peeps in. Closes it quickly.*

ARNOLD
Yes, he's still there.

ROGER
Where?

ARNOLD
In London.

ROGER
Who?

ARNOLD
Digby.

ROGER
You've already told us that, Dad.

ARNOLD
I know. I'm reminding you.

ROGER
You know half the trouble is you've got an agent who's dead useless.

ARNOLD
He is dead, yes… Dead useless, son, you're right. Dead wood. Dead weight.
Dead and never called me mother…

MOTHER
Arnold, we must engage in conversation with these lunatics. Somehow. Doing nothing is not an option.

ARNOLD
Are you a skilled negotiator?

MOTHER
No.

ARNOLD
Then don't make things worse. Something will turn up. They must be looking for them, the authorities.

ROGER
Probably glad to get rid of them. Desperate measures from the board of hospital management to cut financial deficit, allowing dangerous patients to escape.

KATEY
That's funny, Roger… *( laughs )*

MOTHER
Don't get hysterical, Kate.

KATEY
No, Mum.

*FX. Door chimes. Ding Dong. ERIC peers out of window.*

ERIC
It's the rozzers! Right, action stations! We all know the drill. One false move and it's a body rolled out on the doorstep. Right? OK! One every half hour. Random selection.

ROGER
While stocks last. He can't be serious. You are not serious.

ERIC
Try me, son. I'll put 'em back in the cellar.

ROGER
You wouldn't be such a big guy without the gun, would you?

ERIC
Oh aye, I was the only kid down our street without rickets. 'Cos being criminals like, our family, we got the best of everything. I only had to walk in the butcher's shop and he was wrapping up half a dozen lamb chops. That's what I call respect. Where else would you get that? Not at the fishmongers. we had to burn him out.

*ERIC shepherds the family through the cellar door, and exits after them, closing the door behind him.*

*FX : Door chimes. Ding Dong.*

ARNOLD
Leave this to me.

*ARNOLD pours himself a stiff drink. Downs it in one.*
*He goes to front door. Opens it. There is a SHERIFF on the doorstep. He tips his hat.*

SHERIFF
Good-day t' y'all. How's it hanging? I'm sorry to trouble you good folk, you must of heard of the breakout. I'm not here to alarm God fearing people, as if there's not enough trouble in the world with the local factory closing down and the teenage pregnancy rate soaring round this district – but if you happen to have seen two strange looking guys, one in pyjamas who could be mighty dangerous…

*ARNOLD slams door shut. Goes to cabinet. Pours another stiff drink. Downs it.*

*FX DOOR CHIMES.*

ARNOLD
I'll fetch it.

*ARNOLD goes to front door. Opens it. POLICE SERGEANT stands on doorstep (same actor as SHERIFF).*

POLICE SERGEANT
Sorry to trouble you, sir. Two patients from the top security mental hospital have escaped. We are concerned that they might try and hole up locally.

ARNOLD
There's nobody insane in this house, sergeant. I can vouch for that.

SERGEANT
You're to be congratulated, sir. Long may it last.

ARNOLD
Thank you. Was there anything else?

SERGEANT
No, sir. Just be careful, please. And report anything untoward.

ARNOLD
Like what?

SERGEANT
Out of place. Out of joint, sir. These days, who can say? If you read the

literature I do. We could have conversations. Possible cracks in time. A parallel universe or two. Flashbacks. Hallucinations. Eclipses and comets. Blessings and curses...

ARNOLD
And ever filled purses.

SERGEANT
Where would you place yourself in terms of the Big Bang, sir?

ARNOLD
Here.

SERGEANT
When?

ARNOLD
Now.

SERGEANT
Then things aren't so bad, are they? Good-day, sir.

ARNOLD
Goodbye.

*ARNOLD shuts door, firmly.*
*Opens door again. No-one is there. He shuts door.*

*Enter HELEN, wearing a provocative dress.*

HELEN
Arnold, I'm not a girl anymore. I don't know if you've noticed. The biological clock is ticking. I'm not getting any younger. I want to start my own family.

ARNOLD
Oh horror. Helen, family's don't work. The family is an evolutionary concept that has proved to be a backwater. All literature, all drama, supports my contention.

HELEN
With what would you replace it?

ARNOLD
We need to go back to the tribe and start again. The family has become too intense. It can't take the strain, it's the wrong basic social unit – as it has developed in the West. And all the political machinations support the insupportable – family. Because the family has become the prime consumer unit. Therefore big business supports family policies and they are the dog that wags the tail... But did you really want to know all this?

HELEN
You're making excuses to stop me having children.

ARNOLD
In your case it would be a particular disaster. Helen, if you could have a child and give it away I could understand a biological need being met... but you would never ever let go. You'd have a Norman Bates monster that would soak up the social services for years, ending in an Interpol chase across five continents for a sex killer.

HELEN
And if I had a girl?

ARNOLD
Worse. She'd become a Tory MP.

HELEN
You're only saying that because you've failed. As a father.

ARNOLD
If I had succeeded as a father I would have ruined my offspring. Thank God they have no-one to look up to. They are thrown upon their inner resources. The paternal role has been smashed and... And they are free to go.

HELEN
Don't the children need nurturing in the early years, Arnold?

ARNOLD
Ye, but not until they are at an age to turn around and place you in a

geriatric home.

HELEN
I'm not unattractive. I can find another man, if I have to. I have had offers, darling.

ARNOLD
I didn't know you'd been advertising. But go ahead, if you must.

HELEN
I don't have to throw my life away on an older man. You have an option that's expiring.

ARNOLD
I sometimes think it's me that's expiring. Helen, it's depressing, all this talk about age, stop it. You will do what you have to do, and talking's not going to change that.

HELEN
You're impossible.

ARNOLD
Time is something we've invented, Helen. It is an illusion, it does not exist. We can even be like the humble proton – in two places at the same time. Although there must be an observer, or… an audience. An audience? Yes, that is possible.

HELEN
You look down on me. Because I'm a librarian.

ARNOLD
No, I love you Helen. And your mobile library van. It's been a beacon of hope for me, your visits. Ever since I ordered The Plumed Serpent and you brought it out to the cottage. That changed everything. You were nineteen. I've been infatuated by you ever since.

HELEN
You took advantage of me.

ARNOLD
Who wouldn't? Look we've read DH Lawrence together in places – and in positions – that defy belief. We've gone through his entire works together. We did *Lady Chatterley's Lover* in one week, in the Lake District. Remember? I was supposed to be doing a recall on a Barclays Bank advertisement.

HELEN
Are you committed to me, Arnold?

ARNOLD
I am totally committed to you, Helen, and I'll prove it. Here and now. Listen, I've found that comedy thriller I was talking to you about. Written by an obscure hack, once famous now forgotten. Name of Antrobus. We can make something of his work. The miserable bastard is demanding a seven thousand pound commission or he'll take it to the Old Red Lion and direct it himself. Bloody idiot. Put up the seven grand, darling, it's no good clinging on to those pathetic life savings of yours – what life? What are you saving? We can cement our relationship, our partnership, with a business deal, that's practical! It's the first step. And we will build on it. Together. Our first production will lead to others. Each production will be like a child to us. We will have many children, Helen. The West End will be their playground, their nursery. These productions will be our family. Our family, yes. They will spread throughout the world. In many languages, our children will be multi-lingual, Japanese, French, German, Swedish... American.
Look, you can have a kid that craps and keeps us up all night, if you like! With someone. Some evolutionary retard bent upon destruction of the human race. Or you can grab this great opportunity. With me. Just sign the cheque, Helen, and the future is yours.

HELEN
How deep are you into this venture, Arnold? This comedy thriller?

ARNOLD
Up to my neck. I don't know where it's going, from what I've read. It's full of promise but it's yet to deliver. It will take my input...
Well, are you in? Or is it over between us? Must I find financial resources elsewhere, and sleep in another bed?

*HELEN exits.*

*BRIAN is at the window. ARNOLD pours himself another drink.*

ARNOLD
'Tis a consummation devoutly to be wished for. To die, to sleep. To sleep, perchance to dream; Aye, there's the rub, For in that sleep of death, what dreams come?
Ah, Will, my dearest dearest love. My wordsmith, cobbling parts for ill-shod actors, like as me, that is the half of it. *What dreams may come?* Aye, Will, and in the waking what illusion? This trace of dreams, the minefield of memories, penned like sheep inside electric circuits of the brain. A most unreliable device. The brain. Which gives us experience, true. Experience is a common denominator, for you can experience terror in a nightmare, and wake up to a dream, being anxious – grading fear – then shaken awake – nothing! Nothing but the stomach's pit, dark, black. And so we start another jolly day while planets orbit, policemen philosophise, and dogs bark! Add goldfish in a tank, swimming round a rock that they forget existed every six seconds, making their life tolerable.

BRIAN
How do you think we're fitting in to family life, me and Eric, Mr Gosport?

ARNOLD
Exceedingly well, Mr...?

BRIAN
Darey. Mister Darey. Well, soon to be Doctor Darey, I trust. Once I get my recognition, that is. I hope that we are making the right adjustments here, after being hospitalised for so long, against our will of course.

ARNOLD
Oh yes, it is a pleasure having you around, as an extended family, really. With young Eric bouncing about. I think he'd be better without the gun, don't you?

BRIAN
When the trust has built up, sir. It's early days. Twentynine days to go. By the European Convention we will have to be recommitted.

ARNOLD
Now let's get down to brass tacks, shall we? Mr Darey. How did the body

get in here? Into this room?

BRIAN
Which one, sir?

ARNOLD
You mean there's more than one? I'm talking about the body in the window box.

BRIAN
Not the one in the piano?

*ARNOLD lifts piano lid. Let's it drop.*
*Piano note, 'PING!'*
*Hand flops out. BRIAN tucks it back in.*
*ARNOLD sits on window seat. Stands up. Lifts lid and looks inside.*
*ARNOLD closes window seat. Closes it quickly. Sits down.*

BRIAN
Well, we only brought the one, sir. Nurse Arthur.

ARNOLD
That's Nurse Arthur?

BRIAN
Yes, sir. The other gentleman is persons unknown. As he had no means of introducing himself. Unless, sir, you happen to be acquainted with him.

ARNOLD
Why should I know him?

BRIAN
He was in the boot of your car, sir. We brought him in. I assumed, that being a foggy night, you had run him down.

ARNOLD
I have no memory of that. How could that be?

BRIAN
Well, sir, if you stopped at a Little Chef say, for some refreshment, and left

your car unattended, then someone else who had run that gentlemen down – him in the window box – they could have taken him out of the boot of their car and put him in your boot, thus disposing of their unwanted item. It could have been a fridge or a washing machine.

ARNOLD
Yes, I suppose I'm lucky – lucky it was only a body. I'm surprised they didn't empty their ashtrays in my boot, while they were about it.

BRIAN
People are like that these days, sir. No consideration for others.

ARNOLD
So that's what happened?

BRIAN
I expect so.

ARNOLD
Well we can't leave him here, this…

BRIAN
I called him Mr Brown.

ARNOLD
Good idea. Mr Brown, yes…

BRIAN
As a code. In case he happens to be a Russian spy and we are starting to get entangled in an international scandal.

ARNOLD
Yes, I see. In which case we should call him Mr Abramovich. I intend to put Mr Abramovich in the boot of somebody else's car. It may be rather like Pass The Parcel, but if the Cold War is starting up again, we have to leave no trace of our involvement. I expect you to help out. Discreetly, without upsetting the household. Nobody else need know about this.

BRIAN
Very well, sir.

ARNOLD
And I don't want your body left in my piano either.

BRIAN
We could put Nurse Arthur in the window box.

ARNOLD
What would we do with Abramovich?

BRIAN
We could put him in the piano. He might be musical.

ARNOLD
An international Russian concert pianist seeking asylum in the West, you mean?

BRIAN
Possibly.

ARNOLD
This is getting too complicated. We must get rid of both bodies as soon as possible.

BRIAN
Right. Even though Eric is very attached to Nurse Arthur…

ARNOLD
Well Eric better get unattached. If he is planning a necrophiliac weekend with Nurse Arthur in Morocco, he better be quick about it, because bodies don't keep for long. does he know that?

BRIAN
Some facts of life still escape him.

ARNOLD
Look, get it into your head, Mr Darey, that while you are staying with me, I insist on certain Christian principles that we abide by, and one of them is that we are not running a charnel house. Are there any more bodies lying around?

BRIAN
Not that I know about.

*FX. TWO SHOTS, from direction of cellar. Pause. ERIC comes out of cellar door. Slams door shut behind him and leans against it. He holds the gun.*

ERIC
I had to do it!

ARNOLD
God! What next?

ERIC
I was menaced. He was coming at me. I plugged him. Second shot, fair and square. Demolished him, hairy blighter.

ARNOLD
Roger! *He falls to his knees*. This is an expiation, a punishment from the Gods for a monstrous crime, though covered it shouts out, your son has fallen to square the books.

*The window box opens. DIGBY, as a ghost in sepulchral white robes rises and points an accusing finger at ARNOLD. ARNOLD approaches the ghost.*

ARNOLD
Oh ghost, you mock me. Mock me not agent, agent of my doom. Mr Ten Percent plus VAT, that life I took from you is nothing to my fair son, his light extinguished. His was the light of a thousand stars compared to your pale lamp, but thus I am a thousand fold condemned. Oh for fatherhood I shall suffer. For being a father. For being a father, one sperm that became that fertilised egg, that wonder of nativity, that baby boy, my Roger. Roger, translucent, slightly freckled… Hang on, Roger wasn't hairy.

*DIGBY descends, back into window box, closing lid.*

ERIC
It was a hairy spider, mister. It weren't Roger. I hate spiders. Now it's mate'll be looking for me. I ain't going down that cellar again.
Wild horses won't drag me.

BRIAN
*Takes gun from Eric.* Give me that gun, Eric. You mustn't go wasting bullets shooting spiders. It's a disproportionate response.

ERIC
Yes doctor.

*DOOR CHIMES. ERIC crosses to window.*

ERIC
It's the pigs. They're back.

BRIAN
I'll look after the family. You keep an eye on Mr Gosport, Eric. You know the drill.

ERIC
Oh aye. Keep killing to a minimum.

ARNOLD
Let me handle this…

*ARNOLD crosses to front door. BRIAN exit to cellar. ERIC hides. ARNOLD opens front door. SHERIFF is on doorstep. He tips his hat.*

SHERIFF
Hi, y'all. How's it hanging? Sorry to disturb you God-fearing folks, only a neighbour down the lane aways was out exercising his mutt swore he heard a shot coming from this here house. So he reported it and here I am lickertyspit hotfoot and all tooled up for the Big Bust so what's going on?

ARNOLD
Why are you here?

SHERIFF
A shot was reported, sir.

ARNOLD
No, I mean why are you here in this country?

SHERIFF
Good question. It's God's country, sir, with a broad blue sky where heaven reaches down to earth praise be.

ARNOLD
I was opening a bottle of champagne.

SHERIFF
That's good enough for me, sir, all I need's an explanation from you good folk. 'Fore I leave I should mention that these two monsters who broke out the local hospital are becoming more dangerous by the hour because they are not taking their medication. I have a medical report here says they could go plumb crazy.

ARNOLD
Thank you.

SHERIFF
Good-day to you, God bless America.

*SHERIFF leaves as ARNOLD shuts front door.*
*ERIC steps out of hiding.*

ARNOLD
You're familiar with bodies, aren't you?

ERIC
I am. That's right.

*ERIC nudges piano. Hand flops out.*
*FX : « 'Ping!' » ERIC takes sweetie from inside.*

ERIC
This is one of ours. Nurse Arthur.

ARNOLD
You killed him, did you not?

ERIC
*(chewing the sweet)* It was nothing personal, son. We're still good friends,

like. He wanted me to have his sweeties, Nurse Arthur. Mr Darey doesn't seem to understand that.

ARNOLD
Well I do. I know you've got a sweet tooth. But in having all due regard to your desires for friendship, I simply cannot allow you to have your dead pals litter my house. This is not a tomb of the Pharaoh's, Mr Dewitt. This is a family residence. Nor can we afford to have Nurse Arthur embalmed, which might solve the problem. It is no good looking disappointed, pulling that face, we can't afford it, right? We're on a tight enough budget as it is, in this house! No embalming! It is a fact of life and death that bodies rot, Mr Dewitt. They cannot be left lying around. They have to be disposed of, buried, cremated, chopped up, eaten… I don't care! They have to go. The sweeties won't last forever from Nurse Arthur's pocket. Rely on me. I've already promised you pocket money.

ERIC
You're a straight-up sort of chap, I can tell that. Just looking at you. Right, no probs, guv. We got the cleaners coming, don't worry. They'll tidy up. Big Charlie'll take care of it. He's me brother like.

ARNOLD
Your brother's coming here?

ERIC
Oh aye. It's part of the escape plan. See, I'm the brains, I am. Oh yes, I've organised the whole thing. You wouldn't think so, but the breakout and the follow up, it's all down to me. Like, you know that Mr Darey – Big Mouth who fancies himself as one of the men in white coats – he shoots his mouth off a lot, but behind it all, guess who is running the show? Oh aye, I'm watching. Biding me time. No one insults me, what? Tells me when I can have a sweetie. Comes between me and Nurse Arthur, what? Oh no. you can be my new pal, Elephant Bill. I've taken a liking to you.

ARNOLD
It is mutual, Eric.

ERIC
Oh aye.

ARNOLD
Do you think, while he's organising the cleaners, that Big Charlie could get rid of one for me?

ERIC
What?

ARNOLD
A body?

*ARNOLD lifts window box lid. Shows ERIC the body of DIGBY.*

ERIC
Oh easy peasy. You got one as well, have you? Good as gold, he looks. But you're right, they don't last too long in this weather. Consider it done, glad to help. No, probs there mate. He's gone. Two's as easy as one, while you're cleaning up. No probs there.

ARNOLD
Oh splendid.

ERIC
You scratch my back I'll scratch yours, OK?

ARNOLD
Always send the lift back for the next person, yes.

ERIC
You want him under a motorway I can fix it. Right? Big Charlie'll do that, no worries – when he arrives like – when he turns up. I'll speak to Big Charlie – he's me brother. Oh aye, he – he is diversifying into entertainment, something you should know, son.

ARNOLD
Really? You mean your brother might have funds to invest?

ERIC
Funds coming out of his ears, mate. Money to wash, lots of it. From abroad, like. You know, suitcases full of cash, notes, various currencies. You know, from Eastern Europe. Usual thing. We've got to turn it round.

Lose it in investments. it comes out clean as profit. We can even afford to take a loss. Twenty percent, maybe. I'll have to talk to Charlie.

ARNOLD
I'd be interested to meet your brother, Big Charlie. I might be able to put him on to something. Like a film…?

ERIC
Something like Elephant Bill, perhaps? I was waiting for you to say that.

ARNOLD
Indeed.

ERIC
Easy peasy. Always room for another jungle picture, son. If it wasn't for the jungle there wouldn't be any jungle, would there? No. And then where would the monkeys swing, tell me that?

ARNOLD
Yes, true. You say he is coming here? Big Charlie?

ERIC
Oh aye, it's the pickup! The Big One Plan A. I'll make the intros. No probs. No problems there. He's me brother. I think he's me brother?

ARNOLD
And theatre investment? Would that interest Big Charlie? Do you think?

ERIC
On my recommendation, no probs. Oh aye, consider it done. You see, next to him there's me. Anything happens to Big Charlie, I'm next in line. Oh aye, take over, me. Criminal empire. Tentacles everywhere. West End, Strip clubs, pole dancing, Gielgud Theatre, Michael Gambon, he's one of ours!

ARNOLD
That's very interesting. I've always had my suspicions about Michael Gambon.

*DOOR CHIMES.*
*ARNOLD crosses to door. ERIC just stands there.*

*ARNOLD opens front door.*
*POLICE SERGEANT is on doorstep.*

SERGEANT
Good afternoon sir, sorry to trouble you. Only there's been a breakout from the local lunatic asylum.

ARNOLD
Yes, I know about it. You've already been round.

SERGEANT
Not this one, sir, you don't know about this one. There's a dangerous lunatic, a menace to the public, who loves to pass himself off as a Texas Ranger. Or US Sheriff, we're not sure which. He visits households warning people, God fearing people as he puts it, of lunatics escaping from the hospital.

ARNOLD
Thank you, sergeant.

SERGEANT
*Pointing at Eric.* Who's he?

ARNOLD
He's my nephew. Teddy. He's slightly retarded.

SERGEANT
Righto, sir.

ARNOLD
You should concentrate on keeping people inside the asylum, sergeant.

SERGEANT
That's not our job sir. Our job is to round them up once they've got out.

ARNOLD
So how many are on the loose?

SERGEANT
What, including your nephew?

ARNOLD
He's not from the hospital.

SERGEANT
I didn't say he was. It's you that said he's retarded.

ARNOLD
Slightly.

SERGEANT
Full moon tonight, sir. If your nephew's on medication make sure he takes it. We've got enough trouble to deal with tonight. Good-day, sir.

*SERGEANT departs, as ARNOLD closes front door.*

ERIC
You did well, mate. You covered for me there. I'm your nephew, right, Teddy, OK.

ARNOLD
Yes, Teddy dug graves in the cellar. Did you see Arsenic And Old Lace?

ERIC
I get it. Right. You want graves dug in the cellar. I'm your man. How many? How many did you have in mind?

*BLACKOUT.*

## SCENE 4

*LOUNGE. NIGHT. The family.*
*ERIC, to one side, guards with the gun.*

*KATEY plays flute. BRIAN sings :*
*« I think that I shall never see,*
*A rose as lovely as a tree… »*

BRIAN
Thank you, Miss Katey. I am most partial to a musical evening. We used to have them down on the farm. Quite often, if very seldom. My mother was musical.

KATEY
Really? What did she play?

BRIAN
The tractor.

KATEY
Don't you mean she drove the tractor?

BRIAN
That as well, yes. She was a – a big woman, my mother – with a stick.

KATEY
Did she beat you with it? I hope.

BRIAN
Only when evil tendencies showed. But they have been mastered. The devil has been set at naught. Do you think we're fitting in well to your family life, Miss Katey?

KATEY
At the point of a gun, yes.

BRIAN
That's a formality I hope we can dispense with in due course. However we are moving on according to Plan A, when Eric's brother comes to collect us.

KATEY
The sooner the better.

BRIAN
Yes, life must go on, I realise. Nothing is constant except change, stitch it on a cushion. But Miss Katey, I am – and this is the good news – considering activating Plan B.

KATEY
Plan B? What's that?

BRIAN
Well that means we stay here. Thirty days. As it is proving to be so congenial.

KATEY
Forget Plan B.

BRIAN
Then we would go to the European court with your father's glowing references, I trust, to our characters.

KATEY
You have several characters, Mr Darey, all of them unpleasant. You are quite mad.

BRIAN
Contrary Kate. To win a soft word from you I shall have to work harder, I see.

KATEY
I would be willing to recommend to the courts…

BRIAN
Oh good.

KATEY
That you should be chemically castrated.

BRIAN
Putting that to one side, I would like to speak to your father, as my prospects will soon be improved.

KATEY
This is not a BBC costume drama, Mr Darey. You don't get it, do you? As a species of punter you belong in a strip club with the other sad sacks playing with themselves under their raincoats.

BRIAN
I would never visit such an establishment, Miss Kate. To see the topless ladies with their udders swinging.

KATEY
Udders? You're a fucking retard! You think Happy Hour is milking time. Go back to your farm and fuck your favourite sheep! It must be missing you.

*KATEY makes ' Baa, baa ' sheep noise. ROGER joins in.*
*BRIAN takes the gun from ERIC.*

MOTHER
Stop!
Ominous silence.Which way will it go?

BRIAN
These are fractious times. The young are tumbling into adulthood with a clown's instruction….
*(He gives the gun back to ERIC)*
'Tis true, faint heart never won fair lady. I can see I shall have to persevere with this courtship. Love's a game. If music be the food of love, play on …

*'Ping!' Hand flops our of piano.*
*ERIC pushes it back in, and takes a sweet.*
*MOTHER was only one to notice.*

MOTHER
*(To ARNOLD, not to alarm the others)*
Arnold! My God, there's a body in the piano!

ARNOLD
Don't worry, Mother, it's one of ours.

MOTHER
What do you mean, it's one of ours? Are you in collusion with these maniacs?

ARNOLD
No, they are in collusion with me. I am winning them over, Vera. Leave everything to me. I am home. How many more times?

*ARNOLD pours himself another drink.*
*Holds up whisky bottle upside down. It is empty.*

MOTHER
Arnold, what is going on here? Do you know? Have you the vaguest idea? A body in the piano? This is terrible. Where's it going to end?

ARNOLD
I wonder if the off licence is still open?

MOTHER
Everyone is exhausted. This is when mistakes can happen.

ARNOLD
There are no mistakes, Vera. That's a value judgement, your own words. Sticking labels on experience. Where's your famous optimism, when we need it?

MOTHER
I was optimistic, that doesn't mean I should be deluded.

ARNOLD
Don't let circumstances dictate how you feel? Isn't that one of your sayings?

MOTHER
Don't throw my words in my face, Arnold. Please, why are you reproving me? This place could turn into a bloodbath.

ARNOLD
Nothing will be as bad as that month we spent in Eastbourne with your mother.

MOTHER
She didn't keep a body in the piano.

ARNOLD
No she kept one in the kitchen. Your father. The only place he could smoke. Until he went to the crematorium.

MOTHER
That's not funny, Arnold. Why can't you face it? This situation is desperate.

ARNOLD
The Desperate Hours. Humphrey Bogart. Frederick March. A classic. Could redo it as a stage musical. Too many ideas and not enough time for all of them, that's the problem. Ah well. Yes, this is pretty much a rerun of The Desperate Hours. Roger! I want you to pop down the off licence. Ask gay Nigel to put a bottle of scotch on the slate. He'll do it for me. He'll definitely do it for you, use your looks, boy.

MOTHER
You are not sending Roger to the off licence, we've got two murderers running around the house. Let them be.

ARNOLD
They'll respond to my…

MOTHER
No.

ROGER
Am I going, or not?

ARNOLD
I can arrange it, Roger. And get some soft drinks and nuts for everyone.

MOTHER
We've got enough nuts. Roger, sit down. Arnold, behave yourself, please.

Realise that we have two children to look after.

ARNOLD
Children? They're old enough to look after themselves. Cut them loose, for God's sake, Vera.

MOTHER
At a time like this?

ARNOLD
There's no time like the present. Let them stand on their own two feet. They're not babies. Your trouble is you're role playing. You're playing mother and the supporting cast have outgrown you.

MOTHER
This is not the time… Couldn't you stop drinking for one day?

ARNOLD
I don't know. I've never tried.

MOTHER
There must be an answer.

ARNOLD
What's the question?

MOTHER
How do we get help? Without emphasising a hostage situation? Sending Roger off on a bicycle to an off licence is not the way to do it. Even if they would let him go and he alerts the police. These crazy…

ARNOLD
Jazz fiends?

MOTHER
What?

ARNOLD
Black music has unhinged society. Debate.

MOTHER
What's that got to do with these people?

ARNOLD
Exactly. My point entirely. Go on, mother...

MOTHER
Oh my head is splitting, talking to you.

ARNOLD
Of course the police have called round several times.

MOTHER
What did you tell them? Because I knew...

ARNOLD
Nothing.

MOTHER
I knew they had been, and it was difficult when you were being held at the end of a gun. Or we were, in the cellar? I don't know. I'm losing track... You didn't tell the police anything? Wink even...? Gesture? Silently?

ARNOLD
No, I did not gesture. I clammed up, Vera. For safety's sake. And quite honestly I do not want a Police Armed Response Unit turning up here. A van load of rozzers running around the garden, putting a mobile lavatory in the middle of the flower bed. Keeping us awake with their megaphones. And, of course, eventually giving up and smashing our windows and chucking in stun grenades. They'd taser the wrong people when they burst in, they always do. No, and I do not want a police helicopter blowing slates off the roof. We're not insured for any of it, Vera.

MOTHER
Arnold, we need trained hostage negotiators outside. Who understand the minds of these creatures.

ARNOLD
You think I don't? That I don't understand them? I'm building up a trust, a relationship. Because I see them as human, fallen, but in the drama of

life. They see me as a father figure. I'm getting some respect from them – which is more than I get from my own family. It's pitiful. It's pitiful that I have to turn to strangers for some measure of – of self regard. You're turning me into a eunuch.

MOTHER
That is not the issue, Arnold. This is not about you. This situation is not about you.

ARNOLD
From my perspective it is. Everything is about me. That is why the Universe has been created. For me, if nobody else will claim it. Vera, it's a matter of trust.

MOTHER
We've always trusted you, Arnold. Look where it's got us.

ARNOLD
Oh, I'm to blame for all this, am I, now?

MOTHER
Yes, if I hadn't married you this would never have happened.

ARNOLD
Ah, now it's come out. Ah well, that's logical. I was waiting for it. I've devoted my life to this family. And all I get is discouragement, and being continually undermined.

MOTHER
Arnold. I want to believe in you. Not to doubt you. it is me that has kept the flame alive. To be the fuel that ignites your star again.

ARNOLD
I like that.

MOTHER
But I don't know what you're planning to do next. And I panic when I think about it…

ARNOLD
I'm sorry. Really. Now do be a dear old hen and stop worrying. We're coming out the other side, Vera. The worst is over, I promise you.

*Window box lid opens. DIGBY peers out.*

MOTHER
Oh my God...

*Window box lid closes.*

MOTHER
He's in the window box.

ARNOLD
Who?

MOTHER
Digby. You didn't tell me he was here.

*ARNOLD looks in window box, lifting lid, then closing it.*

ARNOLD
No he's not.

MOTHER
What is Digby doing in the window box, Arnold?

ARNOLD
Well, there was no room in the piano. And anyway he's not here. No Digby. It's your imagination, Vera. You're seeing things.

MOTHER
But...

ARNOLD
It's the stress. Everyone's stressed these days. People don't know how to enjoy the moment.

MOTHER
How can anyone enjoy this moment? You're fogging the issue. I saw Digby looking out of the window box?

ARNOLD
Why would he do that? I mean if he was in the window box, and planned a surprise entrance for Katey's birthday, how did he get in there? In the first place?

MOTHER
I don't know.

ARNOLD
Where have you been?

MOTHER
We haven't been anywhere.

ARNOLD
Then he couldn't have got in, could he? You would have noticed. And if he did – sneak into the window box – and if he looked out, which you claim he did, he would spoil the surprise anyway, wouldn't he? That he had planned. If he looked out, he'd jump up and say 'Happy Birthday Katey!' would he not?

MOTHER
I'm sure I saw him, as broad as daylight...

ARNOLD
You didn't. Come and have a look.

MOTHER
No. No, thank you. Is there anyone in that window box?

ARNOLD
No.

MOTHER
It would explain a lot. That Digby had come to the party, and they thought they had killed him and stuffed him in the window box.

ARNOLD
I like that. That's a good explanation. Perhaps he is here after all. Digby.

MOTHER
But you said he wasn't.

ARNOLD
Then he's not. That's settled. You don't need explanations. Explanations are for small people. Faith is your speciality, my love.

MOTHER
Faith? Faith? You talk of faith? I used to have faith. Where's it gone? What's happened to our family life? It was a refuge and strength against the ills of the world. We could pull up the drawbridge…

ARNOLD
It's all gone pear-shaped, Mum. You can't put all your ducks in a row now, right? Get use to it.

MOTHER
This isn't real, is it? Tell me it isn't real.

ARNOLD
No, we've probably been written.

MOTHER
Don't start that Pirandello stuff again! Please. The night's bad enough without Pirandello. There is a body in the piano?

ARNOLD
Yes, but it's not Digby. We must be grateful that it's not someone close to us, Mother. We see so much death on television these days, we become blasé. I don't think the body of a stranger in the piano need concern us overly. I'll get rid of it before it goes off, don't worry. Leave everything to me. I'm home now. I didn't create this mess but I'll sort it out…

*CROSSFADE LIGHTING.*

*FX. FADE UP CLOCK TICKING – FADE OUT.*
*Same scene.*

*All are asleep except ARNOLD. He pours himself another drink.*

*BRIAN, who has dozed off, drops the gun.*

*ARNOLD notices, picks up the gun. He nudges BRIAN to waken him, and gives him the gun.*

ARNOLD
What time is Eric's brother arriving? Soon the cock will crow and the fingers of daylight strangle our dreams. To gut the candles brings no relief. This day's march shall wear out many boots, and who'll cry Harry for England when he's carousing in the brothels of Plymouth.

BRIAN
Is that Shakespeare, sir?

ARNOLD
Cod. We did it backstage at the RSC all the time. Mr Darey, we've got to get rid of these bodies. They won't keep their condition this weather. However fond we are of them. Do you think Big Charlie, when he gets here, will he get rid of them for us? It's a matter of hygiene. I hope you know what that is?

BRIAN
I do, sir. Hygiene is next to God. Stitch it on a cushion. I must report Big Charlie is more likely to add to the body count, Mr Gosport. I have analysed the family background, as one has to when dealing with a patient, namely Eric Dewitt. Everyone in the family has a role in the trauma.

ARNOLD
It's text book stuff, I know. I know that. The family trauma as psychodrama. It's your Greek tragedy. Oedipus as Freudian complex. It's saloon bar talk these days, we all know about it. But none of us can get a handle on it, can we?

BRIAN
Precisely, sir. It's a downward spiral. I can predict that in Eric Dewitt's case – having killed his mother and his father – acting out that is – the drama is incomplete. That leaves the two brothers, you see. So one has to go. It's inevitable.

ARNOLD
Yes tragedy does deal with inevitable conclusions. I, however, choose to believe in absurd outcomes. Does this make me a theatrical modernist?

BRIAN
Undoubtably, sir.

ARNOLD
Does Ionesco mean anything to you?

BRIAN
I've heard of Ian Lavender, sir, but not the other one.

*CLOCK TICKING as BRIAN nods off back to sleep.*
*THE LIGHT CHANGES TO DAWN.*
*FX. COCK CROWS.*

*The window box lid opens and DIGBY climbs out. He comes to the centre of the room, disorientated. He sees the gaily wrapped present, half hidden under a chair, and picks it up. DIGBY wanders out by french windows, singing « Happy Birthday To You »….*

*ROGER wakes – too late to notice exit of DIGBY – and sees that BRIAN is asleep.*

*ROGER jumps on BRIAN, wrestling him for the gun as KATEY and MOTHER wake up. ERIC sleeps through everything.*

*ROGER holds the gun, covering BRIAN and ERIC.*

MOTHER
Arnold! Wake up!

ARNOLD
What's up?

ROGER
It's alright, Dad, I've got the gun.

ARNOLD
So I see, yes. Can't I sleep for a few moments? Roger's got the gun. He's taken over. I see, I can see that.

ROGER
I've got control of the situation.

ARNOLD
Control? You've got control, have you? Don't be pathetic. Haven't we got enough control freaks in this family? Roger's got the gun so we'll all do what he wants now, is that it? We'll all jump when Roger jumps. Do we think that life under Roger with the gun will be any better? Give me that gun, boy.

ROGER
*Not handing over the gun.* You can call the police now, Dad.

ARNOLD
Can I? Dad can call the police. Thanks for your permission. Roger says we should call the police now, I've told you he was taking over. He's making all the decisions now. Weirdo wacko Roger with the gun. Trade it up for a Kalashnikov, my boy – where's the nearest school? Let's have a massacre. If you want to dominate the family, start your own family – but you can't can you – unless you adopt with your pal – because this one's mine. This is my family. So, give me that gun, Roger.

*ROGER reluctantly hands over the gun.*

ARNOLD
Next time we want a regime change we'll let you know.

MOTHER
Roger was acting very bravely, Arnold. To the point of foolhardy.

ARNOLD
I go along with foolhardy. What's he trying to prove? If he's trying to win my affection it's pointless. Of course I love Roger. We all love Roger. But not at the point of a gun.

ROGER
Dad's got Stockholm syndrome.

KATEY
And the rest of Sweden.

ROGER
I give up.

MOTHER
Roger is right. Someone should fetch the police.

ARNOLD
No-one's fetching the police until I say so. We're playing for bigger stakes, right? Don't ask me to explain. You can judge me by results.

ROGER
Explain? When has he ever? Been able to explain. I'm... I'm going to get the police.

ARNOLD
No, you're not. *With gun, threatening.* You're not going anywhere, Roger. Stand back.

ROGER
Are you threatening me?

ARNOLD
What? Yes... No... What if I am? I don't need to threaten you Roger, it's enough that I'm home. I am home! You might try on my big boots while I'm away, but I'm back. Right. So...

ROGER
So?

ARNOLD
What?

ROGER
So what?

ARNOLD
So we don't need to contact the police.

ROGER
Why not?

MOTHER
Arnold, we must…

ARNOLD
Don't take his side, mother. I'll tell you why not. Because these people – call them what you will – but they are human, like us – and they have sought sanctuary in our household. From a hostile environment. They are fugitives. Refugees. And we should treat them as honoured guests. As in the East we should regard them as a sacred trust. It would be a betrayal to turn them into the authorities.

ROGER
The only bollocksy thing about that is that these honoured guests have been on the tipping point of killing us ever since they arrived.

ARNOLD
Because they are frightened, Roger. They are looking for love. We must turn the other cheek. Set an example. Is this not a Christian household? Secular, but imbued with Christian principle. The new liberalism. Do we not listen to Thought For The Day on Radio Four? What I'm saying is, Roger, these people are our responsibility. It's alright to go on demonstrations for Darfur, but when the misery of the world spills over our own doorstep, is that all you can do? Call the police. Lock them up again. None of our business? Is that it? Sweep them under the carpet and get on with our own lives?

ROGER
Fuck. OK. Let them go. Yes, go on. I agree, there's the door. No-one's stopping you, bye bye.

ARNOLD
They can't go yet.

ROGER
Why not?

MOTHER
Arnold, this is gilding the lily. Enough is enough. Get rid of them. This moment is a tipping point.

ROGER
He can't. He's hopelessly compromised.

KATEY
Are we still in a hostage situation Roger, are we?

ROGER
There is no situation.

KATEY
That's impossible. You have to conceptualise in a way that gives you leverage to a reality – however grotesque – that's good, that's modern – so that each character can draw boundaries and inter-relate…

ROGER
Kate, this is not a scriptwriting seminar. Sorry. This is life. I know it's scary but situations can dissolve.

KATEY
They do not dissolve Roger, they have resolution. I'm doing the fucking correspondence course! I know. I do not conceptualise normal, boring – I conceptualise Post Modern Situation Comedy. I have been accepted for the BBC Young Writers Under Twenty-one The Surest Way To Middle Management – Sitcom course.

ROGER
Everyone is under twenty-one at the BBC. It's the new retirement age.

KATEY
Then I'm too late.

ARNOLD
So, here we are! Oh happy day, that our hearts are offered in this act of

hospitality. Yes, the situation is transformed, Katey. We put up our weapons. There… *(lays gun down)* Mr Darey, you are free to come and go as you please, with your friend. Into that naughty night you may choose to go, where all sleep except hostile elements, such as wolves, vampires, ghosts and various apparitions. Including police patrols seeking to restore people to institutions where without trial they shall languish unhappily for days without number, drugged senseless. Or you may rest awhile in our humble abode, where we find ourselves to be also strangers, such as are you. However strong the portals and whatever family lineage we may claim, 'tis but a tent we pitch in this spinning, weird, universe. Nothing is secure, sir. The air we breath is the most substance we know. Without it, our wallets full or empty, mean little. Would you hang on with us? What say you?

BRIAN
Let it be sir, as it is. A fairer offer I have yet to hear. We accept your hospitality. Eric, put this gun away. it shall be decommissioned…

*BRIAN picks up the gun and gives it to ERIC*

ERIC
Aye, when Big Charlie arrives I'll arrange to have another cake baked, and the gun shall go inside it. Back where it came from.

MOTHER
Big Charlie? Who's he?

ROGER
Eric's brother. Did you think it was over? It's just started…

*ROGER sits at piano. Plays and sings,*
*Amazing Grace.*
*The others join in.*

BLACKOUT.

## SCENE 5

*Later, that morning. Sunny. Birdsong.*
*The lounge is empty.*
*Enter HELEN, through French windows.*
*She carries several library books and also a gaily wrapped present.*

HELEN
(Sings) Happy rather late birthday to you…
Happy rather late birthday to you…!
Hello! Anyone at home?

*HELEN looks round, to make sure she is unobserved, puts the books down and climbs into the window box.*
*She shuts the lid.*
*Enter BRIAN one way, then ERIC, from the kitchen – eating a bowl of cereal.*

BRIAN
What are you eating?

ERIC
Wheetabix.

BRIAN
You're eating them out of house and home, you are. Can't you wait till everybody gets up?

ERIC
Where are they? The family, like?

BRIAN
Upstairs. Having a lie in. We are all family now, Eric.

ERIC
Oh aye?

BRIAN
We have been accepted into the bosom of the family.

ERIC
We might have to kill the lot. Body rolled out on the doorstep every half hour till our demands are met. Helicopter to Heathrow like, and a million pounds in untraceable notes. Off we go to South America. Hello rhumba!

BRIAN
We're doing nothing anything like that, Eric. Don't you go dreaming up plans on your own. They are violent fantasies.

ERIC
What?

BRIAN
Where's the gun? Where have you put it?

ERIC
Oh, don't worry about that. Hey, I've got that under control. Reloaded, aye, all ready for action.

BRIAN
You worry me sometimes, you do. I need to to get a structured something or other.

ERIC
Your clinic!

BRIAN
That's right.

ERIC
In Rio de Janeiro, eh?

BRIAN
No, Eric. Not in Rio de Janeiro.

ERIC
Are they locked up in the cellar, the family?

BRIAN
They are in their bedrooms! How many more times? What is the matter

with you? Everything's changed. We are accepted as normal people. Normal people! Get that in your head! Oh dear. Now when your brother arrives…

ERIC
He probably got the day wrong. Or had a job on, you know. Like security van hold up. Simple they are. One car in front, one behind, and plastic explosive blows the door off. I love it! You should see their faces! Oh, he'll be here, Big Charlie! Any time, he'll turn up, don't worry…

BRIAN
He'll have to help us get rid of the bodies, you understand that? Big Charlie?

ERIC
Oh, aye. No probs..

BRIAN
Priority, Eric. Hygiene.

ERIC
Oh aye, stitch it on a cushion. Nurse Arthur can go, as far as I'm concerned. His sweeties are finished.

BRIAN
And Mr Abramovich.

ERIC
Oh, definitely…

*ERIC raises window box lid.*
*HELEN pokes her head out, finger to lips.*
*ERIC closes the lid. BRIAN has not seen this.*

ERIC
It's Mrs Abramovich.

BRIAN
I don't care what you call him.

ERIC
He can't have had a sex change this quick. Like Jimmy Nolan down our street. Mary Nolan now! Oh my God, what a – I mean – out here she is!

BRIAN
It's only a code name for Mr Gosport's body, Eric.

ERIC
Oh aye? Body is it?

BRIAN
That's right.

ERIC
Right you are, I'll soon fix that.

*ERIC produces the gun and fires two shots into the window box. MOTHER appears on the stairs, wrapping a dressing gown on.*

MOTHER
Oh my God! What now? What's next?

BRIAN
Not to worry, Mrs Gosport. It was just Eric being a bit careless with a gun.

MOTHER
You're firing guns in my lounge and you call that being a bit careless?

BRIAN
Mr Dewitt has got emotional problems.

MOTHER
I've got emotional problems. I am in a state of shock. Where is my husband? He wasn't in bed. Have you shot him?

BRIAN
No. Not seen Mr Gosport yet to say good-morning, and to check for the daily round, the common task. Should need to furnish all we ask. Room to deny ourselves a road, to bring us daily nearer God.

ERIC
Stitch it on a cushion, Missus. A big one.

MOTHER
Let's get this straight, boys. There are some house rules here. No smoking. No feet up on the cushions. And no bodies in the piano!
My home is not an undertakers parlour. You get rid of that body this morning, you hear?

BRIAN
You hear that, Eric?

ERIC
Aye. We can chop it up and put it in the furnace.

MOTHER
You will not chop it up and put it in the furnace! Do you have no sense of propriety?

BRIAN
I'll look that word up, Missus. Eric, you've set us back, you have, upsetting the lady of the house. Firing that gun, waking up the whole household. And you ain't exactly made it easy for me to plight my troth with her daughter. Why don't you offer to clean the windows?

ERIC
I've cleaned a few windows in me time. Oh aye, you can see who's at home and what's worth nicking.

*KATEY appears on the stairs in panda one-piece pyjamas, with floppy ears. She has a notebook and pen.*

KATEY
What's going on, Mum? Am I missing some good dialogue?

MOTHER
Katey, I would wish for you to miss everything in this house of horrors.

*Window box lid opens. HELEN stands up. Her dress is bloodstained. She is holding the present.*

HELEN
*(Sings weakly)*
*Happy rather late birthday to you,*
*Happy rather late birthday to you...*

*MOTHER collapses onto settee.*
*Enter DIGBY, holding present, by French windows.*

DIGBY
*(Joins in singing)*
*Happy rather late birthday dear Katey,*
*Happy birthday to you....*

*ROGER appears on the stairs. Crosses to window box.*
*Looks inside.*

ROGER
Who's shot up my can of red paint? I was going to do the kitchen in that colour.

HELEN
Then I'm not mortally wounded?

*DIGBY crosses to window box.*

DIGBY
Excuse me, madam, you are standing in my window box.

HELEN
Oh? I didn't realise...

*HELEN climbs out of the window box.*
*DIGBY gets in.*

DIGBY
Thank you very much.

*DIGBY sits in the window box, and closes the lid.*

*Enter ARNOLD, carrying two plastic bags that clink with bottles.*

*He crosses to cocktail cabinet and puts bottles on it.*

ARNOLD
There's a new spotty 'erbert down the off-licence. He loves all the old films, including *Elephant Bill*, and put all this on the slate. It's our lucky day.

*SHERIFF appears on stairs with gun.*

SHERIFF
Hi, y'all! How's it hanging? How are you God fearing folks doing this fine day? Down on your knees the lot of you! Get down I say, miserable sinners that you are! Only the Righteous shall prevail. And all that is abhorrent in His sight shall surely disappear from the face of the earth. For this mission I have been called by the Archangel Gabriel. I have heard His voice in the night, and in the daytime, calling me to slaughter all in the wicked city, even the cattle shall be slaughtered.

MOTHER
We are not in the city, young man.

SHERIFF
The cattle are here. It is enough. Prepare to die...

MOTHER
Can we not talk?

SHERIFF
Enough talking. Goodbye...

SHERIFF squeezes trigger. A flag pops out of the toy gun. He laughs hysterically.

BRIAN
That's Desperate Dan from D ward. Multiple personality disorder. He wanted to escape with us but I told him he weren't ready for out-patient treatment. He was too agitated. You're not wanted here, Dan. You're pathetic. Go back to the hospital.

SHERIFF
*(In a different personality, high pitched voice, sings)*

Desperate Dan is a multiple of one,
One sick bunny, a rabbit on the run…
He's a fractured fraction,
Looking for the action,
Looking for a bloodbath,
Looking for a good laugh,
Desperate Dan is one of very many,
And sometimes isn't any…one!

*KATEY picks up flute, and accompanies the next verse.*

He's a personality disorder, who has crossed the border,
Of sanity and reason, in the shooting season,
He's a fractured fraction,
Looking for the action,
Looking for a bloodbath,
Looking for a good laugh,
Desperate Dan is one of very many,
And sometimes isn't any… one!

*Ensemble sing with him, KATEY still on flute.*

Desperate Dan hears a hundred voices,
Making him make anti-social choices,
He's a fractured fraction,
Looking for the action,
Looking for a bloodbath,
Looking for a good laugh,
Desperate Dan is one of very many,
(SHERIFF alone) And sometimes isn't any…
(OMNES) … One!

*SHERIFF exits.*

BRIAN
It took him three years to compose that song.

ERIC
If he works on it for another three years he might have a hit.
*BLACKOUT*

## SCENE 6

*THE LOUNGE. Later that morning.*
*DIGBY, HELEN and the family are seated in the lounge.*
*KATEY has wrapping paper around her. She is holding, in each hand, a pair of one-piece pyjamas.*

KATEY
Like, thanks everyone! Happy Birthday, me!

DIGBY
That's only until I can think of something else, Kate.

ARNOLD
You've had twenty-one years.

DIGBY
I've no idea how I got here, Arnold. Complete blank. Domino, double blank.

ARNOLD
Let me fill you in, Digby. You'd had a break-in at your office. Stuff chucked around and the petty cash box pilfered.

DIGBY
I kept two hundred pounds in that.

ARNOLD
Well it had gone but the time I called in to see you. So had the intruder. You were somewhat shaken up so we decided to motor down in my car – for Katey's party – whereupon when we arrived you were set upon by lunatics, left for dead and stuffed into the window box.

DIGBY
Not my day, was it?

ARNOLD
No it wasn't.

DIGBY
I should see somebody.

ARNOLD
A doctor.

DIGBY
No, an estate agent. I'm going to sell this place.

ARNOLD
But I bought this cottage off you.

DIGBY
No, you didn't.

ARNOLD
Yes, I did. I paid with my life. It was an understanding of honour, without documentation. A gentlemen's agreement.

DIGBY
I was not aware of that. I didn't know there were any gentlemen involved.
*MOTHER stands and fetches suitcase (on wheels) from behind settee.*

MOTHER
I've heard enough nonsense for one lifetime. Are you ready, Digby?

DIGBY
What for?

MOTHER
It's been decided. I'm moving in with you.

DIGBY
Who by?

MOTHER
You.

DIGBY
I didn't know that.

ARNOLD
It's a temporary measure.

MOTHER
It's permanent.

ARNOLD
While I sell up the place, you mean?

MOTHER
It's not yours to sell, Arnold. We do not need to continue that fantasy.

ARNOLD
You were sharing a fantasy with me? That's a first.

MOTHER
I encouraged you to live a lie, yes. I regret it. I thought it would be a bridge to – somewhere. I was wrong. It's over, Arnold. Come along, Digby. We'll walk to the station.

DIGBY
Which one?

MOTHER
The local one.

DIGBY
Yes, that's the nearest. Good idea…
*(He stands up)*
Absolutely blank! White canvas! Stark! Nothing! Modernist crap!

MOTHER
He's still concussed.

ARNOLD
It's an improvement. In his present state he could even get me work.

MOTHER
Goodbye, Arnold.

ARNOLD
You're baling out at the wrong time, Vera. We're on the verge of a huge success. New funding…

MOTHER
That's the next fantasy, is it? There's always something wonderful about to turn up, to give us back that brief window of fame we apparently enjoyed so much. In the seventies, was it? Before some war, or after some other war that we were demonstrating against? I don't remember. I don't want back those Jane Fonda days. I want the hours and the minutes of this day…

ARNOLD
Is this a new book you are reading?

MOTHER
Yes, Arnold, I'm as much to blame. I kept the illusion going. I fed it with all my…

ARNOLD
Positive thinking. You Can If You Think You Can, Vera.

MOTHER
I believed what I wanted to believe, to protect the children. But you're right, they're all grown up. I hadn't noticed.

ARNOLD
We can start again. It's ridiculous to dismantle a lifetime's work. I mean we've got grandchildren to look forward to. Maybe not with Roger…

ROGER
I can adopt.

ARNOLD
Thanks.

MOTHER
No. I need to find myself. I'm going to look for Vera.

ARNOLD
The girl I left behind me.

MOTHER
And when I find her neither of us will be returning to you.

ARNOLD
Yes, read lots of self-help books, Vera. I'm sure you'll become very empowered, take up pottery and become a lesbian. I'll send you a pipe.

MOTHER
You're impossible!

DIGBY
What do we do next?

MOTHER
I don't know.

DIGBY
But you said…? Arnold…?

ARNOLD
I don't know. I'm out of words.

HELEN
I've brought you Sons And Lovers, Arnold.

ARNOLD
Why did you say that?

HELEN
To keep the conversation going.

ARNOLD
Improvising… *( Picks up the book )*
That's the fifth time you've brought it here.

HELEN
And Hubert Death's Famous Last Meals. For you, Vera.

MOTHER
I've cooked my last meal in this house, Helen. You can take over if you like.

HELEN
I could never replace you, oh no, Vera. I mean I'd have to be someone entirely different. Like… well like me, I suppose. If I was you I'd go. Definitely. But I'm not it just shows that we none of us know who we are, or what we are capable of. I suppose it depends on the situation, doesn't it?

KATEY
Definitely. Situation defines character. You put the people into a situation and then you find out who they are. That is best BBC comedy script department thinking.

ARNOLD
Someone's thinking at the BBC? That's dangerous.

*A packet drops through the letter box. ARNOLD picks up the packet and opens it. Takes out a script. And finds a letter…*

ARNOLD
*Reading.* Dear Arnold, here is the commissioned play. I have called it Looneys. I think it all works very well, except I do not know how to finish the play. I've run out of dialogue, of things to say. Sorry. I can't work on it any more, it's driving me mad. Don't try to find me. Goodbye…
I knew we'd been written! There's proof…
*He screws up letter.* It was behind every every word uttered. I felt it. I knew it. So that bastard playwright won't see it through. He won't finish our drama. Where's that leave us? Up the creek without a paddle…
That's what happens when you find a writer in a pub in St Martin's Lane – ex-Royal Court playwright – claiming to be a rejected genius. He's abandoned us before the end of Act Two, the wanker. Assuming it is a two act play. If it's three act play we're really in the shit. Even Pirandello wouldn't do that to his actors.

MOTHER
This is the perfect ending Arnold, as far as I am concerned. Nobody could hold this family together any longer. So I've found out I'm not Superwoman, it's a relief…
*She kisses him lightly.* Goodbye Arnold. Good luck…
Goodbye Helen. Thank you for sharing the load all these years. You've got him all to yourself now. Come along, Digby.

DIGBY
Where are we going?

MOTHER
Somewhere else.

DIGBY
To another play? No curtain call here then. Absolute blank. Tate Modern crap!

*DIGBY exits, with MOTHER.*

ROGER
We need to leave home, Kate. We have to make a decision. No-one is going to make it for us.

KATEY
I can't leave Dad on his own, he's hopeless.

ROGER
It's you that's hopeless on your own. Dad'll survive, it's what he does best. He always puts himself first, don't worry. Come with me.

KATEY
What about Elephant Bill? Our movie? Our dream.

ARNOLD
Yes, Katey, you're right. We don't give up now.

KATEY
My script…?

ARNOLD
What is it your mother says?

KATEY
Don't quit before the miracle.

ROGER
The miracle has happened. We're still alive. Come on, Kate.

ARNOLD
We've got to get Big Charlie here with funding. Eric's brother. He's looking for a project. We can wash his money for him. The more the better. I'll write a new ending. A happy ending. That's what people want these days. An upbeat ending, isn't it?

KATEY
What, for us or the film?

ARNOLD
Both. Why not?

ROGER
Why not? He's flipped. Dad can't write our lives. He's done everything else to try to make us happy, except be there for us when it counted. It's a train wreck. Kate, come on.

KATEY
On my twenty-first birthday? Leave with two sets of floppy pyjamas? What's the most upbeat thing that can happen, Dads?

ARNOLD
Truly? Madly? Deeply? Katey? Roger's right. It's best that you shove off and make a life for yourself. Go on, get out. We're finished.

KATEY
You don't like my script? Is that it?

ARNOLD
It's rubbish. Go.

KATEY
Dad, that's not a happy ending.

ARNOLD
Kate... Katey, let's hope you look back one day and say it is. That it is the happiest of endings one could fashion from this jumble. Go somewhere else and write another script. And then another, and another. And another. Keep going. Keep going...
Goodbye, daughter.

*ROGER has gone to the piano and plays.*

ROGER
*Sings from The Animals:* We've got to get out of this place.

KATEY
*Joins in :* If it's the last thing we ever do!

*ROGER pulls KATEY to leave. She breaks away – embraces her father – then runs out. ROGER exits after her.*

ARNOLD
All gone. All gone. I have no family now. I am bereft, a caged bird set free. Into the cruel elements I go, my feathers whipped by winds I have not the strength to ride, nor the practise of it. I am a preening bird, my mirror and my perch I miss. Your eyes, sweet Kate, were my mirror, and Vera's faith, my perch. Roger was the grit. 'Tis true I flew away, but never far, and always returned to my cage. But now I am a cuckoo, the nest is broke. I fall before I learn to fly... No, no, I am a chaffinch, a singing bird trained to sing songs that keep the habit of happiness awake in others. No, I am an owl, a night bird hunting mice. I sit on the high branch, waiting for cautious thought to gain courage and run, and then I swoop to kill all originality. I am what I am, an untold story, abandoned by a drunken sot who's brain has given up. Yet in this tale there is surely enough momentum to put us over the finishing line?

HELEN
I will build you a new cage, and my eyes will be your mirror. And your perch shall be my faith in thee, dear Arnold.

ARNOLD
Sweet Helen. I fear for my sanity. I am unhinged by this script sent through the post. What means it, nurse?

HELEN
It is a plot device. Failed. We continue, as we must, and write our own parts. Parents, teachers, governments and society wrote our scripts, but now we have to manage this work.

ARNOLD
It is a hard won freedom. And hard to retain. How shall we end this act?

HELEN
It will end itself. Listen…

*FX : Sound of gunfire. Shots. Pause.*
*Enter ERIC.*

ERIC
Big Charlie's gone. He's bought it like, gone for a Burton. It was a family quarrel, and no mistake. He had come to put me back in the hospital, think of that. To hide me, the shame he felt amongst his friends. His mind was changed. He would not admit I am the brains of the whole outfit.

ARNOLD
This is good news, Eric. With you in charge we will expand into show business together.

ERIC
Oh aye, the killing's done. The lessons have been learnt, like. The foot soldiers are subdued and swear a new loyalty to me, their Eric. I have emerged as top banana.

ARNOLD
Madness has won the day then.

ERIC
The treasury is yours. I'll put you in touch with our accountant.

ARNOLD
You will not regret this day's work. What is still to be done?

ERIC
There are bodies to tidy.

ARNOLD
Helen, we can use your mobile library van to take a few items up to the quarry and ditch them there.

HELEN
Bodies? In my van? Amongst my carefully chosen books? Literature for an elderly, disabled and demented public? You can't be serious? That van is a local council service vehicle, Arnold. You're asking me to do something immoral, unethical, even criminal.

ARNOLD
That's right.

HELEN
Oh well, just this once.

*BRIAN enters.*

BRIAN
And I will have my clinic out of all this. When I place my evidence of the worst treatment since Dickens in that hospital, the European court is bound to declare us sane.

ARNOLD
If they're consistent, they will. They always have done, so far.

HELEN
Come on then, let's all muck in...

*As HELEN goes to piano to take out body...*
*NURSE ARTHUR climbs out of piano, like a Zombie.*
*Walks a couple of paces, stiffly, then sits at piano and plays...*

NURSE ARTHUR
*(Sings)* We've got to get out of this place,
If it's the last thing we ever do...

*OMNES join in song! BLACKOUT*

**THE END**

www.ingramcontent.com/pod-product-compliance
Lightning Source LLC
Chambersburg PA
CBHW050328230426
43663CB00010B/1785